RECRUITING, EDUCATING, AND TRAINING CATALOGING LIBRARIANS

Recent Titles in
New Directions in Information Management

RECRUITING, EDUCATING, AND TRAINING CATALOGING LIBRARIANS

Solving the Problems

EDITED BY
Sheila S. Intner and Janet Swan Hill

*NEW DIRECTIONS IN INFORMATION MANAGEMENT,
NUMBER 19*

GREENWOOD PRESS
New York • Westport, Connecticut • London

Library of Congress Cataloging-in-Publication Data

Recruiting, educating, and training cataloging librarians : solving
    the problems / edited by Sheila Intner and Janet Swan Hill.
        p.   cm. — (New directions in information management, ISSN
    0887-3844 ; no. 19)
        Proceedings of the Simmons College Symposium on Recruiting,
    Educating, and Training Cataloging Librarians: Solving the Problems,
    held Mar. 10-11, 1989 at Simmons College, Boston, Mass.
        Bibliography: p.
        Includes index.
        ISBN 0-313-26693-X (lib. bdg. : alk. paper)
        1. Catalogers—Recruiting—Congresses. 2. Catalogers—Education—
    Congresses. 3. Catalogers—In-service training—Congresses.
    4. Librarians—Recruiting—Congresses. 5. Library education—
    Congresses. 6. Cataloging—Congresses. I. Intner, Sheila S.
    II. Hill, Janet Swan. III. Simmons College Symposium on Recruiting,
    Educating, and Training Cataloging Librarians: Solving the Problems
    (1989) IV. Series.
    Z682.4.C38R43   1989
    331.12′4102—dc19   88-33643

British Library Cataloguing in Publication Data is available.

Library of Congress Catalog Card Number: 88-33643
ISBN: 0-313-26693-X
ISSN: 0887-3844

First published in 1989

Greenwood Press, Inc.
88 Post Road West, Westport, Connecticut 06881

Printed in the United States of America

The paper used in this book complies with the
Permanent Paper Standard issued by the National
Information Standards Organization (Z39.48-1984).

10 9 8 7 6 5 4 3 2 1

Contents

Preface

Welcome!

Those of us who came up through the ranks as technical services librarians have always recognized the importance of that work which has traditionally taken place outside of the public's eye. Now, more than ever, the role of technical services librarians in general, and cataloging librarians in particular, has taken on new meaning and greater significance. This has occurred, unfortunately, at the same moment when the library and information science professions are facing a crisis in recruiting, particularly in the important areas of technical services and cataloging.

A brave new step to begin resolving this dilemma is evinced in this Symposium. One of my favorite Chinese proverbs is the one that maintains, "The journey of a thousand miles begins with the first step." We, here at Simmons, are pleased that this first step is being taken here and that the Council on Library Resources has recognized its importance through its generous support.

This gathering brings together both educators and practitioners to address the issues. Coordinators Sheila Intner, Janet Hill, and Karen Muller are to be congratulated for their ideas and enthusiasm in planning and implementing the

Symposium. Members of the profession and the people they serve can only benefit from the results.

To all of you here, welcome to Boston, for the next two days the bibliographic capitol of the world, and to Simmons College, a pioneer school in preparing cataloging librarians for a new world--a different and more challenging world than the one into which we were born.

-- Robert D. Stueart, Dean.

Introduction

Sheila S. Intner and Janet Swan Hill

The Simmons College Symposium on Recruiting, Educating, and Training Cataloging Librarians is one of the many creative ideas that owes its origins to the conversations between colleagues that occur at professional conferences. At the 1987 midwinter conferences of the Association of Library and Information Science Education (ALISE) and the American Library Association (ALA), presentation of the report of the ALA Resources and Technical Services Division (RTSD) Task Force on Recruiting, Educating, and Training of Catalogers (chaired by editor Hill) at a special ALISE session elicited much sound and fury, but very little visible movement toward solutions to the problems it documented with painful clarity.

During a luncheon conversation following the session, however, editors Intner and Hill agreed that the work of the Task Force needed to be carried forward by more than just a task force or a single event, but by an ongoing series of activities that would: (1) raise the consciousness of all members of the profession regarding the concerns of cataloging librarians; (2) build on the work of the Task Force by establishing a research-based body of knowledge about cataloging recruitment, education, and training; and, (3) identify viable solutions.

One response by editors Intner and Hill was to form a Special Interest Group in ALISE dedicated to discussing the issues of technical services education. This group, which had its first meeting at the ALISE conference in San Antonio, continues to consider specific educational problems, both curricular and extra-curricular. A second encouraging response was the decision of RSTD and its Cataloging and Classification Section to change the status of the Task Force (which was ad hoc) to a regularly-constituted standing committee of the section, currently under the leadership of Heide Hoerman, a Symposium participant. A third response by Intner and Hill, in which our co-coordinator Karen Muller participated, too, was the formulation of the proposal for this Symposium and its subsequent implementation.

The people who were invited to participate in the Symposium represent a gathering of practitioners and educators having two things in common: Expertise in one or more of the areas of concern, i.e., cataloging recruitment, education, or training; and, a solution that they wished to share with their colleagues intended to address an identified problem in one of those areas. Each participant was asked to document the solution carefully in a paper of limited length to be presented at one of the Symposium's sessions.

This book, comprising the papers prepared for the Symposium, is intended to be used in two ways: First, by library administrators, to stimulate experimentation in applying its solutions to the real-life problems being encountered in their institutions; and, second, by professional educators and students to help them gain greater understanding of a critical set of issues and to meet the institutional needs of the library and information science program. *The Simmons College Symposium* is also important for practicing catalogers in suggesting ways that they might become proactive participants in solving the problems they experience and understand so well.

In order that this book might appear simultaneously with the Symposium itself, the papers in it were prepared well in advance of the event. As a result, the discussions by Symposium participants that followed their formal presentations could not be captured for inclusion here. Another publication will have to record the creative energy contained in those discussions.

That the idea for the Symposium has come to fruition is attributable to the efforts of many more people than its three coordinators. Chief among those whose good counsel and support aided us were Henriette D. Avram, Ching-chih Chen, Robert M. Hayes, Deanna Marcum, Lucia Rather, Robert D. Stueart, Ben R. Tucker, Richard P. Smiraglia, Robert Vosper, and members of the Executive Board of the Resources and Technical Services Division of the American Library Association. The valuable critique from members of the Council on Library Resources provided to the coordinators helped to focus the Symposium sharply on solutions, rather than problems already well-defined, and the Council's generous financial support helped bring it all to reality. The editors are grateful to every one for their contributions.

In addition, many people helped in the preparation of the book itself, including Alexandra Herz and Linda Willey of Simmons College, and Donna Cody and Tom Rose of the Medical Area Service Corporation (MASCO). James Hill lent his special expertise with word-processing software and Jonathan Intner solved problems with flagging disk drives and power supplies. Mathew Intner's mastery of logistics was especially important in helping us to meet our deadlines successfully.

A special word of thanks is due to Mary R. Sive, who demonstrated extraordinary confidence in the book and who arranged for its timely production.

-- Sheila S. Intner and Janet Swan Hill, Editors.

RECRUITING, EDUCATING, AND TRAINING CATALOGING LIBRARIANS

The More Things Change . . .

Robert M. Hayes

INTRODUCTION

For some reason, Sheila Intner thought that I could provide a keynote speech that would start this symposium with a suitable frame of reference. Since I am not a cataloger and indeed have never even taken a course in cataloging, you might well wonder what she could possibly have had in mind. Certainly I have wondered and, indeed, have had difficulty in determining what would be a suitable frame of reference, one that would both be meaningful to you and appropriate to my own qualifications.

In that light, then, I want to set a context much broader than the title of the symposium would imply. While you will be focused on recruiting, educating, and training cataloging librarians, I hope you will do so with recognition of the appropriate role of "cataloging" as part of the curriculum for education of librarians and information scientists whatever their ultimate professional responsibilities may be. I think such a context is important because I see cataloging as a critical part of the fundamental theory of the field, as something that need be understood by all information professionals, theoretically and even scientifically, as well as operationally. I am consciously using the concept "science", and find no anomaly in doing so. The definition I am using for it is from *Webster's Dictionary*:

1 a: a possession of knowledge as distinguished from ignorance or misunderstanding; b: knowledge attained through study or practice.
2 a: a department of systematized knowledge as an object of study; b: something that may be studied or learned like systematized knowledge.
3: knowledge covering general truths or the operation of general laws.

I bring to that view a history of experience in trying to reconcile and integrate the various aspects of our field, with cataloging a central focus of concern. I bring a professional and technical interest in issues represented by cataloging. I bring the perspective of nearly fifteen years as dean of a school in which cataloging has been regarded as the very foundation of the educational program. In my comments today, I want to cover each of those three points of view in a way that I hope will be meaningful to your own deliberations.

Before doing so, though, I should pay at least passing attention to your own agenda. I suspect that Sheila wants at least some reference to why you all are here. Basically, I guess we need to ask whether "Recruiting, Educating and Training Cataloging Librarians" is really all that necessary. Indeed, haven't the online cataloging services eliminated the need for catalogers? Haven't many of the library schools eliminated instruction in cataloging as a core course in recognition of that perception?

The answer to the first question, in my view, unequivocally is NO. Now, in saying that I recognize that increasing proportions of cataloging work in individual libraries is being done by clerical or technical staff, and that is surely to the good in terms of efficiency in library operations. But those staff must be supervised by professionals who know what is needed. The basic data, as generated by the Library of Congress and the major resource libraries of the country must be created by professionals. The range of materials and differing formats for them that need to be cataloged is steadily increasing; each of them requires the highest level of professional qualification.

Turning to the second question, frankly I am least concerned with the last of the three objectives of your program. "Training" cataloging librarians is important, but in my view hardly at the level of import of the first two objectives. The need for professional catalogers requires recruitment and education; training may be of value to them and clearly is necessary for clerical and professional staff. I emphasize the word professional, of course, because that is where the role of education is critical. That is why I am personally concerned about the extent to which library school programs have abandoned a requirement for education in cataloging. But beyond that, and the point of my asking you to consider the larger frame of reference as well as the narrow one reflected in the title, is the importance of cataloging to the professional librarian and information scientist, whatever the specialty. So now let me turn to that larger context in which I hope you will view you own efforts.

HISTORY

First, I want to present some bits of personal history, because they provide a context for discussing some of the issues that I think are important to the deliberations of this symposium. Specifically, I want to discuss the process by which I have come to see cataloging as an essential component of education for our field, including the problems I have faced in doing so, the difficulties I had in reconciling the proper role of cataloging, the means for resolution of those difficulties, and the resulting revelations amounting to a near religious experience. I have seen the light! Cataloging is the answer!

Some thirty years ago, I taught my first course on computer-based information storage and retrieval at UCLA. It was offered through University Extension as a two-week short course, with an intensive eight hours per day of lecture and discussion. It was subsequently offered for about a dozen times both at UCLA and at a number of other places in the country. Its purpose was to introduce the concepts of information storage and retrieval, especially as needed in the application of computers to reference data base files, to persons from both the computer field and the documentation field.

It was my view at that time, as it still is today, that the two fields of librarianship and computer science (note that I am saying "computer science", not "information science", the latter term then still to be born and even when defined something quite different) had much to gain from each other. That view was, to say the least, not widely held by either group. Only a few librarians saw significant value in use of computers, and even ten years later there were many who regarded computers as comparable to the emperor's clothes. And even fewer computer specialists saw any value at all in what librarians knew or even did.

But still, I held that view, and with respect to the contribution that librarianship could make to computer science I saw cataloging as central to it. In that frame of reference, then, I approached Lawrence Clark Powell and asked him for help in planning one of the days of the course I was developing. It is clear evidence of my naivete that I chose Larry, not realizing that he of all persons regarded the computer with anathema. But Larry has vision and, at the very time I approached him, along with Andy Horn was laying the foundation for the UCLA library school. Something in what I said struck a responsive chord in both of them, and Andy did indeed participate in the course, presenting the approaches and methods of the librarian.

Here, though, arose the first of the many problems I have faced in achieving my vision of an integration of library and information science. What I had wanted was a presentation of theoretical structures underlying cataloging--and I knew enough to know that that was what I wanted--and reference. What Andy presented was an historical overview of the development of the field, a beautiful presentation but at best peripherally related to my objectives in developing a formal basis for applying computers to information storage and retrieval. Things might have gone differently had I known enough to ask Seymour Lubetzky, though I suspect the students in the course--none of them with any knowledge of library science--would have been totally at sea in trying to grasp the fundamental significance or even the relevance of the "main entry". (Today, I find the concept still to be exceptionally important, with profound effects upon online file structures, provided we give it highly generalized interpretation.)

The relevance of this historical anecdote is the fact that it exemplifies two problems I hope you will consider, along with your examination of the recruitment, education, and training of catalogers: How do we present cataloging to students whose objectives are information science specialty in ways that make it relevant and meaningful? How do we assure that all librarians, whatever their specialty, have an appreciation of the importance of cataloging?

The next bit of history moves forward about six years, when I became a full-time member of the faculty of the UCLA library school. My responsibility was to establish a program of education in information systems analysis within the context of that School--that being my focus of concern in both computer science and information science. My preference was to integrate it with the professional MLS degree program, since I regarded systems analysis as a professional activity parallel to and supportive of the general programs of the School, as well as having its own domain of application, including areas outside of librarianship as such.

However, I faced three problems. The first was length of program; one calendar year simply was not enough to encompass the essential technical content required for effective systems work. The second was the requirements for admission of students; there needed to be much stronger qualification especially with respect to mathematics and computer competence if the program was to accomplish its objectives. The third was in the substance of required courses, and this is the one of immediate relevance to your discussion.

I will be frank. At that time, in 1964, I naively saw cataloging as the problem, not the solution. I did not then see the things I have since recognized. To me then it was a diversion of time and effort to require students concerned with the technical needs in systems analysis and design to learn the rules of cataloging and to learn how to deal with specific examples of cataloging requirements. I saw it as far too specific to library operations and not sufficiently generalizable to provide systems analysts with the tools they would need.

The result was the development of a proposal for a new degree program, a Master Science in Information Science, that was approved and implemented starting in 1965. It was a two-year program, with extensive requirements for admission and for graduation. It was not integrated with the MLS, though even then we were beginning to advise students to develop an integration.

And now I come to the revelations resulting from discussion with Seymour Lubetzky and Betty Baughman and, in later years, with Elaine Svenonius. I am not sure whether I had any effect upon them in those collegial discussions, though one debate did lead to a paper jointly written with Seymour. The relevant point here is that I began to see the essential relationship between cataloging and my own technical and professional interests more and more clearly.

By the time the School decided to make the MLS program two calendar years in length, it had become clear to me that cataloging was indeed essential to information systems analysis and design, and not simply in terms of library applications. It was, therefore, easy to make a decision that the time was right to effect integration of the two degrees. Not only would the increased length and the added admission requirements for the MLS program permit it, but my experience of near religious conversion made it possible to envision effective relationships between the MLS program and my own objectives. I will go into some detail about all of that in a moment, but before doing so, there is one other bit of personal history to present.

Becoming a Dean is less a religious experience than simply a exercise in balancing problems. And cataloging was central among those problems. Indeed, one of the early concerns was how the School would fill Betty Baughman's crucial role if, for whatever reason, she could not? I went so far as to sit in on her class in order to prepare myself for the eventuality that I might need to fill in for her. Frankly, the very thought or perhaps threat was sufficient to keep her as healthy as was possible and wishing to teach at the highest level.

But again, from sitting in on her classes, I gained an appreciation of the nature of cataloging, of her methods of instruction, and of my own potential approach if indeed I were to try to teach cataloging. That was virtually a second revelation. And I will also go into that as well.

Aside from my own near religious experience, the responsibilities of being dean do require that one understand the role of each faculty member, of each course, of each requirement. That in itself gave me added appreciation of the importance of cataloging and of the necessity to maintain the highest possible quality in that area of our program. I think we have succeeded well in doing so.

PROFESSIONAL AND TECHNICAL INTEREST

Now, let me turn from nostalgia and personal history to substance. There are three primary points I want to make. The first concerns the role of cataloging as the theoretical foundation for library science. The second concerns the specific issue of "complexity". And the third concerns the relationship of both to systems analysis and design.

In my view, cataloging is the fundamental basis for a theory to our field. It is here that information organization and structure become identified and the means for handling them specified. The structures embodied in cataloging are the basis for all subsequent retrieval, including reference. Even the substantive tasks in library management revolve around the structure provided by the catalog. As in Panizzi's day, it is the tool for management of the collection. Obviously, these are operational issues, but they must have a theoretical foundation and that resides in the catalog.

Those highlight the theoretical significance of cataloging to the library, as such. But in my view, it has theoretical significance even beyond the bounds of librarianship.

When I taught my first short course on computer based information storage and retrieval, in 1958, I used as one of my primary examples the Federal parts catalog. That's cataloging, of course, but of a dramatically different nature, on the surface anyway, from library cataloging. I don't know the extent to which any of you may have knowledge of that data base, but it covers millions of Federal stock numbers and for each of them provides a means for description of the part. The means for doing so is a set of some 15,000 "descriptive patterns"--as I visualize them, primitive MARC formats--by which individual parts are described in standardized formats. The system was created to meet perceived needs to coordinate inventories among the agencies in the Department of Defense; it required development of a standardized vocabulary, of the several descriptive patterns, of the procedures for determining whether a new item was already in the file or not, and of the procedures for input and validation of new entries.

Now, my point is that this data processing example embodies all of the problems involved in library cataloging, though at a primitive level (except for size of file) of complexity, as I will discuss in a moment. The concepts of authority, of classification and categorization, of formats and rules for entry, of validation--all are exhibited in this example. Such file systems are characteristic of all of data processing, and the concerns of library cataloging potentially provide the theoretical underpinning for them.

I say theoretically because I think one of the serious lacks in cataloging instruction and theory is the failure to see beyond the specifics of the library. If there is one thing I would urge it is to extend the scope of our cataloging theory to encompass the full range of data base design problems, wherever they may occur, at whatever level of complexity they may represent. The literature of data base design--relational data bases, data dictionaries, data formats and data structures--all should be encompassed within the scope of our cataloging theory and courses.

A primary reason for that view is represented by a term I have used now several times: complexity. There is a dramatic difference between the problems in library cataloging and those in the data bases typical of more general data processing. Library data are far more complex and in a variety of ways. They are substantively more complex, embodying variable formats, variable fields, variable numbers of entries. And they are operationally more complex, needing to deal with the irrationalities and idiosyncracies of the real world in ways outside the scope of standard data processing.

I would like to explore this issue in some detail, since I consider it to be fundamental to understanding the role of cataloging, both in theory and in practice. I call it the "problem oriented" approach to in contrast to the "rule based" approach to cataloging. I do not know the extent to which you, as cataloging faculty or as practitioner-teachers, explicitly and consciously provide a problem oriented structure to your instruction, but that's the one I would use, for both descriptive and subject cataloging. Let me briefly illustrate it:

Consider a matrix, the rows of which are individual fields and sub-fields of a MARC record and the columns of which are categories of "problems". Without being inclusive or prescriptive, let me illustrate with some examples of problems in descriptive cataloging:

- Multiple values for a field (e.g., multiple authors, multiple imprint imprints, multiple titles)
- Missing data for a field (e.g., no author, no imprint, no title)
- Invalid data for a field (e.g., incorrect author name on title page, invalid imprint, incorrect title)
- Foreign data for a field (e.g., foreign name for author, for imprint, for title)

The point, of course, is that cataloging rules are designed to deal with the problems and the number of rules reflects the product of the number of problems and the number of fields.

I have illustrated with descriptive cataloging because the rules are so well developed there and so clearly tied to solution of problems. But I think comparable approaches to characterization of classification and subject cataloging are evident.

The beauty and value of library cataloging is that it has identified and dealt with these problems, allowing us to handle complexity, to deal with the real world and its uncontrollable irrationalities rather than by forcing it into fixed, controllable requirements. This is the great contribution both to theory and to practice in data base design and operational practice.

Now, I turn to my own area of professional interest-- systems analysis and design. The task here is to determine requirements (for data, for information, for a system), establish the specifications for both data structures and procedures to meet them, design alternative means for meeting those specifications, and evaluate them in terms of effectiveness and cost.

In that process, we need to work in contexts that may not be well defined at the time. They may require establishing new data structures and new procedures for data entry and validation. They may require new file structures and organizations. They should be able flexibly to deal with ambiguity, complexity, and divergent conditions without breakdown and failure. They should include interfaces that can handle a wide range of knowledge on the part of the user, again without breakdown or failure.

But these requirements in systems analysis and design are precisely those which library cataloging has had to deal with. The experience, the theoretical and practical knowledge are there. The need is to make evident that these are what instruction in cataloging can provide the student.

DEAN-LIKE VIEW

Let me turn now to the third of my points: the perspective of fifteen years as a dean. I want to raise three issues:

- How do we bring students to cataloging?
- How do we bring cataloging to students?
- How do we increase the theoretical content of cataloging instruction?

It is evident to me that there is a problem in attracting students to cataloging. In some way, we must either convey the sense of excitement that cataloging ought to represent. Or we must confirm that there are real needs to be filled by catalogers.

Or we must make it a requirement, to be taken whether they like it or not. In my own School, I think we have done all three, so the result has been graduates all of whom have had cataloging, many of whom have gone into cataloging positions, and at least some of whom have "seen the light!"

I must say, though, that each year we face rejection by some students, and especially among those that I think should benefit most--those specializing in information science. In some way, we must convey to them the views I've have tried to express here.

With respect to delivery of cataloging to the students, first of all I think it should indeed be required of all students, whatever their level and whatever their specialty, including information science. Clearly, though, there are the ones specializing in cataloging, and for them we preserve a special place in heaven or at least in the curriculum.

My greatest concern though is how to increase the theoretical content of cataloging and of the courses by which we teach it. The theory is there; the breadth of applications of it is there; the need in the curriculum is there. But the nature of cataloging instruction, I think even in my own School, is heavily based on practice. Can we separate instruction in theory--the science of our field--from instruction in practice? Are the two so inter-twined as to be inseparable? Does professional practice as a librarian in every specialty require the same level of experience in practice as it does for catalogers? Is it possible to develop cataloging courses that emphasize the data base design implications, with cataloging as a prime example, the most complex example perhaps, but not the only one?

My great wish as a dean and, now, as just a faculty member with my own specific interests, is that answers to those questions can be found and that they will indeed make the scientific basis for our field evident.

CONCLUSION

In this talk, I have tried to highlight the importance with which I view your concerns in this symposium. I could not possibly deal with the substantive issues--Recruiting, Educating and Training Cataloging Librarians. That is your role. I hope, though, that I have set a larger frame of reference so that you will also consider a number of other issues. I have used some personal history to exemplify those issues and I have expressed very personal views concerning them. They are indeed important to me, as I hope they will be important to you.

PART I:
SESSION ON RECRUITING
CATALOGING LIBRARIANS

Recruitment: The Way Ahead

James M. Matarazzo

Every so often, librarians and employers of librarians gather together in large and small meetings to lament the shortage of librarians and to propose solutions to recruiting large numbers to the profession. In the last 40 years, librarianship has had three periods of shortages and two corresponding periods of what appeared to be an oversupply of professional librarians.

We meet again at this conference under similar circumstances to the meetings held by our predecessors. We meet as they did to try to solve the problems associated with the recruitment of students. As in the past, various proposals will be put forth for better recruitment materials and unique approaches to recruitment. These ideas and proposed procedures will be presented in an effort to reach greater numbers of potential students of librarianship. Meetings such as this one have another purpose, aside from the discussion of solutions, which is to further spread the word about the shortage of staff. In the past, as the word about staff shortages has spread, enrollments have increased, the number of graduates has increased, and the pendulum began its inevitable swing. All this has occurred in the past and should happen again. At least, this is one educator's interpretation of what has happened over the past four decades as I have studied the issue in preparation for this conference.

THE 1970S

In order to best understand where we are now, a review of the recent past is essential.

In 1975, the Bureau of Labor Statistics (BLS) published a study entitled, *Library Manpower: A Study of Demand and Supply.*[1] This study was conducted because of concerns raised by the library community that an apparent oversupply of librarians was competing for a limited number of vacancies. On the whole, the BLS report provided the kind of data needed by the profession. BLS told us that in 1970, for example, 115,000 librarians were gainfully employed in American libraries. Between 1970 and 1985, 168,000 new librarians would be needed--47,000 for the growth in new positions and 121,000 to replace those who left the field because of retirement and for a variety of other reasons.

BLS projected that to meet the demand, an average of 9,000 new professionals would have to enter the profession each year and an additional 2,200 librarians would enter the field annually after some earlier delay. Since BLS had predicted 168,000 vacancies over the same 15 year period, 1970-1985, supply and demand would be somewhat in balance. The BLS report did caution, however, that for new entrants and non-graduate degree librarians, job prospects would be limited.

Also included in the report were an array of incredibly valuable statistics in table after table on or about the profession. Several of these tables are crucial to understanding what appears to be dramatic swings in the supply and demand of librarians. The most important information provided by BLS in this study was the fact that nearly half of the librarians in the United States were 45 years old or older in 1970. BLS could and did safely conclude that nearly half the female librarians and one-fourth the male librarians would be approaching retirement (or would have retired) by 1985. This meant that in excess of 50,000 new librarians would be needed over the 15 year period just to replace the librarians who had retired.

The BLS report was published in 1975, although conducted in 1972. The three years between the study and publication allowed for the necessary preparation of the report and comment from the various library associations and individual librarians as well as consultants, educators, and the like. Thus, the report itself represented a consensus on the matter of supply and demand by all concerned.

A cornerstone of these projections rests on the availability of 9,000 new graduates per year from all library education programs, i.e., accredited master's degree programs, non-accredited programs, bachelor's degree programs and school library certification programs. Until 1978, these projections appeared to hold. In 1978, a decline in the output of all of these degree and certificate programs began to emerge and this phenomenon continues today. However, in 1975, BLS's advice to the library schools in light of its projections was as follows:

> Library schools may choose to reexamine their curriculums from the viewpoint of the principal growth areas for librarians through 1985--school librarianship, media-audiovisual technology, library administration, library automation, and community outreach librarianship. Library schools which traditionally have placed a large number of their

graduates in academic and research libraries, for example, may opt to place greater stress on preparation for other areas of librarianship, where future employment growth is expected to be somewhat stronger.[2]

And, BLS added by way of advice:

Library schools concerned about the career satisfaction of past as well as current graduates may opt to curtail expansion. Some schools already have done so.[3]

1980S AND BEYOND

A 1982 King Research Study prepared for the National Center for Educational Statistics and the Office of Library and Learning Technologies offered a projection of supply and demand for professional librarians through 1990.[4] Unlike the earlier BLS study, which had access to the latest census data, the 1980 census data were not available for the King Research project, so the base line census data on the number of librarians in 1980 was not included in the report.

The King investigators did discuss the material collected by the Current Population Survey of BLS, which placed the number of librarians in 1980 at 182,000, and explained the reasons these data were not selected. The researchers elected to use the data collected by another BLS group, Occupational Employment Survey, which placed the number of librarians at 134,000, a figure this author believes was much too low. The information used, however, in the King report on the census of librarians was probably the best available at the time.

The King study detailed the decline in the total number of graduates of accredited master's degree programs from a high of 6,323 in 1974 through a decade of declining numbers of new degree holders per year. Along with the decline in the number of accredited degree graduates, declines in the total numbers of persons graduating with undergraduate degrees in library science, nonaccredited master's degrees and school library certificates were also documented. The King researchers report in graphic form the dramatic 35 percent decline in graduates of library education programs between 1977 and 1981 alone.[5]

At the same time, the researchers at King projected a modest increase in vacancies in the early 1980's and a leveling off through 1990. Increases in vacancies were projected in public and special libraries, while decreases in the number of vacancies were projected for academic and school libraries. Overall the King report forecasted small changes in the number of library school graduates and a tightening job market in the late 1980s.[6]

All of this new data led the King group to offer the following advice to employers:

> For employers of librarians, this study implies that, on the average, they will not be hiring many librarians. Such job openings as they have will result from retirements and from current employees changing jobs, not from expansion. Although supply will be below its past levels, it will still exceed demand, resulting in a buyer's market. The low level of turnover, however, suggests that libraries will have to place an increasing emphasis on staff development. Unable to create new positions, and with fewer people leaving voluntarily

greener pastures), libraries will have to rely more on retraining and less on hiring to bring in new skills in changing areas such as automation of library processes and of information storage and retrieval.[7]

And King's researchers provided the following advice to the library schools:

The study also has implications for library educators: MLS program enrollments are projected to increase, but slowly, during the 1980's and enrollments in BLS and school library certificate programs are expected to decrease throughout the 1980's. Responses are needed to new patterns of demand for librarians. There appears to be potential for programs currently offering any level of library training to also take on the training of information professionals for non-library settings.[8]

All of this advice was couched against the following backdrop:

While only very small changes are projected in the number of graduates of library education programs and in librarian employment, differences in the rates of change suggest that the job market will improve modestly in the 1982-1986 period and then tighten in the latter part of the decade. This statement reflects the job market for traditional librarians, and could be counteracted by increased movement of library program graduates to non-library information professional positions.[9]

It could be that we all read in the King report and similar reports in the library press, and/or used our own judgment to arrive at the same conclusions about the lack of job opportunity in librarianship, because the reality is that there have been fewer and fewer students in the schools and fewer graduates.

KEY DATA

It is most unfortunate that the results of the 1980 census were not available to the King research group. Nowhere in the King data do we have any clue about the number of retirements to come or the ages of the library professionals. These key data are missing from this report, but one can see how, with the projections available, the King study recommends that library schools examine the potential for the training of information professionals for non-library settings knowing that "traditional job opportunities for librarians are in short supply."[10]

Since I had responsibility for recruiting and placement at the Simmons College Graduate School of Library and Information Science, as soon as the King report was published, I called the Bureau of the Census for its 1980 data. In a short time, I was provided the data I believe is the key to the problem before us. The census data for 1980 reveals 183,000 working librarians.[11] One year later, the Census of Population publication, *Earnings by Occupation and Education*, provides confirmation to the higher number--a number nearly 50,000 higher than the King data.[12] (See Figure 1.)

The census data also contained the information most critical to educational planners and employers: probable retirements. It is clear that between 1980 and 2000, approximately 70,000 librarians will reach retirement age (or will have retired). (See Figure 1.) These 70,000 likely leave the labor force for other reasons. In 1975, we should remember, BLS projected 121,000 vacancies would occur between 1970 and 1985 due to deaths and retirements out of a base number of librarians of 115,000 in 1970.

Without trying to determine the numbers who will leave the profession for reasons other than retirements between 1980 and 2000, all of the library education programs in the U.S. cannot produce enough graduates over this 20 year period to replace the numbers of librarians who appear likely to retire. This is the single most critical fact before the profession at this time. (See Figure 2.)

THE NEW ENGLAND VIEW

At Simmons, we have made a sincere effort to collect data on vacancies in the six New England states (Connecticut, Maine, Massachusetts, New Hampshire, Rhode Island, and Vermont). I believe it is as complete as it can be, but it undoubtedly does not include all of the vacancies that have occurred in the six states. Vacancies posted at Simmons increased from 440 positions in 1981, to 770 positions in 1985, to over 900 vacancies posted in 1987.

In 1981, when available advice suggested that a surplus of librarians existed, we began to post increasing numbers of vacancies for the New England area, while a large number of vacancies were mailed to Simmons from around the United States on a daily basis. Clearly, something was wrong with the reports of surplus librarians in the literature in the face of the increased activity in placement at Simmons.

For the past six years we have also collected vacancies by specialization for the New England area. What began as an effort to document the increases in vacancies for youth services librarians, eventually expanded to include over 40 specializations.

At the very time that children's services vacancies were highlighted as an area of local and national need, vacancies for cataloging librarians were as numerous or more so on a year-to-year basis than nearly all other specializations. (See Table I.) While all vacancies posted at Simmons provided unparalleled opportunities for new graduates, employers were very vocal in their disappointment over the small number or, in some cases, the complete absence of applicants for posted vacancies. It was clear to me and to others that a dramatic swing had taken place from 1979 to 1981 alone. More vacancy notices than were reasonable, in light of all of the projections, appeared to be arriving at my desk for posting at Simmons.

While we may not wish to remember it, many people were asking, then, what else we could do with our library degree. At the same time some of the graduate schools were positing programs to produce information professionals for nontraditional placements. Others argued strongly that the skills taught in schools of library and information science could be and should be applied outside library settings. Much of this activity occurred when the market for librarians appeared to have diminished and library education programs, eager to survive, attempted to justify the skills of their graduates elsewhere.

THE VAN HOUSE EFFECT

A portion of the King report was completed by Nancy A. Van House. In her chapter entitled "Projections of Supply,"[13] Van House traces the number of accredited master's degrees awarded from 1954 to 1980. One of the approaches taken was to project the number of graduates as a function of market conditions over that time period. Under this approach, salary and market conditions are considered variables for people's decisions to enter the profession. For example, an increase in demand for librarians with no increase in supply will tend to increase salaries, while a larger number of librarians with low demand will decrease salaries.

Van House provided a detailed analysis of the past and demonstrated very clearly that increases in the number of graduates of accredited library schools are a function of starting salaries. Next, she provided still more convincing evidence of the strength of the relationship between the numbers of graduates and starting salaries by adjusting starting salaries for inflation.[14] (See Figure 3.)

I doubt that many paid attention to her supply analysis in 1983. In the same chapter, Van House reminded the profession that the shortage in the 1950s lasted a long time in spite of the fact that librarians were in great demand. Demand notwithstanding, the shortage did not end until salaries improved enough to make the career decision reasonable. Van House did not suggest that salaries were the only reason that individuals enter librarianship, but she agreed that it was a significant variable. More important, she proved her point.

In a second study published in 1985, Van House expanded on the thesis about the relationship between salaries and career decisions to enter librarianship. In this later study, she investigated the master's degree as an investment in terms of the time spent and the money expended to earn the degree. She concluded that, since the salaries paid to librarians are low, the decision to invest in the degree provides a poor payoff. Van House reasoned further that it would be difficult to retain experienced staff and to attract new staff as long as salaries were low. Low salaries also seemed to affect the librarian's self image.

Once again, Van House's warnings appeared to have little impact. It is most unfortunate that this is so, since she was right on the mark. Perhaps we did not want to hear or to think about what she said. But two or three years later when the shortages have become obvious, we are all asking why.

RECRUITMENT

Some library education programs make an effort to recruit students to their programs. They do this by attending career fairs at local colleges and universities, by participating in nationally sponsored career days in major U.S. cities, as well as by the usual array of colorful brochures sent in response to inquiries. It has been my contention, however, that the single most important source of recruitment has been referral by professionals in the field.

In my days as a college student in the Boston area, I worked in an academic library along with many other students. My supervisor went out of his way to interest me in the profession. By the time I was a junior in college, he was taking me along to local professional meetings and referring articles of potential interest to me about the profession. In my senior year, he called Simmons for me, scheduled my interview, and actually took me to the College for the interview.

I was not the only one in whom he demonstrated an interest. Every single student who worked for him was poked and prodded to consider librarianship as a career. It was obvious that he was pleased with his career choice, and eager for others to explore its possibilities. It seems to me that this zeal for the profession on the part of practitioners seems to have been missing for a good many years. And, I believe the result has been fewer and fewer students entering the schools and, of course, fewer graduates.

A recent survey of all of the students enrolled in library and information science programs was presented at an ALA preconference entitled, "Recruiting for the Profession," in July of 1987.[16] This survey revealed that the students' decision to go to library school was highly influenced by practicing librarians. While not the only reason potential recruits are attracted to the profession, or to a graduate library education program, this survey certainly confirms my personal experience.

THE WAY AHEAD

John Berry, Editor-in-Chief of *Library Journal*, warned in an editorial that "the shortage of librarians is back."[17] He suggested that salaries were rising as a result of the shortage and he also scolded the accredited schools for being "caught off guard again as they were with the last shortage."[18] Yet, as I have implied in this article, the projections provided to employers and educators alike did not suggest the need for additional students or graduates. Indeed, in 1975, and again in 1983, those projections provided every good reason for librarians to be cautious in making referrals of potential master's degree seekers, and for the schools to branch off and find alternate career paths for the students enrolled in their programs.

We can develop all of the recruitment brochures and schemes we have time to produce. Our past record on recruitment suggests that we concentrate on another area: salaries. The sooner that   salaries are more realistic for those entering the profession and those we wish to retain, the sooner the shortage will be reversed.

For a more graphic view of salaries, a comparison between the Consumer Price Index (CPI) and librarians' salaries is most illustrative. The starting salaries for special librarians are often thought to be the highest, if not among the highest. By using the data collected by Special Libraries Association and comparing the starting salaries reported to the CPI, however, it is clear that even these salaries have not kept pace. (See Figure 4.)

Cataloging librarians face one additional hurdle, if the data presented in the recent survey of library schools is accurate. Responses to queries about their area of specialization indicated that the majority of students in graduate school will seek positions in reference services, not in cataloging. Nearly two out of three new library school students, according to Moem's large survey, appear to favor the area of refernce above all functional areas, leaving the remaining third to consider all of the other types of vacancies.[19]

Solutions to the recruitment of a new generation of librarians in general and cataloging librarians in particular must address problems on several levels. Our best recruitment tool will be to bring librarians' salaries up to a level where we can attract new and needed members to the profession and retain our experienced members for longer periods of time. With reasonable salaries those in practice might demonstrate again their traditional and necessary role not only as zealous recruiters to the profession, but as the greatest single source for the future propagation of the profession.

NOTES

1. U.S. Bureau of Labor Statistics. *Library Manpower: A Study of Demand and Supply.* (Washington, D.C.: U.S. Government Printing Office, 1975).
2. *Library Manpower*, p. 51.
3. Ibid., p. 50.
4. King Research. *Library Human Resources: A Study of Supply and Demand.* (Chicago: American Library Association, 1983).
5. *Library Human Resources,* p. 55.
6. Ibid., p. 110.
7. Ibid., p. 123.
8. Ibid., p. 123.
9. Ibid., p. 110.
10. Ibid., p. 6.
11. U.S. Bureau of the Census. *1980 Census of Population.* (Washington, D.C.: the Bureau, 1983).
12. *1980 Census of Population*, v. 2 "Earnings by Occupation and Education." (Washington: the Bureau, 1984), p. 54.
13. Nancy A. Van House. "Projections of Supply" in *Library Human Resources 1983,* p. 88-109.
14. Ibid., p. 95-96.
15. Van House. "MLS Delivers Poor Payoff on Investment." *American Libraries* 16 (Sep. 1985):548-51.
16. W. E. Moen, "Library and Information Science Student Attitudes, Demographics and Aspirations Survey: Who We Are and Why We Are Here," in *Librarians for the New Millenium.* (Chicago: American Library Association, 1988), p. 91-109.
17. John N. Berry, III, "The Shortage of Librarians Is Back," *Library Journal* 113 (May 1, 1988):4.

18. Ibid.
19. Moen, p. 107.

The author is grateful for the assistance provided by Richard Feldman, Artemis G. Kirk, Paula Olsen and Linda Willey in the preparation of this manuscript.

Figure 1:
Total Librarians in the United States

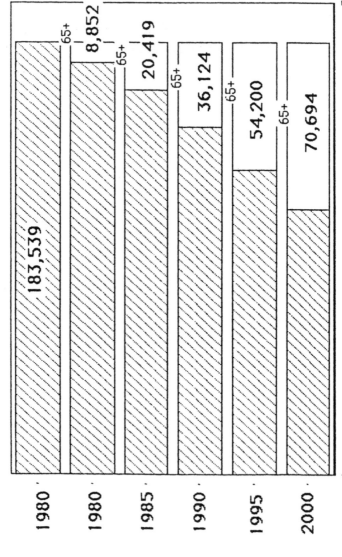

Source: U.S. Bureau of the Census.

Figure 2:
Bachelor's/Master's Degrees Conferred, Library and Archival Science

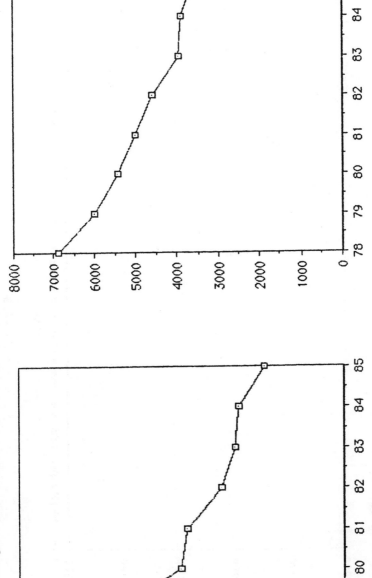

Source: U.S. Department of Education Center for Statistics.

35

Figure 3:
Relationship between Deflated Starting Salaries and Accredited MLS Degrees, 1950-1980

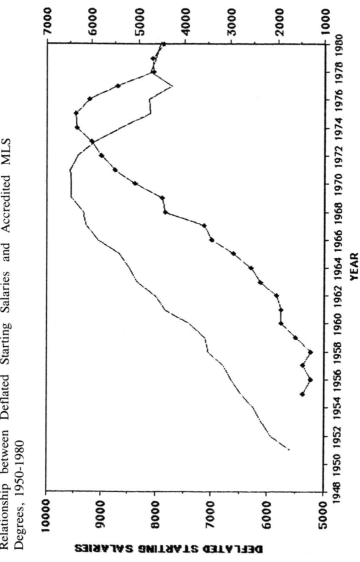

Source: Library Human Resources, 1983. A merger of data from two tables into one by James M. Matarazzo.

Figure 4:
CPI and Librarian Salaries

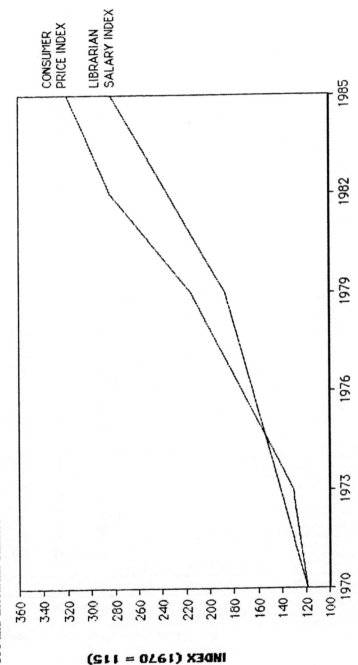

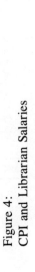

Source: Special Libraries Association Annual and Triennial Salary Surveys.

37

Table I:

New England Job Vacancies by Specialization

Job Area/Title	1983	1984	1985	1986	1987	TOTAL
TOTAL						
1. Acquisitions	5	3	9	8	12	37
2. Administration—Academic Library	29	2	19	20	31	101
3. Administration—Public Library	45	64	41	68	67	285
4. Administration—School Library Media Center	1	5	7	5	5	23
5. Administration—Special Library	5	17	3	15	21	61
6. Administration—Youth Services	12	2	0	0	3	17
7. Archivist	6	17	9	14	22	68
8. Art	5	4	4	1	3	17
9. Audio-Visual Media (non-school)	8	7	8	9	1	33
10. Bibliographic Instruction	3	4	2	2	19	30
11. Bookmobile	0	2	0	2	0	4
12. Cataloger	44	87	74	60	72	337
13. Children's	53	44	66	67	87	317
14. Church or Temple	1	0	2	0	2	5
15. Circulation	5	16	11	21	23	76
16. Collection Department*	15	7	5	9	9	45
17. Community Information & Referral	4	9	8	5	1	27
18. Conservator/Preservation	0	1	6	3	4	14
19. Correctional Institution	5	1	1	6	2	15
20. Editor	4	2	7	1	2	16
21. Government Documents	4	3	5	11	3	26
22. Information Specialist/Researcher**	46	56	45	42	50	239
23. Inter-library Loan	1	4	3	1	5	14
24. Indexer	4	1	2	1	3	11
25. Law	19	13	17	21	26	96
26. Medical	16	21	22	27	20	106
27. Music	9	5	6	6	15	41
28. Network	3	4	4	2	3	16
29. Records Management	1	1	5	5	7	19
30. Reference—Academic***	61	80	88	69	93	391
31. Reference—Public****	56	75	100	61	76	368
32. Reference—Special*****	5	21	18	12	49	105
33. Sales/Marketing Representative	2	7	11	5	1	26
34. School Library Media Center-Elementary	24	14	23	18	19	98
35. School Library Media Center-Secondary	41	24	42	23	20	150
36. School Library Media Center-Combined E/S	5	13	14	5	20	57
37. Serials	6	18	6	13	8	51
38. Service to the Handicapped	1	0	0	0	1	2
39. Special Collections******	7	8	8	6	8	37
40. State Library Agency	6	6	9	8	5	34
41. Systems/Automated Specialist	23	29	11	43	29	135
42. Technical Services	38	44	36	42	53	213
43. Young Adult	12	7	10	8	15	52
44. Youth Services (Children & Young Adult)	4	3	4	18	3	32
TOTAL POSITIONS IN YEAR	644	751	771	763	918	3847

* includes Subject Bibliographer
** in Special Libraries & Information Industry
*** includes Public Services Librarian
**** includes Adult Services, Generalist, Information Specialist & Reader Services
***** exclusive of Information Specialist (22)
****** includes Rare Book & Map Librarian

Recruiting, What Next?

Liz Bishoff

Directors of technical services departments, heads of cataloging and library directors in almost every type of library for the past five years, have expressed concern about the lack of catalogers, most particularly, the lack of well qualified catalogers--catalogers who not only have the traditional cataloging skills and knowledge, but who also are technologically savvy with strong management and leadership skills. At the same time, we have heard similar cries from libraries requiring children's services, or expertise in science and technology. The shortage of librarians in these fields was the topic of the October 15, 1988 *Library Journal* editorial[1], and has been the focus of a Library Services and Contruction Act funded study in California, and the source of preconference and conference meetings for the past 12 to 18 months. This seminar focuses on the many issues related to recruiting, educating, and training catalogers, and practitioners are faced with the problem of filling the cataloging and technical service librarian positions they currently have.

BACKGROUND OF THE PROBLEM

Before we consider solutions to recruiting candidates for today's cataloging positions, a review of the conditions that created the current shortage is required. The library recruiting environment, in the late 1980's, is a result of library activities of the past 20 years. Through the mid-1960's, libraries were relatively stagnant and growth was limited, particularily in school and public libraries. Interlibrary loan and resource sharing was limited to information provided in the *National Union Catalog* and educated guessing, and federal and state funding was practically non-existent. In the mid-1960's, support for libraries began to be fueled by the Library Services and Construction Act. There were dramatic increases in the number of libraries, the role of libraries in all sectors, the number of titles acquired and a dramatic increase in resource sharing. As a result of the increased support for libraries, there was an increase in the need for libraries to catalog the large number of titles being added to their collections. In response to the increased demand for librarians, library school enrollments increased and new library schools were established and accredited.

By 1975, there was a surplus of librarians. Libraries were faced with financial constraints pushed by double digit inflation, reduction in staff due to automation, and the looming effects of legislated funding reductions, such as California's Proposition 13 and Massachusetts' Proposition 2 1/2. At the same time, alternative career options for our traditional pool, college educated women, were being offered. The fields of law, medicine and business began to attract many college educated women. Concurrently, the bibliographic services, OCLC, WLN, and RLIN were developing. Libraries discovered that they required fewer catalogers as paraprofessionals were trained to handle Library of Congress (LC) cataloging copy and eventually member contributed cataloging. Typing and sorting cards was eliminated, while revision of copy or blanket acceptance of LC copy have changed staffing patterns and requirements.

With the decreased demand for professional cataloging librarians, there was a decline in library school enrollment, most notably in cataloging. Students and library schools learned quickly that the cataloger's role in the library was reduced in proportion to the original cataloging required, and fewer jobs meant a reduction in the need for new catalogers. Library schools no longer counselled students to become catalogers; rather they directed them into public service, online database searching, records management and library administration. Other responses to this perceived decrease in need for catalogers was the elimination of required cataloging courses which made room for the new courses needed to prepare students for the areas where jobs were available. At the same time, the content in the remaining cataloging courses grew larger, including training in MARC formats, new cataloging rules, and a new emphasis on the management of technical services departments.

The growth of the bibliographic services was followed closely by the beginning of local systems development. In 1973, the first turnkey circulation system was introduced. In these early days, the role of the technical services librarian was limited to directing the retrospective conversion of the collection, but that limited involvement was short lived. As the availability of these circulation systems moved out to the reference desks, the need for standardized records containing more information grew. These early systems evolved from their brief records to full MARC cataloging, with author, title and subject access. The creation and management of these systems required knowledge of how to organize, retrieve, and display information, the skills possessed by catalogers and technical service librarians.

By 1988, there were many local systems on the market and an ever increasing number of libraries procuring these systems. The April 1, 1988 *Library Journal* reported more than 1400 local systems had been installed in U.S. libraries.[2] The vast majority of these systems are based on MARC formatted bibliographic and authority records, are supported by tapes and records transferred from bibliographic services. Where the cataloger or technical service librarian's involvement was originally limited to the retrospective conversion of the records, they are now involved with the design of the system from the Request For Proposal stage through to installation and user training. The demand for the expertise and knowledge of the technical services librarian has grown along with the growth of local systems.

At the same time that libraries need the expertise and knowledge of the cataloger, so do the local system vendors, publishers who provide automated support to libraries, networks, and the bibliographic services. These organizations are hiring technical services librarians for system design and analysis, user support, product development, sales and project management. So while the supply of catalogers was low coming into the mid-1980's, the demand was escalating. Catalogers were now needed to fill their traditional role of original cataloging, department management and staff training, as well as new responsibilities in system administration, design and system analysis.

RECRUITING FOR THE LIBRARY MARKET

Libraries have used the traditional approaches to recruiting, including advertising in local newspapers and professional journals, notifying graduate school placement offices of available positions, on-campus recruiting, placement services at library conferences and word of mouth. Depending on the level of staff required for the position, different recruiting options are selected. Although recruiting is a year-round activity, one sees greater activity around the time of the national library conferences, especially the American Library Association, Special Library Association and Medical Library Association. Activity also peaks for academic and school libraries in the spring and summer months, assuring staff availability by the start of the academic year. While these approaches to recruiting are successful during periods of high supply and low demand, a more creative and assertive approach to recruiting is required during times of low supply and high demand.

WHAT ARE WE RECRUITING FOR?

Recruiting approaches will vary with the position the library or organization needs to fill. Entry level catalogers can be recruited through graduate school placement programs, conference placement services and job ads in local newspapers and professional journals. Heads of cataloging, assistant directors for technical services will require more far reaching recruiting including advertising in newspapers with a nationwide circulation, in professional journals, through specialized journals, as well as joblines. In many cases, the most effective means of recruiting this level of personnel is through word of mouth. One mentions to a colleague that a position is open and ask if they know any well qualified candidates. Other strategies include writing personal letters to potential candidates announcing the availability of the position, and asking the individual who is not interested to pass the notice of the position along to another qualified librarian. The more specialized expertise that is required, the more difficult it may be to fill the position, and the more creative the recruiting must be. Local system vendors are hiring librarians who ran installations of their system or heads of technical services to provide user support, training and system design in the cataloging and authorities services. Libraries are also hiring good staff members away from other libraries with the same system.

Today libraries are looking for individuals with experience in online cataloging, local systems, system design experience, experience in management of the procurement procedure, and management of technical services. The November, 1988 *American Libraries* listed cataloging positions with the following requirements:

(1)   For an entry level cataloger for an academic library: "...Knowledge of MARC formats, AACR2, LC Classification, LCSH, and automated systems. Preference will be given to candidates with experience in ... Automated systems, and with a demonstrated interest in cataloging;"[3]

(2)   For the position of head of automated cataloging in an academic library: "...Demonstrated supervisory skills. Knowledge of MARC formats, *AACR2*, LC rule interpretations, and *Library of Congress Subject Headings* required. Must have experience with OCLC or similar

bibliographic utility. Experience with NOTIS desirable."[4]

(3) For a technical services division manager in a public library: "...management experience in a technical services operation and working knowledge of computerized circulation and online cataloging systems and OCLC.... Experience with or knowledge of systems analysis techniques highly desirable."[5]

(4) For the staff of a local system vendor: "...working knowledge of library automation; 2-5 years technical services experience; excellent verbal and written communications skills."[6]

Technical services librarians are now supervising cataloging, acquisitions and processing departments, automated services, and sometimes circulation and interlibrary loan. Clearly, the range of responsibilities of the cataloging and technical services librarian has grown from what it was in the mid-1960's and our recruiting approaches must also change.

CREATIVE RECRUITING

Today recruiting must be multi-faceted. We cannot expect to post a position at a conference and obtain a sufficient pool of candidates to make a selection. The rules of the game and the situation have changed. Recruiting is now a year-round activity. Libraries cannot wait until individuals complete their graduate training to attract them to cataloging. Libraries need to work closely with graduate schools on a regular basis, providing information on career opportunities in cataloging at their individual library. This can be accomplished by arranging to talk to the cataloging classes or the graduate student campus recruitment. Scheduling the presentation the day before the interviews will assure a larger pool of candidates for the next day's recruiting activities. While some of these students may not be appropriate for your current position, they may be likely candidates for future openings.

Another approach is to meet with the library school faculty to discuss the opportunities at your institution. Arrange for a visit to the library, showing the various activities that the staff are involved in. Offer to make presentations to library classes on different activities. For example, if you have installed an online public access catalog, a presentation can be made on the design of the screens, or discussion of the installation process, staff and user training, or the procurement process. Library school faculty are eager to a have 'real' librarian meet with their classes.

Developing a strong working relationship with the faculty of area library schools will benefit both the library and the library school. The library school faculty will be able to recommend graduates that will meet the library's particular needs. Word of mouth recruiting between the library school and the library is very successful, especially when the library school faculty understand the libraries' staffing requirements.

Exposing graduate students to the different opportunities available to them is another non-traditional means of recruiting. While many library schools offer practicum programs, which place students in libraries under closely supervised conditions, these programs are generally viewed as a curricular activity, not as a recruiting activity. During the spring of 1987, the Pasadena Public Library, Los Angeles County Public Library and the Lancaster Public Library hosted approximately 35 graduate students from UCLA to a one-day tour of the three libraries. UCLA had been placing a large number of graduates in academic and special libraries, but few students were interested in public librarianship. In order to increase their recruitment of UCLA graduates, the three libraries felt the students needed exposure to public libraries and librarians. Each library focused on a special program--children's services, online reference services, outreach services. I was given the opportunity to describe technical services and automation activities during the bus trip between libraries. The libraries hosted a luncheon at the Rose Bowl, various brochures were distributed, the students were given brief exposures to the variety of activities in the public library and were introduced to practicing librarians.

MORE ASSERTIVE RECRUITING

With the shortage of librarians, position postings and advertisements need to be made more attractive. In recent months, libraries have been placing notices of open houses to be hosted when a conference is in their city. Librarians interested in the institution are introduced to its career opportunities at these receptions. During American Library Association annual and midwinter meetings major libraries and library organizations set up permanent tables at the placement centers, staff them with representatives knowledgable about the organization and its staffing needs. Glossy brochures are prepared, showing the programs and activities of the library, discussing the benefits of joining the organization, as well as job descriptions and application forms. Other libraries have developed eye catching posters announcing career opportunities. Broad-based distribution of position postings between colleagues have become commonplace at committee meetings, discussion groups sessions, and user group meetings.

To obtain candidates for more senior positions, those with extensive managerial or technical expertise, libraries are using executive search firms, called head hunters. These organizations identify the exact skills and requirements of the position, potential sources of candidates, and develop a recruiting and selection program. Search firms will employ a variety of standard recruitment activities, however, the most effective tool is contacting people in the field and asking for names of individuals who might be suited for the position. These firms do the time consuming preliminary interviewing and will present a final list from which the library can select a finalist. The cost of this type of recruiting varies and generally is justifiable only for the most senior positions.

Recruiting for a non-library organization is not dissimilar from recruiting to fill a library position, except that it is more difficult. Catalogers do not see that their cataloging skills can be transferred to system design, project management, or user training. The challenge in recruiting for positions in this type of organization is communicating to the candidate or potential candidate that the non-library position could fulfill many of their career goals. For example, during a recruiting visit to a graduate school, I interviewed a graduate student with eight years of experience in retrospective conversion. During our discussion she indicated that she enjoyed planning the retrospective conversion projects and looking for new approaches to solve retrospective conversion problems. I was seeking a product support specialist in cataloging, but this person appeared to be an excellent candidate for the retrospective conversion marketing representative, where she would meet with libraries interested in retrospective conversion. Ultimately, this recruiting visit was considered a success, as she accepted the marketing representative position.

OTHER OPTIONS

In addition to alternative recruiting options, libraries are also examining their selection criteria. In general, all cataloging positions require knowledge of current cataloging standards, *Anglo-American Cataloguing Rules, Library of Congress Subject Headings*, Library of Congress classification, and the MARC formats. Language requirements and additional subject master's degrees could be required for some positions, while local systems and retrospective conversion experience might be required for other positions. Some of these skills must be acquired in graduate programs, while others can be obtained on the job in a professional or a paraprofessional position. Traditionally, OCLC has recruited librarians with extensive cataloging and format experience. When we found that we could not fill positions with format expertise, we began looking at our requirements. Could we hire generalist catalogers? Could we hire individuals who were recent graduates, but who had extensive paraprofessional experience? Could we establish a program of 'growing our own' catalogers, bringing in entry level catalogers and developing a program of internal career growth. The internal training program could be modeled on the programs established by large corporations. Selected graduates of business administration programs who have identified an interest and potential in management, are placed in a lengthy training program. Management trainees enter a six to twelve month program where they spend one to two months in each department. At the end of the training period, the trainee can select the area of greatest interest for their permanent placement.

Availability of this type of program would allow organizations that require cataloging to hire recent graduates and train them for their particular needs. Clearly all three options are needed to meet the increased demand for qualified catalogers.

CONCLUSION

I have attempted to identify some creative recruiting ideas to solve the current problem of availability of catalogers and technical services librarians. Certainly, they are not a comprehensive list, but rather some options that librarians can try if they suit their situation. Additionally, I hope that they will cause everyone to rethink their recruiting approach.

I hope I have demonstrated that we need to smooth this roller coaster ride of supply and demand. We need to develop recruiting programs that will not leave us in the situation we find ourselves today--significant demand that has been growing for the past five years, and a supply that is insufficient for both today and the near future. For, where today we cannot find entry level catalogers, system designers, or acquisition librarians,in five years, we will not have a sufficient pool of qualified managers, senior designers, and trainers. Today's deficits will have a ripple affect and be felt for years to come.

NOTES

1. John N. Berry, III, "Salaries and Shortages: If You Can Get Away With It, Give 'em the Money!" *Library Journal* (October 15, 1988):4.

2. Frank R. Bridge and Robert Walton, "Automated System Marketplace 1987: Maturity and Competition." *Library Journal* (April 1, 1988):33-44.

3. Beverly Goldberg and Debbie McDade. eds., "Career Leads, American Libraries Classified Ads." *American Libraries* (November, 1988):861.

4.   Ibid, p. 872.
5.   Ibid, p. 875.
6.   Ibid, p. 879.

Recruitment, a Positive Process

D. Whitney Coe

Recruitment is a very personal activity. It allows the technical service librarian to approach the problem of the shortage of qualified catalogers with a variety of creative techniques to reach a successful solution. An analysis of the recruitment practices followed at the Princeton University Library over the past five years indicates that recruitment may begin with the encouragement of promising members of the library support staff and continues with the development of closer relations with neighboring library schools.

DEVELOPMENT OF SUPPORT STAFF

One strong pool of candidates for recruitment into the profession is the library's support staff. The individual often already has made a decision to seek employment in this particular environment. The work experience, when utilizing his or her skills appropriately, may confirm those original impressions. Then, if the institution can provide support either with financial aid and/or compensatory time, a strong candidate for a future vacancy can be developed.

The library must rely upon its institution's benefits policy in this situation. Most academic institutions provide for some kind of educational program for its staff. Princeton University, normally not accepting part-time graduate students, introduced a new program for staff educational assistance, effective July 1, 1988: "The new plan will be a reimbursement program which will cover tuition expenses up to $3000 per year. After successful completion of a course, 85 percent of the tuition will be reimbursed. The plan will cover courses which are job related or which may be job related in the future. Other plan parameters include a limit of two courses per semester and elimination of coverage for books and fees."[1] This permits a library staff member to pursue the MLS while working. The Personnel Librarian explains these benefits to any support staff member who expresses an interest in pursuing the MLS as well as to any individual seeking a position on the support staff with a similar interest. It is made clear that there is no guarantee of appointment to a professional position upon completion of the degree.

In the past five years, two vacancies in the Catalog Division were filled by individuals who were in the process of completing their master's degrees. One cataloger was hired in a part-time position after seven years on the support staff in the Technical Services Department. During the final three years, she attended library school on a part-time basis. The second cataloger was hired after serving for four years as a support staff member in two public services positions in branch libraries. Again, the library degree took three years to complete. Although it was not her original goal to enter technical services, the value of cataloging was continually emphasized by her supervisors so she was attracted to the vacancy in the Catalog Division when it occurred. We at Princeton anticipate that support staff will continue to provide a strong pool of candidates for future vacancies in the Catalog Division.

The role model presented by the professional cataloger can have its effect upon another category of non-professional library worker—the student assistant. Many library careers were initiated under the tutelage of an interested professional librarian.

One technique used to encourage interest among the support staff and to make them aware of the possibilities of a career as a professional librarian is inviting a faculty member from a neighboring library school to talk about program requirements and courses. An informal setting, such as the brown bag lunch, offers a suitable format.

RELATIONSHIPS WITH THE NEIGHBORING LIBRARY SCHOOL

Recruitment to cataloging, in particular, requires a close relationship between the professional cataloger and the library school faculty. A number of techniques can be used to strengthen these relationships. The visit to the library school by a member of the Catalog Division of the Princeton University Library has been one basic and successful practice. In the most recent visits, the cataloger has presented a two-pronged approach—why the library school student should seek a job in cataloging; and, secondly, why consider a job in the Princeton University Library Catalog Division.

The professional cataloger has a number of positive elements to emphasize when speaking to prospective catalogers. First, the shortage of qualified catalogers is an advantage for them. There are more job opportunities available in cataloging than in public services and, since the size of the pool is smaller, the applicant's individual qualifications can surface more clearly. Second, cutting-edge technology is most apparent in technical services. Since this technology is often still in its formative stages, catalogers have a unique opportunity for direct input and can have an important impact on system design. As systems move from generation to generation, this opportunity will continue to exist. Third, cataloging, as an intellectual process, offers much variety. Cataloging problems may result from similar situations, but no two problems are exactly the same. Good detective work often is a necessity and analytical skills are essential. Fourth, because the size of the staff is larger in technical services and there are more levels of staff, there is more potential for developing one's managerial skills. Finally, the skills developed in cataloging are highly transferable. Career paths are open for advancement in either technical services or public services. Technical services skills, especially cataloging, remain central to successful service in any information retrieval system.

The second part of the presentation emphasizes what the Princeton University Library Catalog Division offers the new library school graduate. Chief among the points described is the training the Catalog Division will provide. It is not expected that the new graduate will be immediately productive as a cataloger, and approximately one year of intensive training is anticipated. This is a major commitment on the part of the Library and the University since it involves not only the cost of the new cataloger but also that of the trainer/reviser. New catalogers are trained in all aspects of cataloging, including description, subject analysis and classification, and MARC tagging. The level of detail and the attention and close adherence to national standards imparted by this training is a result of Princeton's participation in the Research Libraries Group (RLG) and major national projects as the National Coordinated Cataloging Operations (NACO).

Princeton also offers considerable exposure to several automated systems and the cataloger can expect extensive experience and training on each: Geac for acquisitions and circulation; RLIN for cataloging and interlibrary loan; and Carlyle for online public access. These skills, once learned, are all transferable.

The organization of the Catalog Division into Cataloging Teams is described. The facts that the Catalog Division is not a static group and has an atmosphere of change that creates opportunities for further growth and development are emphasized. Library school students are advised of any specific job opportunities available at the moment as well as the general requirements necessary for employment: working knowledge of at least one European language, flexibility and self-motivation. Procedures for applying for a vacancy are covered, including the role of the resume and cover letter. These presentations usually are given before a technical services/cataloging class, but arrangements are made for individual students who are not in that class or who want further information. They can talk privately with the cataloger.

A reverse visit can be equally effective, i.e., the visit of the technical services/cataloging class from a neighboring library school to Princeton's Firestone Library. This allows students to observe first-hand the work flow in a functioning technical services department. Such a visit might begin with the Order Division, covering the automated acquisitions system for monographs and serials, explanation of the operation of the approval plans, claiming, and invoicing, and the sorting for distribution of newly arrived titles. This would be followed in the Catalog Division with an analysis of the work flow and holds of the Cataloging Teams, online cataloging, quality control and authority work, and the role of the Online Processing Unit that catalogs titles with LC copy directly upon receipt. Also included should be a description of the Database Management Section with record creation and maintenance, and database interface. It should conclude with an examination of the catalogs, both card and online, and the circulation, shelving and reserve book departments. This exposure gives students a context for the more theoretical nature of their course work. Details to be covered in such visits should be determined mutually by the librarian and the library school instructor.

INTERNSHIPS IN THE CATALOGING DEPARTMENT

The library school internship has offered another route for students to professional cataloging jobs. The carefully designed internship offers a balance of work accomplished for the library and practical experience gained by the student. This work must be meaningful and supervision attentive to the student's needs. The potential intern is screened and given a thorough interview, which helps insure the program's success. In the past five years, the Princeton University Library Catalog Division has worked with three library school interns.

The first intern lived in the Princeton area and knew she wanted to work in a large academic research library. She encouraged her library school to contact Princeton and then divided a total of about 140 hours of work between the Database Management Section and the Serials Division. When a vacancy occurred six months later, she was a strong and successful candidate for the Slavic/Germanic Languages Cataloging Team. The second intern filled a cataloging vacancy in the Gest Oriental Library. There was no appropriate cataloging vacancy, however, when the third intern initially sought employment; but, the experience was a positive factor in the intern's search. Thus, library school internships have been beneficial both to students and to Firestone Library.

CATALOGER AS FACULTY MEMBER

A rare opportunity exists when the practicing cataloger can teach a course in the neighboring library school. This occurred recently when a new Princeton cataloger with a Ph.D. in Linguistics and two and a half years of teaching experience was asked to teach a course in cataloging for large libraries in a neighboring library school. The benefits for everyone involved are obvious.

All of these techniques depend upon a close relationship between the library and the neighboring library school. Any of them can be initiated by a concerned professional from either institution.

OTHER OPTIONS

An individual librarian can work with regional or state library associations, too. For example, a local organization, New York Technical Services Librarians (NYTSL), annually sponsors a student reception so that library school students can meet and talk with members of the profession. (Occasionally, the local chapter of the American Library Association's Association of College and Research Libraries co-sponsors this event.) Also, a student from each of the neighboring library schools is invited free of charge to NYTSL's fall and spring meetings, which are highlighted by an informal social hour, dinner, and a guest speaker who addresses a topic of concern to technical service librarians. The value of personal relationships in gatherings such as these can never be ignored.

RECRUITMENT AT PRINCETON UNIVERSITY LIBRARY

Today, the process of recruitment can be discouraging. Without question, the size of the pools for cataloging vacancies has steadily declined in the recent past and the number of qualified candidates appears more limited. Ten to fifteen years ago, pools of 75 to 100 applicants for a cataloging position were not unusual. It was a difficult task to select the top candidates who would be invited for the interview from those very good candidates who could be held in reserve. Now, the luxury provided by such numbers has evaporated. In the past five years, the size of the pools has varied from 38 for a beginning position with a general modern European language requirement to only three for a beginning position with a very specific (and more esoteric) language requirement. Generally, the pools have fluctuated between ten and fifteen applicants. The entire process has become much more competitive.

Nevertheless, a vacancy should be treated as an opportunity. It permits the administrators in the Catalog Division to reassess its cataloging needs and priorities and to reexamine the work flows within the Division. Flexibility in staffing is essential, allowing free movement of the current staff to meet new work assignments. Over the past five years, it would have been considered unusual if there was not some shift in personnel to allow for adjustments to meet current priorities as well as to take advantage of the opportunities resulting from a particular candidate pool. It is important to remember that candidates for each vacancy will bring different qualifications to the position and only an organization with flexibility can benefit from blending any particular mix of new talents with the existing talents on its staff.

It is critical that the general library administration support such flexibility. Having this commitment, the administration of the Princeton University Library Catalog Division will not hold a vacancy indefinitely until a qualified applicant is found. For example, three months after the date of a resignation, if no suitable candidate can be identified, the search for a replacement staff member is re-evaluated. The possibility of internal shifts is examined. Current needs are reassessed and the job description may be rewritten. Then, when a candidate qualified for the original vacancy does appear, every means is taken to fill the gap in expertise as quickly as possible. The most important first step, however, is the reassessment of divisional needs.

The second major step in recruitment, following assessment of the division's needs, is the drafting of the vacancy announcement. Normally, this announcement includes the position title, date of availability, job description, qualifications, benefits, salary and rank, the cut-off date, and the name of the individual to whom the application should be sent. The Personnel Librarian then sends each vacancy announcement to the following institutions: all accredited library schools; all Association of Research Library member libraries; and approximately twenty minority recruitment agencies (both nationally and locally). The annual list of American Library Association-affiliated organizations with minority focus, prepared by the ALA Office for Library Personnel Resources (OLPR), is most useful in minority recruitment, to which Princeton University is committed. All vacancy announcements also are sent to the *Chronicle of Higher Education* and *Library Hotline*. They are also circulated to members of the Princeton University Library staff.

If the vacancy requires a special expertise, then the appropriate association is contacted, e.g., the Music Library Association (MLA) for a music cataloger, Middle East Studies Association (MESA) and Middle East Librarians Association (MELA) for a Near East cataloger, and American Association for the Advancement of Slavic Studies (AAASS) for a Slavic cataloger. The Personnel Librarian does not maintain a list of persons who have expressed an interest in obtaining a professional library position at Princeton, but these people are advised that they may contact the Library Personnel Office to check on available positions at any time. When someone first contacts the Personnel Librarian, this procedure is explained and any current vacancies are identified.

Interviews with the 13 catalogers hired in the past five years and still on the Catalog Division staff illustrate the effectiveness of Princeton's recruitment procedures and also demonstrate another powerful factor at work in the recruitment process: the role of personal relationships. Two catalogers first became aware of Princeton vacancies during their student days through job postings at their respective library schools. Two more benefited from the practices of the Personnel Librarian, one checking the listing of library vacancies in the Personnel Office until a cataloging vacancy occurred and the other receiving a response to a letter inquiring about possible vacancies. Our music cataloger saw the job announcement in a listing of the Music Library Association. Another was informed of the vacancy by a friend who knew she was interested in changing jobs. The two former support staff members arrived at their positions by different routes. One saw the announcement as it was circulated to the Princeton University Library staff and the other, seeking a part-time position, inquired to find that another cataloger returning from child-bearing leave also wanted a part-time position. Accommodating both people, the position was split.

The personal element was basic in filling the other five cataloging vacancies. Two successful candidates were contacted directly by Princeton librarians—one a cataloger and the other a bibliographer—when vacancies occurred. Two others had applied for other positions in the library and were asked if they would be interested in applying for the cataloging vacancy when the original position was filled. The thirteenth cataloger was found when he visited the library, and, once it was determined that he would be interested in cataloging at Princeton, a position was funded by the Near East Department to permit the search to be conducted. Personal contacts were most significant when the vacant position required exceptionally rare language skills. A willingness to remain flexible made it possible to fill the most challenging vacancy when the opportunity arose.

These are the success stories. A look at the failures and our responses to them also is revealing. During the winter of 1986 and the spring of 1987, two searches were unsuccessful and resulted in a reassessment of the vacancies. One search yielded two potential candidates, but both ended up rejecting the employment offer, so the search was merely reopened. The second job description included a requirement of modern Greek, which appeared to complicate the search. Finally, the requirement had to be dropped. A careful review of the vacancy announcement was done at this time and a major change in the wording was deliberately made (see Examples 1 and 2). As shown by comparison of Examples 1 and 2, a new paragraph was added to the job description. Its intent was to emphasize the positives the Princeton University Library Catalog Division could offer the prospective cataloger. Among the advantages pointed out are: the strong foundation for a career in academic librarianship which is offered by an entry-level position in cataloging; the extensive training which will be provided by the Catalog Division; and the experience with various technologies that would be available. Interviews with the five most recently hired catalogers show that these were important factors to the candidates in their consideration of Princeton. Four were particularly influenced by the promise of extensive training and two were strongly influenced by the prospects of online cataloging opportunities. A job announcement that shows the candidate what the library and, in particular, what the cataloging group has to offer has positive effects.

Princeton University Library has not utilized the American Library Association placement services in any recent searches beyond giving these services any current vacancy announcements. Generally, it is a matter of timing—midwinter and annual conferences have not coincided with any vacancies. Interviewing prospective candidates at these conferences would only be an exploratory meeting and would not replace the interview on campus.

While vacancy announcements are being distributed, a small search committee is established, chaired by the appropriate Cataloging Team Leader. The committee reviews all the applications and determines which candidates will be invited to campus for the interview. The Catalog Librarian remains involved on a consultative basis to make sure the process is kept moving and that the interests of the Division in retaining its flexibility are considered. Arrangements are then made for several candidates to visit Princeton.

The candidate is given a full one-day interview (see Example 3). Not only is the Princeton University library administration and staff interviewing the candidate, but the candidate is interviewing the library. The candidate meets with library administrators as well as with those individuals who will be responsible for direct training, supervision and evaluation. An online cataloging demonstration and a tour of Technical Services help to provide the candidate with a sense of the environment in which he or she will be working. Most importantly, time is scheduled for the interviewee to have an opportunity to relax and meet, informally, some of the individuals with whom he or she will be working. Again, the process reflects the role of personal relationships in effective recruitment.

When the process of recruitment—whether it is recruitment to the library profession as a whole or to cataloging as a professional activity specifically, or is recruitment to a particular library's catalog department, is viewed as an opportunity which can be influenced by one's personal involvement, the result will end as a positive, not a negative, experience.

NOTES

1. "Benefits News," (Princeton University, Personnel Services,Spring 1988), p. 1.

EXAMPLE 1

1985 VACANCY ANNOUNCEMENT

PLEASE POST
PRINCETON UNIVERSITY LIBRARY
PRINCETON, NEW JERSEY

Position: CATALOGUER, ROMANCE LANGUAGES CATALOGUING TEAM, LIBRARIAN I or II

Available: Immediately

Description: Responsible for original cataloguing (descriptive and subject) and classifying of monographic publications in Romance languages and a variety of formats covering all areas of the humanities and social sciences. Prepares cataloguing for input into the RLIN computer database. Revises and modifies RLIN member copy to conform with Princeton cataloguing. Performs related tasks such as correction of catalogue records as conflicts arise. Assists in general department duties as necessary.

Qualifications: MLS from ALA accredited library school required. Strong reading knowledge of one or more Romance Languages: Spanish, French, Italian, or Portuguese. Broad subject background in the social sciences and/or humanities. Knowledge of Anglo-American Cataloguing Rules, 2nd edition, and Library of Congress classification and

	subject headings. Ability to work effectively with other Library staff.
Benefits:	Twenty-four (24) vacation days a year, plus eleven (11) paid holidays. Annuity program (TIAA/CREF), group life insurance, health coverage insurance, and disability insurance, all paid for by the University.
Salary and Rank:	Dependent upon qualifications and experience.

Applications, including resume and the names, titles, addresses and phone numbers of three references to be contacted, should be postmarked by November 15, 1985, and sent to:

Cataloguer Search Committee
c/o Maria G. Gopel
Personnel Librarian
Princeton University Library
Princeton, NJ 08544

PRINCETON UNIVERSITY IS AN EQUAL
OPPORTUNITY/AFFIRMATIVE
ACTION EMPLOYER.

EXAMPLE 2

1988 VACANCY ANNOUNCEMENT

PLEASE POST
PRINCETON UNIVERSITY LIBRARY
PRINCETON, NEW JERSEY

Position: CATALOGER, LIBRARIAN I, Modern
                   Greek and Romance Languages
Available: Immediately
Description: Performs original subject and descriptive
                   cataloging of monographs in modern Greek
                   and the Romance Languages using the RLIN
                   database, AACR2, Library of Congress
                   subject headings and classification. Prepares
                   authority records for input to the Library of
                   Congress Name Authorities File. Revises
                   RLIN member copy to conform with
                   national cataloging standards. Resolves
                   problems, performs general departmental
                   duties and participates in special projects as
                   needed.

                   This is an entry-level position on the
                   Romance Languages Cataloging Team
                   offering a strong foundation for a career in
                   academic librarianship. Princeton
                   University Library is a major research
                   library which catalogs approximately 70,000
                   titles a year with a cataloging staff of 25
                   professionals and 12 support staff. The
                   Catalog Division provides extensive training

for new staff in all areas of cataloging and is a leader in NACO participation and in the development of online cataloging applications. Princeton is a pilot library for the Carlyle online catalog and is heavily involved in the development of this exciting new system.

Qualifications: MLS from ALA accredited library school required. Subject background in the humanities, social sciences or area studies preferred. Strong working knowledge of modern Greek and the Romance Languages required. Applicants should have a strong interest in bibliographic control of library materials, good analytical skills, the ability to adapt in a rapidly-changing automated environment and the ability to work effectively with other library staff.

Benefits: Twenty-four (24) vacation days a year, plus eleven (11) paid holidays. Annuity program (TIAA/CREF), group life insurance, health coverage insurance, and disability insurance, all paid for by the University.

Salary and
Rank: In a range having a floor of $22,000, depending upon qualifications and experience.

Applications, including resume and the names, titles, addresses and phone numbers of three references to be contacted, should be postmarked by October 15, 1988, and sent to:

Cataloger Search Committee
c/o Maria G. Gopel
Personnel Librarian
Princeton University Library
One Washington Road
Princeton, NJ 08544

PRINCETON UNIVERSITY IS AN EQUAL
OPPORTUNITY/AFFIRMATIVE
ACTION EMPLOYER.

EXAMPLE 3

Interview Schedule for
James L.
Friday, April 29, 1988

9:00-9:30	Online Cataloging Demonstration with Gabrielle Arno, Cataloger, Slavic/Germanic Cataloging Team
9:30-10:00	Meeting with Don Thornbury, Assistant Catalog Librarian
10:00-10:45	Coffee break with: Patti Kosco, Cataloger, Sci-Tech/Social Sciences Cataloging Team Luisa Paster, Database Management Section Librarian Richard Phillips, Leader, Romance Languages Cataloging Team Kathy Van de Vate, Cataloger, Near East Cataloging Team
10:45-11:15	Meeting with Donald W. Koepp, University Librarian
11:15-11:45	Meeting with Glendon Odell, Deputy University Librarian
11:45-1:15	Lunch with: Nina Shapiro, Leader, Slavic/Germanic Cataloging Team Alan P. Pollard, Slavic Bibliographer
1:30-2:00	Meeting with Richard Schulz, Catalog Librarian

2:00-2:30   Meeting with Nancy S. Klath, Associate University Librarian for Technical Services

2:30-3:00   Tour of Technical Services with David Johnson, Leader, Serials Cataloging Team

3:00-   Interview with Search Committee — Slavic Reading Room: Nina Shapiro; Gabrielle Arno; David Johnson Rhoda Kesselman, Cataloger, Sci-Tech/Social Sciences Cataloging Team

Are We Teaching Dinosaurs to Forage: Recruiting Catalogers to the Profession

Elizabeth Futas and Fay Zipkowitz

INTRODUCTION

Our approach to the recruitment of catalogers into the profession comes from the library educators' point of view. It has two major directions, both based upon outreach from the library school (specifically, the University of Rhode Island Graduate School of Library and Information Studies) to the library community. The first is a direct appeal and a presentation, particularly in a library setting, to potential students; the second is an appeal to library professionals whose work settings are the breeding ground for career decisions. These librarians have professional contacts and professional activities where their attitudes, competences and behaviors are carried out of the work place and into the wider library setting, and perhaps beyond to the general public in the world at large.

THE PROBLEM

There is general agreement within the profession, bolstered in recent years by a spate of articles and advertisements for positions, that there is a genuine shortage of librarians entering the area of cataloging as their specialty. It is not the only area of shortage (witness children's and young adult librarianship and school media specialists) but it is one which is becoming increasingly important in the age of technological advances in this specialty. The need for newly educated professionals who have been trained both in the new technology and in modern cataloging standards and responsibilities, whose vision goes beyond what catalogers of twenty years ago dreamed of becomes urgent for the twenty-first century.

Library educators have known for some time that the number of students entering the cataloging field is decreasing, and that electives in the area of cataloging are regarded by students as among the more esoteric courses in the library school's curriculum. Many library schools have dropped the cataloging requirement altogether, and therefore general library school graduates are ill-equipped to apply for cataloging positions, because they do not even have the basic coursework upon which to build a foundation of further on-the-job training. Cataloging is not viewed as the place to be for today's professionals. It can be argued that these statements are too one-sided: many library schools still do teach cataloging as a requirement (ours, for one), many advanced cataloging courses do still exist in library school curricula (as they do in ours), and the increased availability and use of cataloging copy from bibliographic networks reduces the need for individuals who can do original cataloging. These arguments are all true to some extent, but perceptions of shortages of catalogers are seen to be more than just perceptions when viewed against the job ads section of almost any issue of *American Libraries* or *Library Journal*, where there are many listings for professionals with just these skills and with just such training. Employers know that these positions are difficult to fill. One library in New England recently searched for months for a cataloger and eventually hired someone from Texas-- something that for them had been unheard of only a few years ago. For whatever reason, the perceptions have become a reality and appear to be self-perpetuating.

Whatever the causes-- bad press, low self-esteem, lack of organizational recognition, "fear of inputting" (as Richard De Gennaro has phrased it), lack of feedback for successful work (as Herbert White has described it), to name but a few--we believe that they can be addressed in two major ways. The first is to get out the message to prospective students by direct appeal from the library school; and the second is to focus on the library work setting, and the librarians in cataloging and other technical services positions and how they can stimulate interest and create opportunities in cataloging. Our work as library educators concentrates on these two aspects for a solution to the problem.

SOLUTIONS

As library educators, we have begun direct appeal to prospective students in a number of ways. We do, as all library school personnel do, go to conferences, meetings, institutes, symposia and workshops to make ourselves and our school visible within the community of professionals. There we talk, cajole, ferment, and generally try to stimulate other professionals into going back to their institutions and really looking for interested people for our program. This one-on-one type of recruitment is time consuming, but the payoff in students can be tremendous given the right circumstances and the right librarians. Some people are wonderful recruiters, and since they do not work in library schools often do not recognize it in themselves. The job of the library educator is to pinpoint these professionals and give them the impetus to recruit their own replacements. Library educators have a vested interest in attracting new students, not only to fill their classrooms, but also because it stimulates thinking and growing in teaching. Library practitioners have a vested interest in attracting more people to the profession, because as they climb the hierarchy into the management of technical services departments at their institutions, it gives them a pool from which to draw the people who will replace them as catalogers.

Another method that we employ is to talk to undergraduates who are either in their last year of a bachelor's degree program or who are out of school and still searching for career opportunities and direction. Our school is part of the College of Arts and Sciences at The University of Rhode Island and we often go to student career days within our college (being part of the College makes it easy for us to get invited to participate, and we are expected to be there, although it is doubtful, since we are only a graduate program, whether our absence would be commented upon). One weekend every year prospective undergraduate students from high schools are invited on the campus. We go to these programs as well, and if we don't wind up attracting future library science students at that early age, we sometimes get their mid-life career changing parents. Besides possibly attracting students to our graduate program, participating in the College's career days also helps us to be visible on the campus, which is very important to our funding and status as faculty members, and which may inspire other faculty to direct potential students to us.

In addition to our recruiting on our own campus, we began, about three years ago, a series of "recruitment teas" all over the New England region. We go out on Saturdays. We send notices to all the area libraries to post where their public and support staff can see them, and in effect we invite the neighbors in to have a look at us. We usually do not go overboard on the formality of the situation, we bring a cake, some cider, a cookie or two, and provide coffee and tea. We spend some time in a formal talk (15 minutes or so depending on the size of the group), and then we talk individually to the people who come. Many of them work in libraries, and all of them use libraries (or else how would they have seen the notice!).   There are usually three of us who go out on these forays, and perhaps it isn't surprising that all three of us have been catalogers and have taught cataloging at one time or another. Perhaps it is not just coincidence, but rather reflects the need that the three of us who have been in cataloging feel about the importance of replacing ourselves in the work place and the enthusiasm that we feel toward the specialty.

The final point in direct appeal, whether it be to prospective students or to librarians in the field, is to discuss honestly with them the topics of types of work, opportunities in the field, and most importantly, drawbacks. Every specialty within every field has its drawbacks. Every job has its moments of frustration, its periods of boredom. The point is not to de-emphasize these, but to put them in perspective with other professions. We truly believe that our profession is the best in terms of quality of worklife, and the enthusiasm we feel is bound to come through in one-on-one discussions of career choices. We don't understand how we lucked out into this profession, and we don't understand why, given the opportunity, everyone wouldn't want to be a librarian in general, and a cataloger in particular. That attitude is a must for recruiters.

Most of the studies done on recruitment of librarians and the reason why they chose the field have determined that librarians and library working experience are the most significant factors in attracting students to study to become library professionals [1] While we may not know exactly what precipitated a career decision in each case, clearly a positive or appealing person, performance, or situation signaled to the decision-maker that this was her/his direction to take. Occasionally, people may also see the potential for growth or intellectual reward beyond the immediate setting, and make that leap of faith into the profession, but that is very difficult to achieve without considerable experience or very direct, detailed and credible advice from someone in the field. More likely potential and future librarians will react to what they see, experience and anticipate. We may conclude that in the settings in which they find themselves, the cataloging positions, with their status in the organization, work place, potential for involvement in the profession outside of the institution, job content, recognition factors, personalities, and a host of other variables, simply are not attractive to new professionals.

We accept the premise that a potentially valuable source of cataloging professionals should be the cataloging units of libraries, and the corollary to that premise is that any negative impressions in the working experience or observations of those potential recruitees steers, nay, drives, people away from seeking careers as catalogers, and away from concentrating on cataloging in library school. Further, insufficient education or inspiration in library school precludes placement of new graduates in cataloging positions. Finally, lack of training, challenging experiences and defined interests in pre-professional and beginning professional jobs, or in internships while in school, eliminates promotional possibilities for up and coming professionals. A sidebar to this last point is that the higher someone goes in the profession, the less inclined that person is to retreat, move sideways or otherwise fill in the gaps in his or her experience and start over in another area.   If we do not succeed in getting support staff people from cataloging departments into the profession as catalogers, we don't stand a chance of getting support staff personnel from other areas within the library into cataloging.

What can we do to address our problem? First, forget the "image" and go for reality. Steer potential library professionals to articles in the literature and to conferences which detail the need for and the skills needed by catalogers. Expand the horizons of recruits beyond the narrow area of their present tasks in clerical or paraprofessional positions. In discussing possible careers, in orientation sessions, in outright buttonholing of promising candidates, describe other settings, rapid change, technological developments, intellectual challenges, and similar characteristics in a positive way, as if they are *good* for you. (They are!). Remember that professional is as professional does, Forget about "image." Look at what we do as catalogers, how we do it, and what attitudes we broadcast about what we do. Staff and students see us as we are. We *are* role models whether we like the term or not. Catalogers should be positive role models, serious about their work, continuously evaluating its effectiveness in the larger library context. We should present a cataloger as a professional who knows what the library is for, and strives to keep that mission in front of any preoccupation with parochial matters. Catalogers should display concern with issues and trends in the field and discuss them intelligently with staff. If we are involved in research, we should share that information as well. Catalogers can and should demonstrate leadership, responsiveness to challenges, interest in developing standards, and willingness to direct and accept change.

A second area for activity by catalogers in the field is in recruitment by nurturing. Catalogers should respond to interest and potential present in beginning or budding catalogers, and provide incentives. Wherever possible, recruit from within the organization for professional catalogers from among junior staff (even from elsewhere in the library, if possible; don't hesitate to invade someone else's turf. They would do the same to you, and have been doing so for years). Provide opportunities. and involve paraprofessional staff in special projects, task forces and other situations where they can get information about the profession and feedback on their potential. Encourage them to look at existing routines and practices with a fresh eye, and be willing to make appropriate changes to bring them into the mainstream of the cataloging unit. This next statement may sound obvious, but needs reinforcement: encourage people with talent and interest to go to library school and to specialize in cataloging. Develop career ladders or other incentives which will provide support for their graduate education.

Do not limit your recruiting to cataloging departments. All interested library staff should have the opportunity to become aware of career options. Some ways to do this might be with in-house staff development seminars, and continuing education opportunities geared to professional growth.

Improve the working environment of catalogers. Find ways to make jobs more challenging on a day-to-day basis, and as a long term prospect. All library staff should be able to take advantage of interdisciplinary activities, job exchanges, cross training, and policy formulation processes to develop their sense of the importance and appeal of cataloging. Every cataloger and paraprofessional should have duties that go beyond "just cataloging", even if some organizational restructuring is necessary. Such restructuring may well have long term beneficial results for the library as a whole, and may more than repay the investment of time, money and talent. In the largest of library organizations, the trend is toward a blurring between the public and technical service areas, and now may be a good time for reorganization and expansion of the cataloger's job responsibilities. Lizbeth Bishoff describes many areas of use for catalogers' knowledge and experience in her 1987 article "Who Said We Don't Need Catalogers?" [2]

By involving staff in some activities beyond "just cataloging," we can highlight the transferability of cataloging skills and the impact those skills may have on administration, planning, project supervision, consulting, cooperative activities, evaluation of resources, and the provision of information services. Catalogers who understand the structure and composition of catalogs and databases are in a good postion to evaluate technological and telecommunications options the library faces. The expertise of catalogers must be recognized by the library administration, not only for an the catalogers' sake, but also for the message that such recognition sends to the entire staff, and to the governing structure.

In an article in the *Journal of Library Administration*, Gisela Webb states that we should begin to recruit by "examining the past and letting go of unnecessary assumptions, traditions, procedures, by experimenting with automation and management practices, by taking risks, by thinking globally and holistically, by creating opportunities for ourselves and providing them for colleagues and staff, by being accountable and ethical." [3] She also mentions "instilling new visions and values, setting a good example and encouraging each person to become the best clerk, the best paraprofessional, the best librarian they [sic] can be." [4] But don't leave it at that. Clerks become paraprofessionals and then librarians. And some librarians become catalogers. *Good* catalogers. But only if we do our part.

To conclude, our approach to recruiting catalogers moves in two directions--outreach from the library school, and recruitment within library settings. Both directions involve high visibility, a positive and strong impression, and a sense of professional responsibility to attract and retain bright, hardworking, creative and dedicated new professional catalogers for our libraries.

REFERENCES

1.   See, for instance, the *LISSADA* study undertaken by the Louisiana State University School of Library and Information Science, 1988, and its references to earlier studies.

2.   Lizbeth J. Bishoff, "Who Says We Don't Need Catalogers?" *American Libraries* 18 (September 1987): 694-6.

3.   Gisela M. Webb, "Educating Librarians and Support Staff for Technical Services," *Journal of Library Administration* 9 (Fall 1986): 111-120.

4.   *Ibid.*

A Network of Professionals Recruiting
(In Lieu of a Staff of Professional Recruiters)

Heidi Lee Hoerman

The Library and Information Science Student Attitudes, Demographics and Aspirations Survey (hereafter referred to as the LISSADA Survey), which polled library school students in the Spring of 1988, confirmed that most library school students attend accredited library schools in their home state or move from one state without an accredited library school to another to attend an accredited program. Less than three per cent of library school students responding to the survey chose to pursue a graduate degree in library and information science before graduation from high school and less than 17% chose to pursue an MLIS before completing their undergraduate educations. The LISSADA survey also implies a demography for library science students which is not growing and changing to meet the new millennium. Less than seven per cent had degrees in the biological or physical sciences, representing little change in twenty years. (Moen 1988)

Recruitment of undergraduates through college placement centers and career fairs concentrates on enticing individual undergraduates to specific openings. A list of participants at a recent career fair at Montana State University included only employing corporations or agencies and a single university law school. Montana State University admissions recruiters (who attend many career fairs) and MSU career counselors (who are familiar with those who come to our campus to recruit) report that they see very little recruitment by professions as distinct from recruitment by particular corporations or graduate schools.

Individual graduate library schools recruit at undergraduate institutions most likely to supply students for their programs. And the LISSADA study has shown that these institutions are the ones in their own state. The economics of traditional recruitment counsel such concentration of recruitment efforts in the areas most likely to produce immediate, concentrated results. (Bickers 1986) Might recruitment of librarians by library schools be inadvertently reinforcing the unchanging demography of graduate library school students by concentrating on those areas most likely to produce results? There exists no graduate library science program in the State of Montana nor in any state bordering Montana. Individual graduate schools of library and information science can ill afford to devote the financial and personnel resources necessary to recruit students from MSU and other institutions like it. In recognition of this economic fact, this paper proposes a "network of professionals recruiting" to reach out to undergraduate career centers in smaller universities and colleges, especially those in states without an accredited graduate library education program, participate in career fairs, and aid in the development and classroom utilization of career materials for elementary and secondary schools in states without library schools.

Finding solutions to image and visibility problems are key to developing recruitment programs. Years ago I had a second or third generation photocopy of a cartoon depicting a slick career counselor suggestively leaning over his desk and telling a hunched, bunned, bespectacled woman, "Stick with me, babe, and I'll get you into libraries." Career counselors use batteries of interest inventories and interviews to help students find careers in which they may thrive. Counselors cannot help but be affected by their perceptions of careers available and the characteristics they believe necessary to succeed in those careers. Local career counselors immediately suggested that candidates with bachelor's degrees in English were probably what I would be seeking for positions in libraries. If librarianship in general is not immediately evident to career counselors as a possible profession for science and engineering students, cataloging and technical services are very rarely evident as possible careers at all.

Visibility and career awareness are particular problems for cataloging and technical services. Many of the smaller public libraries with which students may be familiar have no full time technical services personnel. Few of those employed in the smaller public and school libraries share the "common education that is monitored through stringent reviews," as Heim (1988) describes American Library Association accredited programs. Catalogers and other technical services librarians, by the nature of their positions have little direct contact with the public. Often, when I tell people on campus that I am a librarian, they respond, "Really? I've never seen you there," almost indignant that I am not at the reference desk.

In small, rural states, there are very few full time catalogers at all, easily less than a dozen in the State of Montana.

Career awareness forms an important part of career choice. Career education and development are part of human development and can start in preschool years. (Dianna 1985) Over 73% of those who participated in North Dakota high school science fairs in the fifties, sixties, and seventies, indicated that participation in the fairs influenced their choice of career. The more education the respondent had, the more likely was it that this high school experience had influenced career choice. (Olson 1985) Career awareness or visibility is key to recruitment.

The formation of a "network of professionals recruiting" will allow the enhancement of image and increased visibility required to make librarianship, especially less familiar aspects of librarianship like cataloging, a possible career choice for a broader spectrum of students.

An invitational preconference on recruitment sponsored by the American Library Association Office for Library Personnel Resources (OLPR) Advisory Committee (held in New Orleans, Lousiana, 7/8 July, 1988) had as one of its goals the development of a network to market the profession. The preconference brought together librarians representing a wide range of constituencies who were charged with embarking on the road to recruitment upon leaving the preconference. I represented the Montana Library Association but am also a cataloger-at-heart and "charter member" of the RTSD CCS Task Force on Education, Training and Recruitment for Cataloging. Preparation of this paper and subsequent action on its suggestions will help me begin to fulfill my obligation to help librarians to "Each One Reach One" and actively recruit librarians.

What follows is a design for establishing the network of professionals recruiting for librarianship in a state without a graduate library school. This recruitment network differs from recruitment by a particular graduate library school, recruitment for cataloging in particular, or recruitment to the work force of a specific library or group of libraries, in that it risks seeking librarians in the sources which have not in the past proven to provide the highest yield. It seeks to address recruitment through establishing career awareness before completion of undergraduate study. The steps involved are loosely based on the general marketing plan in Doyle Bickers's "For College Marketing Success, Plan, Plan, Plan!" (1986) Bickers lists five steps: problem definition, research, planning, implementation, and evaluation. As Bicker's steps assume the existence of admissions personnel (professional recruiters) to implement the plan, they are preceded with establishment of a network professionals recruiting.

ESTABLISHING A NETWORK OF PROFESSIONALS RECRUITING

The network of those who share an interest in recruiting librarians may best be started through local library associations and the assumption of responsibility for being a catalyst for recruitment efforts by one or more concerned individuals. Once you have decided to become that catalyst, ascertain who else in the state or region is interested in recruitment and whether such a network already exists. Organize a meeting on recruitment at the next conference of the local library association inviting all who may be interested to a brainstorming session. During the process of education for recruitment, network members may find others outside of librarianship who will be valuable members of the recruitment network: career and guidance counselors, placement officers, college admissions recruiters, and community leaders. These individuals can provide the outsider's perspective which may enhance the network's ability to optimize its effectiveness.

A project undertaken to improve career guidance training in Pennsylvania found that a variety of participants with varying work experiences enriched the process of developing local career guidance networks. Each unique group found its own best network/collaboration design but common to all was the sense of linkage established by the process of sharing differing viewpoints. Priorities varied from region to region but each group set its own priorities without negating the validity and importance of the priorities of other groups. Project results indicated that quality of counseling competence may be directly related to involvement in a viable training network established and maintained by network participants sharing information and enhancing professional development. (Ciavarella 1987)

DEFINITION OF THE PROBLEM

Although the need to recruit more people into librarianship is generally acknowledged, J. C. Bennett's (1988) arguments to the contrary in *American Libraries* notwithstanding, a successful recruitment program requires the definition of specific problems which may be addressed as units. Although each network will establish different priorities, they may generally fall into the following categories: enhancing the public image of librarians, conveying the variety of careers available in library and information science, and heightening the public awareness of librarianship as a career. Broad concepts may then be discussed and specific needs which may be addressed as units defined. Agenda and calendar can then be established with nodes of the network assuming responsibility for individual units.

OF PRIMARY IMPORTANCE: RESEARCH AND EDUCATION

Research and education are the keys to successful program planning. Research is the gathering of information needed to efficiently design an effective program. Education for recruitment is a natural outgrowth of the sharing of research findings of network members. Study the information available on the recruitment dilemma in librarianship. Know what the issues are. Find out what information is being distributed by library associations and graduate library schools. Know what programs and specialties are available. Read about career education and recruitment. Seek the help of recruiters in graduate library schools and university admissions offices to become a better volunteer recruiter. Review the materials in career centers and attend career fairs. Investigate possible funding sources.

Keeping in contact with national associations, library schools and large employers throughout the life of the network can have long lasting benefits. Recruitment efforts are being attempted and sharing of information by program planners will help those in one region avoid pitfalls suffered by another. Smaller networks may benefit a great deal from the work of larger associations. Very few local recruitment efforts will have the resources to do the level of research or create the kind of promotional materials that the California Library Association has produced and is willing to share.

PLANNING NETWORK ACTION

Only when adequate research has been done and information has been shared by network participants can the plan for network action be formalized. The agenda and calendar first developed in the problem definition phase can now be expanded into a master plan consisting of individual goals. Each goal of the network's recruitment efforts may have long-, intermediate-, or short-term aspects. Another way to view the three categories of the network agenda may be as mission , goals, and objectives. Short-term goals or objectives may be viewed as a list of tasks. Whatever way the items are defined, each one will have a target audience and will need a strategy designed for its completion.

Recruitment of undergraduates to librarianship, especially cataloging and technical services, by college career guidance centers.

Develop awareness of the possible careers available in and a positive image of librarianship with local college career guidance centers.

College career centers attempt to maintain well balanced libraries of information on the universe of careers available to students. Examine the materials related to librarianship at local college career centers and try to view that information as a prospective student would. Is the information on careers in library and information sciences attractive and up-to-date? How does the information on librarianship compare with that on other fields?

Ascertain how local career center personnel obtain their information about careers. Offer to help career center personnel with updating the information they have with information from local and national library associations. They may be missing very basic information you can easily obtain.

(The MSU Career Services notebook on librarianship lacked the list of ALA accredited programs.)

Make an appointment to discuss the wide range of opportunities available in librarianship with career counselors. Describe your own position in a library. Many have never met a technical services librarian.

Offer to serve as a career counseling resource for students who may be interested in librarianship.

IMPLEMENTATION OF THE NETWORK RECRUITMENT PLAN

The responsibility for accomplishing the goals of the recruitment plan rests with individual network members. No committee or organization can force individuals to maintain the enthusiasm necessary to accomplish the long-term goals of recruitment into the field of librarianship. Individual network members have a two part responsibility. They not only need to maintain their own involvement but to encourage each other to maintain network activity. Mutual positive reinforcement is key to continued action. Remember, everyone involved is a volunteer and the accomplishment of long-term goals will be a long time in coming and hard to recognize.

EVALUATION OF PROGRESS

The overall network plan should include evaluation of progress toward the accomplishment of the goals established by the plan. Formative evaluation, or evaluation which serves to assess progress and make suggestions for future actions, is vital to the ongoing success of the recruitment network. Such assessment may be quantitative or qualitative, but in either case it is important to record and distribute the evaluative data.

Formative evaluative data is simply a report of progress which helps form and reform future progress. Simply assessing the time allotted for an activity, for example, setting up a booth at a career fair, and reporting that assessment will help others more effectively plan for the next career fair. Assessing fair participant reaction to materials presented will help development of a more polished display.

Formative evaluation and sharing of evaluative data helps to redefine problems and bears a striking resemblance to research, turning network recruitment activities into a loop: Problem Definition/Research--Planning--Implementation--Evaluation/Problem Redefinition/Research--Adjustment of Plan--Further Implementation--Evaluation, etc.

CONCLUSION

William Moen (1988) suggests that LISSADA Survey results "may help us find ways to inform and entice all those other people who have never given a thought to the possibility of being one of the librarians of the new millennium."   In his keynote address to the OLPR Preconference, Vartan Gregorian (1988) spoke of a world drowning in detail yet starved for knowledge, a world in which less than 10% of information is inaccessible.   Catalogers are organizers of information. As information explodes, the world's capacity to absorb experts in information organization will be immense. As the scope of the information grows, our need for cataloging experts in every field of knowledge will increase.

Veaner (1985) stated that the characterization of cataloging and the management of library materials as rule-bound may "hold a natural attraction for those who enjoy regimen." Whereas, on the contrary, new librarians will need to be those who can take risks, develop new methods, experiment, and, on occasion, fail. Veaner recommends that we work with "college and university placement officers to depict a profession that is deeply intellectual and highly technical--not an employment opportunity for those who 'love books,' or 'enjoy reading,' nor a 'game room' for those who love computers." If we work together, as a network of professionals recruiting into librarianship, we can and will attract the brightest and best to help society face the information age.

BIBLIOGRAPHY

Bennett, J. C. "Charge of the Library Brigade: Recruits to the Profession are being Misled by 'Wildly Improbable' Reports of a Librarian Shortage," *American Libraries* 19 (September 1988): 724- 725.

Bickers, Doyle. "For College Marketing Success, Plan, Plan, Plan!" In *The Admissions Strategist: Recruiting in the 1980's* (New York: College Entrance Examination Board, 1986).

Ciavarella, Michael A. *A Plan to Implement the Recommendations of Counseling Personnel who Participated in Six Pennsylvania Regional Workshops Designed to Update Counselors' Competencies and Skills in the Area of Guidance. Final Report* (Harrisburg, Pa.: Dauphin County Technical School, 1987), ERIC ED 288094.

Dianna, Michael A. *Career Education for Elementary Grades.* 1985, ERIC ED 248404.

Gregorian, Vartan. Keynote address presented at the preconference of the American Library Association Office for Library Personnel Resources, New Orleans, La., 7-8 July, 1988.

Heim, Kathleen M. "Librarians for the New Millennium." In *Librarians for the New Millennium*, edited by William E. Moen and Kathleen M. Heim (Chicago: American Library Association Office for Library Personnel Resources, 1988).

Moen, William E. "Library and Information Science Student Attitudes, Demographics and Aspirations Survey: Who we are and why we are here." In *Librarians for the New Millennium.*

Olson, Linda Sue. *The North Dakota Science and Engineering Fair--Its History Land a Survey of Participants.* 1985. ERIC ED 271325.

Veaner, Allen B. "1985-1995: The Next Decade in Academic Librarianship, Part II," *College and Research Libraries* 46 (July 1985): 295-308.

Recruiting Catalogers: Three Sets of Strategies

Thomas W. Leonhardt

INTRODUCTION

This paper is about recruiting library catalogers, not about library education, at least not directly. But it would be impossible to talk about how libraries recruit catalogers without touching on how we recruit new librarians into the profession and how we mold them while they are in library school.

In 1947, Ernest J. Reece, then Melvil Dewey Professor Emeritus of Library Service, Columbia University, conducted a field investigation on "The Task and Training of Librarians".[1] In this work, Reece detailed the attributes and attitudes he found fundamental, calling them, "the personal qualities without which, in any intellectual calling, knowledge can have little value and skills cannot be productively applied. They may be impartible only in limited measure; but it seems agreed that authorities concerned with training bear a responsibility at least for nurturing them where they exist, and for discouraging aspirants who show small sign of possessing them."[2]

Reece undertook a field study, using interviews and a uniform set of questions in order to "enquire whether the responsibilities of American libraries call for intellectual equipment not possessed by library school graduates. The answer might indicate whether new intellectual elements should be added to the preparation of librarians, and perhaps whether the material for a truly professional program of instruction exists."[3]

The debate continues to this day and will be addressed in part during this symposium. My point in citing this study is not to discuss the education of librarians except to say that the higher the quality of entry level librarians, the greater the opportunities for recruiting top-notch catalogers. We need the proper raw material in order to do our jobs.

The other reason I cite this study is that the qualities considered important to recruiting to the profession (Reece's attributes and attitudes) are equally important in recruiting any librarian and especially, for today's discussion, cataloging librarians. Without those qualities we should not consider any library school graduate for any library position.

Reece found six attributes and attitudes worth mentioning:[4]

     (1) Liking for people;
     (2) Intellectual capacity and interest;
     (3) Judgment and the open mind;
     (4) Confidence and animation;
     (5) Professional responsibility;
     (6) Some homely virtues.

When recruiting catalogers, I recognize three levels on which to base my strategies: entry level; midcareer/section head level; and department head/manager level. Each level requires its own strategy that goes beyond preparation of the position listing. To ignore the differences among the levels can be passed on to candidates and the wrong messages are received. A faulty search process can lead to the loss of an otherwise interested candidate.

Before addressing the differences I wish to cover the commonalities that should be part of all efforts to recruit cataloging librarians. Some of these common elements surface again in specific ways at each level of recruitment, and it is important for the good of the library and the profession that these aspects of recruiting cataloging librarians be recognized in principle and in practice.

No matter what level of cataloger you are recruiting, there needs to be a recognition by the library administration from the director on down that cataloging is a professional responsibility and an intellectual activity that is based on intellectual skills, a theoretical education (not training), and a keen intellectual curiosity about knowledge and its organization. This is what Reece calls intellectual capacity and interest. Reece claims that, "Mediocrity in key positions slows the pace of an organization as a whole. Staff members of low capacity and mental tepidity may serve to keep a library or other institution running respectably and for a long time, yet in too stable and static a condition. The hope of obviating such cases probably influenced those who emphasized the need for high intellectual talent and propensity in candidates for librarianship."[5] In the instance of cataloging librarians, I see all their positions as being "key."

Members of the administration and cataloging department need to recognize, too, that catalogers are not librarians who are unsuited for work with the public. If they are not suitable for dealing with library patrons, why should we think they are acceptable in a close working environment where good interpersonal communications skills are essential? And, even if they do not have direct contact with the public, catalogers should have a service orientation. Furthermore, they should be able to work well with all levels of staff, since they often are called upon to give service to their colleagues.

Contrary to the stereotype, catalogers are not misfits, recluses, or detail-oriented compulsives who cannot see the forest for the trees. It has been my experience that people fitting those descriptions do work in libraries but not only as catalogers. According to Reece, his consultants, "gave a high place to regard for humankind. Basically this seemed to mean a warm and free-hearted nature, which might be evidenced by sympathy, responsiveness, satisfaction in having people about, the wish to serve, zeal in bringing books and people together, readiness in sensing clients' needs, and tact in dealing with all who come to a library."[6] People without those qualities ought not be in librarianship at all.

It is worth stating what Reece's "homely virtues" were, too, because it seems to me they should be kept in mind when recruiting cataloging librarians. He said:[7]

> Contributors to the study emphasized a number of non-intellectual requirements, some of which doubtless are implied in qualities already discussed. They saw need, for instance, for a higher average of emotional stability, as made possible by correct adjustment and maturity. They called for physical fitness and for patience and perseverance, together with the graciousness previously mentioned. On the dynamic side, the consultants desired energy, enthusiasm, and industry, without which presumably the requisite degree of initiative could not be maintained. They thought it worth while even to urge courtesy and a well-groomed appearance.

This may sound difficult and demanding and, perhaps, unrealistic. I do not think it is; moreover, I think that such an approach is good for cataloging and for librarianship. There may be an analogy in the strategy of the University of Tennessee football coach. Back in the 1960s, he tried to recruit as many quarterbacks for his team as he could with the idea that high school quarterbacks are generally the best all-around athletes and should be able to play virtually any position, with a few exceptions. Like most analogies, this one breaks down when applied to librarianship, but it is useful to keep in mind when recruiting catalogers at any level. Especially at the entry level, the primary consideration should be the quality of the applicant. For this reason, a rich candidate pool must be sought. This is done most successfully by means of a national search. It may cost more than a local or a regional search (in the long run, it might not, either), but such a strategy indicates the importance attached to the position and that quality is a foremost consideration. A case can be made for recruiting library school students, even those without hands-on cataloging experience, when they are the best and brightest of their classes.

In deciding on who to invite for an interview it is important to carefully and closely review the cover letters of application, the curriculum vitae, and the letters of reference. This is an obvious point but those involved in the hiring process should consciously talk about these areas and critically examine what they expect to get out of them.

The letter of application can be an excellent and accurate indicator of the type of person who authored it. Ideally, it should be well-organized, neat, and exhibit a sense of understanding of what the job is all about. The presence of typographical errors, as such, must be evaluated with common sense and the understanding that everyone makes mistakes. The guiding principle should be consistency, not perfection.

An applicant's curriculum vitae should not leave any unexplained gaps in the employment history and it should be organized sufficiently well that it is easy to read and understand. It should be evaluated with firmness, but humanity, just as the cover letter was judged. If the candidate does not demonstrate an understanding of the importance of these documents, you probably do not want to consider him or her any further.

For the entry level applicant, one can examine what other kinds of work the person has done. This may help the evaluators to judge the person's suitability for the particular position in this particular place of work. Finding the best qualified person is more than just accumulating related training and experience. We should never forget that it is the whole person in the whole work context that we are hiring. We should not think of ourselves as hiring just a cataloger; there should be no such thing, and to search on that basis is to invite a mistake. Hiring mistakes at any level cannot be tolerated.

Letters of reference submitted on behalf of the candidate should be treated similarly. Read between the lines but do not read too much between them. If there is the sense that a reference is trying to say something circuitously, call that person and ask about that particular point and any others you think will help bring out more of the truth about the candidate's capabilities. Look, especially, for remarks about leadership, resourcefulness, the ability to do quality work, and the ability to work with others in a harmonious way.

Once a short list is compiled, i.e., a small group (e.g., fewer than five) of qualified candidates with good potential, call their references and ask about the applicants. If you know the references, so much the better, but call anyway. You may be surprised at what you learn. If there are doubts about any of the candidates as a result of these calls, those people may be relegated to a back-up list or, occasionally, dropped entirely from consideration.

The next step is to call the applicants on your short list and talk to them. At this point, you are probably ready to invite people for interviews. Be ready to do so, unless there are still doubts about who the top candidates are. If a candidate is still interested in the position and sounds reasonable on the telephone, go ahead and invite him or her for an interview.

The length and structure of the interview will vary according to the position. Differences will be explored later, but first, those interview components that apply to all levels should be mentioned. The interview is a crucial part of the recruitment process. The interview is for the mutual benefit of the candidate and the library staff. Each party should be trying to learn as much about the other as possible and each should be trying to make a good impression without being deceitful. The interview can be stressful for the candidate, but it is no less pressured for those doing the interviewing. Recognition and acknowledgement of those facts in advance will smooth the process and help ensure that interviewers make a good impression on the candidate.

Each interview should have an agenda, delivered in advance to the candidate, if possible. In each schedule, a social hour should be scheduled, when the candidate can be put at ease and where both parties can find out about common interests outside of actual job responsibilities. Care should be taken that those not involved in other kinds of interview sessions do not turn the social hour into a grilling session, but keep the tone unpressured and informal. Not only does the candidate need a chance to relax a little, but members of the library staff need to find out what kind of a colleague the candidate might be.

Once the finalists have been interviewed, make a decision as quickly as possible. It is rare that a search must be delayed because no consensus can be found. In most instances, a stalemate means that the library administration has not done an adequate job of preparing the staff or has not been clear about criteria for the job. If you want a good person, you must not make him or her wait too long. Your institution may be judged inadequate if you dally and there is always the possibility that another library may make a quicker, better offer. To lose someone to a better offer is understandable, but to lose a good librarian because of procrastination is to have confounded the recruiting effort.

ENTRY LEVEL STRATEGIES

A national search should be conducted for entry level cataloging librarians. This means mailings to library schools; it means telephone calls and personal contacts with library school faculty. A national search also means advertising in American Libraries, if no where else. If the position is for an academic library, it would not hurt to run at least one advertisement in *College & Research Libraries News*. In addition to these steps, I also talk to colleagues at institutions with library schools to try to find out who their top interns and student employees are. Lack of cataloging experience does not rule out an entry level librarian from a cataloging job, but having cataloging experience   as   a   student   employee,   intern,   or paraprofessional/classified staff is the ideal. This experience should be gained in a reputable institution under the guidance of professionals whose work can be trusted. Experience alone is not enough, either; the personal qualities mentioned earlier must also be considered.

This aggressive first step in recruiting an entry level cataloging librarian is meant to provide the largest, deepest pool of applicants possible. Many students do not know what kind of librarian they want to be, so some may apply for a cataloging job without really knowing just what a cataloger does. They just want a job. If they are good people, however, do not be discouraged if the only cataloging experience they have is from a single course and a laboratory using one of the bibliographic utilities. Be glad that you have the opportunity to hire from the very best in the pool.

If you can, you should visit a library school and interview students nearing graduation. This step is not a substitute for a national search nor for an on-site interview, but it provides a chance to talk to library school students about cataloging, what it really is, how it fits into the larger service context of your library, and what career opportunities it offers. This approach gives you the opportunity to interest some students who would not normally apply for a technical services job, but who might have been told to interview for the experience. A bright, ambitious prospect should be pursued regardless of professed preferences in librarianship. Such visits can help all of us in our recruiting of cataloging librarians.

The interview schedule for entry level positions should not be as long or as intense as it would be for more experienced librarians, but it should be sufficient to enable you to make a determination about the candidate's poise, intelligence, and their genuine interest in the position. One day should be enough time to meet with all the librarians who need to get a good look at the candidate. If the candidate is unfamiliar with your city, some time should be allotted for him or her to look around.

Most of the candidate's time should be spent with members of the catalog department. It may be more appropriate for the candidates to give an impromptu introduction of themselves, their reasons for becoming librarians, what they liked and disliked most about library school, and so on, rather than to prepare a formal presentation to be given to the whole library staff or the whole cataloging department.

Entry level candidates should also meet with members of the library administration, technical service heads, and cataloging section heads. The head of technical services and the head of cataloging will want to spend time alone with the candidate as will the supervisor of the unit in which he or she will be working. The candidate must get a feel for how he or she is going to participate fully in professional activities inside and outside of the library. It must be clear that a cataloger is also a librarian with the rights, privileges, and responsibilities that apply to all librarians.

While restricting the entry-level interview to these basic elements, it is still important that the library director be included because it is the director who must ultimately decide that the candidate fits into the order of things in that system. Disagreements among the director, the head of technical services, and the chief cataloger, if there are any, must be worked out. If those three are in agreement from the very beginning about the type of person being sought, these end-of-interview disagreements ought to be infrequent.

MID-CAREER/SECTION HEAD LEVEL

Although a national search should be conducted for a section head level position just as it should for an entry level position, qualified candidates are likely to exist within the department. Without promising anything but fairness, good cataloging librarians with the right experience to apply for promotions should be encouraged. If the internal candidate wins the position, it tells that person and others in the library that the successful internal candidate really is good and not a fair- haired favorite of the administration or of the staff. Internal candidates must also be prepared for possible disappointment. In the event they are unsuccessful in obtaining the appointment, they should continue being encouraged to grow through administrative assignments that show trust and assume their responsiblity and maturity. Professional development programs in a library should build on strength and ensure continued strength for the profession as a whole.

For midcareer positions in academic libraries, the library' should place advertisements in *American Libraries, The Chronicle of Higher Education, and College & Researc h Libraries News.* Special and public libraries might place their advertisements in other journals and newsletters that attract a readership interested in those types of libraries.

At this level personal contacts can be vitally important. Call your colleagues and ask who they know who is ready to move up and who has the kinds of skills and qualities that you want. You can send letters, too, but they will elicit mixed results.

Use time at American Library Association annual and midwinter meetings to talk to people who have been recommended, with whom you have worked on committees, or heard when they spoke at a discussion group or program. The placement center at these meetings fulfills an important function bringing together prospective employers and employees with no previous knowledge of one another, but the personal contact with known quantities is a more reliable way to find good candidates for cataloging jobs.

Once a short list has been identified from the pool of applicants (and at this level, a respectable pool might be somewhat smaller), two day interviews should be scheduled, including extra time to be spent in the department so the candidate can get a better feel for the routines, the personalities, and the challenges. It is assumed that, at this level, the person hired will have supervisory responsibilities or will have a demanding staff responsibility such as principal cataloger.

It may not be appropriate for someone at this level to speak to the entire library staff, but, at a minimum, candidates should present a prepared talk for members of the cataloging department and be ready and able to answer questions from the audience. If this position includes liaison with persons or groups outside the cataloging department, a library-wide talk is in order.

Candidates should be told in advance that they are expected to speak before a group. They should be given an appropriate general topic and it should be explained that the purpose of the talk is to demonstrate thought processes, verbal abilities, organizational skills, and poise. Explain that such a talk allows the candidate to set the tone for the rest of the interview. Try to set the talk for as early in the interview schedule as possible so that everyone has the benefit of hearing their remarks before other interview sessions take place.

Midcareer candidates should spend time with the cataloging department administrative group, with technical service department heads, and with the library administrative group including library-wide department heads.

Once a decision has been made, it is wise to extend the offer of employment quickly, even though it is possible that the candidate is not actively seeking a new job and less likely a delay might cause the loss of a good candidate. Negotiations for the salary, benefits, and other conditions of employment tend to be more important at this level and these take time. Also, the successful candidate needs time to notify the current employer of their decision to move.

MANAGERIAL/DEPARTMENT HEAD LEVEL

This position is very important to the whole library, not just to the cataloging department, and very difficult to fill. The fact that this position has been difficult to fill in recent years says two things: First, that we have raised the standards for what we want and will accept; and, second, that the pool of qualified applicants has shrunk. The applicant pool has shrunk for several reasons. One important reason is that it reflects a shrinking population of qualified catalogers as well as a reluctance on the part of qualified catalogers to move. Moving is expensive and traumatic and the salary improvements may not make it worth while. Library administrators must face the fact that they will have to pay for good people. They must also provide clear opportunities for responsibility and growth, because those interested in moving up and on probably aspire to being a head of technical services and director of libraries.

Personal contacts when recruiting a head of cataloging are vitally important. You may have to convince people that they ought to apply. This is an accepted and acceptable method of recruiting, i.e., to go after a most-qualified person who is not actively looking for a change. You may also have to implore your colleagues to suggest names even though it would mean the loss of valuable employees.

We should not forget our own cataloging department when recruiting a department head. If we have been doing our jobs right, we will have furnished section heads and general catalogers with the chance to grow and mature, and to develop managerial skills. We may not always want to hire an internal candidate, especially when a change in direction and perspective is needed, and, perhaps, this should be clarified when search is opened.

Advertisements for the position should be placed in the same publications as for the midlevel positions. Great care should be taken in how the position is described. Requirements that have nothing to do with the job should not be requested. When I think of a head of a cataloging department I think of a manager, not someone who will be actively cataloging. The department head will oversee the activities of catalogers and not necessarily be responsible for training and for interpretive duties that are more appropriate for an assistant head or a principal cataloger. In academic libraries, unless there is an institutional mandate, do not require a second master's degree; do not require a foreign language (even though most catalogers will have one); do not require anything that is not necessary for the successful execution of the duties of this office.

There are things that should be included in this description, beginning with a clear indication that the head of the cataloging department will have a voice as strong and important as other department heads in the library. See to it, too, that the salary is commensurate with the duties, responsibilities, and expectations of the job. This seems obvious, but a perusal of want ads for heads of cataloging will show that the importance of the position is often overlooked, if salary and statement of responsibilities are any indication. For example, in a recent packet of position descriptions, a head of collection development was offered a salary of $4,500 more per year than was offered for a head of original cataloging. Part of the salary difference had to do with divisional responsibility versus departmental responsibility, but in reality, the truly qualified manager of cataloging will be as hard if not harder to recruit than the collection development manager. We may be confused about what is truly important and what is not, mainly at the expense of catalogers. The properly qualified head of a cataloging department in this age of automated online catalogs and integrated systems is invaluable and, like invaluable books, should be considered rare and much sought. Judging from the number of extended and re-opened searches for heads of cataloging in recent months, qualified candidates could peddle their services much as free agents do in the sports world, reaping benefits far beyond what they now get.

The processes of winnowing the applicant list, checking references, and conducting on-site interviews are similar to those for section heads. The pool is likely to be smaller and each step of the process must be done carefully, thoroughly, and without haste. In particular, the interview might stretch over a longer period and include more attention to the strengths of the institution, attractions of the location, and possibilities for real challenge. The candidate should meet with top administrators in the library and the institution and should be prepared to make both formal and informal presentations covering topics of general interest as well as those issues the candidate believes are important to this library. The less formal aspects of the interview might take place at a party given for the candidate or at an invitational dinner.

Following the interview period, decisions about this position should not be made hastily and negotiations for the terms of employment will have to be conducted. The list of strengths and weaknesses of each interviewee should be matched carefully with the library's needs and wants. The candidate's total salary-benefit package in their current job must be considered in putting together a successful offer.

CONCLUSION

How we recruit cataloging librarians at every level has an effect on every other level as well as how we regard ouselves and each other. Cataloging is too important to relegate to the back room and hire accordingly. Recruit the best no matter what the job. You cannot always get exactly what you want, but do not settle for anyone below average. Once you hire an entry level cataloger, develop the full potential of that person. Excellence begets excellence. We must never forget that.

NOTES

1. Ernest J. Reece, *The Task and Training of Librarians.* (New York: King's Crown Press, 1949).
2. Ibid., p. 34.
3. Ibid., p. 85.
4. Ibid., p. 34-39.
5. Ibid., p. 36.
6. Ibid., p. 34.
7. Ibid., p. 39-40.

The Evolving Public/Technical Services Relationship: New Opportunities for Staffing the Cataloging Function

James G. Neal

Advancing technology in libraries has spawned a series of important changes in staff relationships and roles. One area ripe for attention has been the traditional division between public and technical services. The consolidation of the databases with which both service areas must work, and the automation of many public and technical services activities has enabled the distribution of the professional aspects of technical operations, and the recruitment of individuals to cataloging within the collection and service environment. This paper will describe these trends, and the successful experience in the Libraries at Pennsylvania State University in the assignment of cataloging responsibilities to public services staff.

Organizations and people often find themselves in conflict. Organizations have typically valued clarity, stability and order, while people tend to be untidy, have strong feelings and change more rapidly than the organizations in which they live and work. The perennial question has been, how can the wants of people and the needs of organizations be better matched so that people are satisfied and organizations are successful. Recently, it has seemed that technological change is turning this pattern upside down: it is the organization that has become untidy and is evolving more rapidly and creatively than its members can cope with.

The stages of technology adoption are familiar. Initially, technology is used to do traditional things, but much faster than was previously possible. At some point, technology is used for new applications, and ultimately produces changes in the fundamental style of operation in an organization. Technology thus promotes important changes in the nature of work and the scope of career opportunities: what a person does in a given job, what training and experience are required, and what opportunities exist for job redesign and upward mobility.

Information processing work can be divided into three categories: operational, control and strategic. With precomputer systems, most staff activity was devoted to the preparation and manipulation of operational information. Strategic information processing, planning activity for example, was allocated the least resources and was dependent on relatively limited and difficult-to-secure information. With advancing computerization, much larger amounts of information can be processed at all levels, the computer takes over an increasing percentage of the operational and control activity, and more employee time is devoted to strategic activities.

It is into this maelstrom of organizational fluidity and employee role blending that a series of workforce planning challenges for libraries have been introduced. Libraries are increasingly facing unprecedented difficulties in recruiting and retaining professional catalogers. A 1986 study by ALA's Resources and Technical Services Division documented in a dramatic fashion these troubling trends.[1] In a three month period, 94 positions with cataloging responsibilities were identified in library job advertisements. Seven months after their postings, 56 percent of the positions were still vacant and 64 percent were either readvertised or extended. These cataloging positions attracted 30 or fewer applicants in 89 percent of the cases and fewer than 11 applicants in 41 percent of the recruitments. Managers rated the applicant pool as "very disappointing" over 50 percent of the time. And 65 percent of these advertised cataloging positions included a significant non-cataloging component. These data are symptomatic of a more general and devastating workforce trend in the overall decline of library school graduates and the increasing percentage moving into non-traditional, non-library positions.

The RTSD study cited a series of factors affecting the availability and stability of cataloging staffs: The complexity of cataloging and the increasing information needs for its effective performance can no longer be adequately covered in the library school curriculum, and libraries are assuming expanded responsibility for completing the training. With the growth of bibliographic networks and the increased availability of cataloging copy, cataloging is viewed as an obsolescent occupation. Cataloging is often identified as an entry-level assignment in librarianship, with the possibility of cataloging as a long-term career choice discouraged. The image of cataloging as a dull occupation performed by antisocial individuals does little to attract new practitioners. Serious attempts to increase the visibility and attractiveness of cataloging will require creativity in designing crossover assignments, plus willingness to accept changes in cataloging production levels. Technical services functions remain relatively invisible, with the image of a librarian being that of a person serving readers and providing information and guidance.

The typical and traditional organizational structure of libraries, built along the basic split between public and technical service functions, has reinforced and perpetuated these conditions. It is automation, however, that has unleashed extraordinary opportunities to undermine these trends and to reshape and revitalize the work and service environment in libraries.

Observations on developments affecting the shifting public and technical services relationship confirm the need for new approaches to roles and organization. The technical services staff no longer controls understanding of online system design and the intricacies of the bibliographic record. As this knowledge has been distributed, so has the ability and responsibility to establish bibliographic policies and priorities. As bibliographic processes have been automated and turned over to an increasingly clerical workflow, catalogers have faced far more limited scope for the use of full bibliographic skills and subject/language expertise. The traditional centralization of bibliographic control responsibilities curtailed opportunities for public services staff to influence system development and processing priorities. The rapid conversion of local records and expanded access to network/utility and LC-MARC files have generalized use of a library's union database and eroded the tyranny of the card environment. Automation can make bibliographic information instantly available throughout a library, to be used directly when needed and to be updated directly from the point where new information is available or generated.

The expansion of bibliographic expertise in public service areas will encourage the conversion and online management of formats and materials traditionally not represented in manual catalogs, including maps, government documents, archives, manuscripts and analytics information. The public service experience of working with database search services will promote successful integration of gateway capabilities as part of library online systems. As librarians with cataloging responsibilities are involved on a day- to-day basis in the service and collection development programs of the library, they are in a better position to respond to exceptional bibliographic needs and to establish cataloging priorities which reflect patron requirements.

It is the convergence of these trends and opportunities that is reinforcing the interrelatedness of functions between technical and public services units, and giving rise to structures in libraries which emphasize the natural and logical flow of activities and information. And it is in this environment that recruitment of public services professionals to cataloging activities offers new, creative and effective means of staffing positions which are increasingly difficult to fill and stabilize.

The development and implementation of an integrated online system in the Libraries at Pennsylvania State University provoked significant pressures for change and provided opportunities to overhaul traditional roles and relationships. Starting in 1975, the public services staff at Penn State participated on broadly representative consultation teams to develop system specifications and prepare recommendations on various automation matters. True understanding of system design and the complexities of the bibliographic record remained the province of the technical services staff, and with this knowledge went the ability and responsibility to establish bibliographic policies and priorities.

The introduction of the online catalog to the public and the completion of retrospective conversion in 1983 produced a new benchmark in the public-technical services relationship. The flush of challenging assignments for catalogers faded and public services staff consciousness of bibliographic control issues was raised. Catalogers were experiencing increasing frustration and dissatisfaction with their work. As part of an automated, largely clerical workflow with hierarchical supervision, they lacked opportunities for professional responsibility, leadership and recognition. But only as cataloger vacancies occurred and difficulties in recruiting satisfactory replacements became obvious was it recognized that an innovative approach was essential.

The Penn State Libraries faced increasing distrust between the creators and staff users of the database. There was concern about having the knowledge of sophisticated bibliographic control techniques and complex workflows so strongly focused in the organization. Intensive and long-term use of the system was seen as control of the system, and ability to influence processing priorities and system development was viewed as very limited. Despite welcome improvements in productivity and reductions in cataloging backlogs produced by the automated system, apprehensions focused on the perceived sacrifice of judgment to procedure, the default setting of priorities and policies based on system rather than library needs, the loss of "special case" treatment of cataloging problems in the mass shuffle, and the difficulties in mastering the language of automation sufficiently to influence policy and procedure.

It was concluded that the decentralization of original cataloging would help establish cataloging as a function which is part of, rather than the entire focus of a professional assignment. This action was seen as a necessary and positive response to the expanding staff frustration being observed and to several important developments. Cataloging was changing in ways that encouraged expanded subject specialization. Automation was promoting the assessment of work patterns that had been centralized because of dependence on centralized tools and staff support, and encouraging an understanding of the interrelatedness of library functions and services.

After a careful analysis of the volume of original cataloging work to be produced by projected acquisitions rate and availability of cataloging copy, it was determined that four full-time catalogers or twelve catalogers with one-third time original cataloging responsibility could handle the load. Librarians, rigorously trained in local cataloging policies and practices, were assigned to public services units where they continue to serve as subject specialists and cataloging practitioners. In addition, a number of original catalogers were retained in technical services, Bibliographic Resources and Services in Penn State parlance, where they serve as bibliographic experts and carry out research, training, standards or staff supervision assignments.

Cataloging is thus performed largely in the context of a public services unit, language collection, subject collection or collection defined by format. Each librarian has opportunities to provide reference services, participate in bibliographic instruction programs, conduct database searches, and develop the collections. Cataloging responsibilities include original cataloging of titles in subject, language or format fields, including authority work; addition of classification numbers, subject headings or series headings for items referred from copy processing; assessment and maintenance of database quality; and establishment of bibliographic policies and priorities in the assigned fields. These librarians have administrative homes in the public services unit, but are also responsible to a bibliographic services unit which provides training, oversight and performance assessment. Early in the process, arrangements in several areas were worked out: commitment to extensive cataloging training before assignment to public services units, availability for participation in cataloger meetings, establishment of annual flexible cataloging workloads, automated system and terminal support, bibliographic tool availability, and various workflow procedural details.

In this public services assignment, the catalog librarian becomes a subject specialist with a complex of related duties. The public services units gain staff who are knowledgeable in technical services and effective system use, who have a formal role in cataloging policy and priority development, and who can serve as the focus for extension of distributed processing functions into public service areas for materials not yet supported by the automated system.

A recent assessment of this organizational development at Penn State confirmed its benefits and the validity of positive expectations. This integration of public and technical services responsibilities has not: eliminated or reduced in importance the cataloging function, produced lower quality or sub-standard cataloging, permitted conflicts in duties and impossible time management conditions, encouraged conflicting directions from several supervisors, or led to the development of mediocre generalists or "holistics". It has enabled the Penn State libraries to recruit to the cataloging function professional staff members with outstanding credentials and experience, and to turn around the trend to disappointing and inadequate candidate pools. It has provided positions with higher levels of flexibility, variety and autonomy. As a result, the Penn State libraries are implementing online information systems more responsive to user needs, offering a more exciting and challenging work environment, and improving service programs in a highly competitive electronic market place.

REFERENCES

1. American Library Association, Resources and Technical Services Division, Cataloging and Classification Section, "CCS Task Force on Education and Recruitment for Cataloging Report, June 1986" *RTSD Newsletter* 11 (1986): 71-78.

Beneath the Stereotyping: Matching Recruitment to Reality

Jill Parchuck, with Carol Mandel and Robert Wolven

The position of catalog librarian is firmly established in librarianship. In contrast to such newcomers as database searchers, information specialists, or preservation administrators, catalog librarians can trace their ancestry to among the first library service professionals. The maturity and general recognition of this branch of the profession would seem to imply that its functions and requirements are well-known and well-understood. In fact, however, familiarity with the title has bred not only contempt, but also a superficial view of what it encompasses. The nature and demands of the position of catalog librarian are regrettably poorly understood by many of those responsible for educating and recruiting them. And, even when an individual the job is well-described, frequently little attention is given to analyzing the skills and aptitudes that enable success in the position. Instead, the stereotype of the lone scholar-cataloger, with a zest for arcane research, an aptitude for memorizing detail, knowledge of ten languages, and a compulsively orderly mind prevails. While these may be admirable qualities, the stereotype has become a too-convenient tool for busy recruiters, and is the only image visible to potential candidates. Successful recruiting must instead be based on an accurate assessment of the skills required for a position under recruitment. This paper attempts to provide that assessment for the position of catalog librarian.

First, a definition of catalog librarian is in order. The term catalog librarian is used in this paper to mean the professional, MLS-holding librarian who catalogs. This librarian may be expected to be able to perform a full range of professional responsibilities including catalog record creation; review and development of procedures; maintaining current knowledge of local and national cataloging standards; workflow planning; revision and training of support staff and professionals; equipment operation and routine maintenance; collegial communications with all library staff; and transport of cataloging materials. This definition is necessary because the term cataloger alone can denote a number of different job contents depending on the employing institution and its personnel terminology, and may be used to refer to anyone involved in cataloging efforts including copy-catalogers, catalog editors, those involved only in catalog maintenance tasks, as well as professional librarian catalogers. It may even, as at the Library of Congress, refer to an individual who performs only one specific facet of catalog record creation. Although similar skills may apply to some degree for all these types of workers, this paper will discuss only the interests and skills that can reasonably be expected in the professional catalog librarian.

The first step in filling any employee position is recognizing the need for one. Implicit in the need for an employee are the need for product or service, tasks required for its creation or delivery, and realization that a human being is necessary to accomplish those tasks. That human being, or prospective employee, must have the interests for and mastery or potential for mastery of the skills necessary to complete those tasks. Just as the tasks involved define a job, so the interests and skills or aptitudes needed to accomplish them define the employee. Just as employers should review and verify the current validity of the tasks, responsibilities, and expectations detailed in a job description each time a position is created or re-filled, so should employers review and verify the current accuracy of the necessary interests and skills or aptitudes that are being sought in candidates.

At a basic level, a recruitment to fill a position is a quest for someone who possesses the right combination of skills and interests for the job in question. From the employee's point of view, "a job is a particular kind of work in a particular field, where you set your hand to particular tasks using particular skills ... [and] they are the essence of what you have to contribute to the world of work."[1] If the basis of successful recruitment in the short term, and successful employment, in the long term, is a matching of needed interests and skills or aptitudes to an individual who possesses those attributes, it is essential to know what these interests and skills are.

To find success and a good person-to-job fit, people seeking employment are instructed by professional or by self-directed methods of career planning to assess their interests and skills before pursuing fields of work or specific jobs. Formal interest-inventory measurement tests offer the taker choices of likes or dislikes in areas such as careers listed by title, academic subjects, and professional or leisure activities, and preference selection between sets of tasks. Test results indicate levels of interest in specific categories of occupation types--for example artistic, scientific, clerical, and social--or in relation to specific occupations. Skills may be assessed either by having the candidate list actual experience training or coursework, and indicate the level of success or failure therein, or by using tests which measure numerical, computational, verbal, analytical and other skills. The results of such skills-assessments report an individual's level of ability in specific task-related groups. Job seekers may then use the combined results of these two types of assessments to focus on fields of study or careers in which their interests and skills meet, and in which they therefore have the greatest potential for satisfaction and success.

To accurately identify the interests and skills that are necessary for success in a particular position, and subsequently to use that precise list to describe a position and attract and evaluate appropriate candidates, we might apply a similar assessment to the position itself. This paper concentrates on skills assessment and attempts to assess the position of the contemporary catalog librarian by making use of the list of 24 skills used in the U.S. Government publication, *The Dictionary of Occupational Titles* as expanded to 40 skills in the popular self-planning monographs *What Color Is Your Parachute?* and *The Three Boxes of Life* by Richard Bolles. These tools very commonly used by career and vocational guidance professionals as well as by self-directed career and work planners making their own individual investigations.

The *D.O.T.*, as the *Dictionary of Occupational Titles* is known, defines a universe of 24 specific skills and divides them into three groups. The three groups are: skills primarily with people, skills primarily with information or data, and skills primarily with things. The categories are not entirely separate, as there is some element of skill with things included in the people and information or data categories, and some element of skill with information in the things category. Each group is arranged hierarchically, with the least complex skills at the bottom.   Skills positioned higher on the list usually include or involve most of those below.   The *D.O.T.* list was compiled in 1977, and uses fewer and more general terms than are present on the list used by Bolles in his works.   Table 1 shows Bolles' expanded list, which is the one that will be used here.   The numbers on the list are a non-relevant numeration of the 40 skills.   The numbers are arranged in bottom-to-top ascending order in each group to represent increasing complexity from bottom to top within the group; no attempt is made to compare the complexity of tasks across groups.

Table 1:

Basic Skills List from *The Dictionary of Occupational Titles* as Expanded by Richard Nelson Bolles in What *Color Is Your Parachute?*

14 SKILLS WITH PEOPLE DATA	15 SKILLS WITH INFORMATION	11 SKILLS WITH THINGS
14 Working with Animals	29 Achieving	40 Repairing
13 Training	28 Expediting	39 Setting Up
12 Counseling (holistic)	27 Planning, Developing	38 Precision Working
11 Advising, Consulting	26 Designing (vehicles)	37 Operating
10 Treating Synthesizing	25 Creating, (Equipment)	36 Operating

9	Founding, Leading Adapting	24	Improving, (Tools)	35	Using
8	Negotiating, Deciding	23	Visualizing	34	Minding
7	Managing, Supervising	22	Evaluating Emptying	33	Feeding,
6	Performing, Amusing	21	Organizing	32	Working With The Earth or Nature
5	Persuading	20	Analyzing	31	Being Athletic
4	Communicating	19	Researching	30	Handling (Objects)
3	Sensing, Feeling	18	Computing		
2	Serving	17	Copying, Storing & Retrieving		
1	Taking Instructions	16	Comparing		
		15	Observing		

As might be expected, the skills listed in the information or data category all apply to cataloging librarians. The abilities to analyze, observe, compare, research, evaluate, and organize are vital to the tasks of subject analysis and classification, especially when using the comprehensive but complex LC systems. Visualizing, synthesizing, storing, and retrieving are necessary to the knowledge and application of descriptive cataloging rules, policies, and procedures. Information storage and retrieval, in fact are what cataloging is all about. Creating, expediting, and achieving relate to the actual complete and timely production of the bibliographic record. Computing is needed for the routine tabulation of inventories and statistical reports and is indirectly related to the mental ease with numbers necessary for the knowledge and application of MARC coding and interpretation and application of classification systems. Planning, developing, designing, improving, and adapting are skills basic to efficient production and workflow. They are also skills needed by the professional cataloger in order to make a contribution to the necessary, dynamic development of policy, procedure, workflows, workforms, systems, supervision, and training. These skills, all of those listed in the category of skills with information or data, are fundamental to the processing of bibliographic materials for the creation of complete and effective bibliographic records.

The bibliographic record communicates information about a work and its contents, and thereby requires the communicating skill in written form, which is listed in the skills with people category. Also included in this group is the skill of serving, or attending to the needs or requests of people. For cataloging librarians, this skill relates to the fulfillment of users' information needs through the access and organization that is provided by bibliographic records by means of subject headings, classification, standard numbering, associated name entry points, physical descriptors, key words, and a number of other possibilities afforded by cataloging rules and MARC field tags. The information access and organization furnished is the catalog librarian's part in "public service". The ability to take instructions, the first on the skills with people list, is essential in any position in which an employee receives some level of training, work revision, or assignment. The entry level catalog librarian, of course, is thoroughly provided with opportunities to take instruction. As experience in the job, and independence from intensive training and revision is gained, the catalog librarian will most likely continue to experience review of work performed as part of a quality control process. It is also characteristic of cataloging that work assignments are frequently dynamic, and instruction in new techniques, requirements, rules, or formats may take place at any juncture.

Advising and consulting, also found on the skills with people list, are routine activities for the catalog librarian who operates in association with other professional and non-professional catalogers, under the direction of a manager, and in coordination with public services and collection development librarians. The ability to train both non-professionals and professionals in various tasks, or in the full range of a position is one required of the catalog librarian to assist in meeting the demands created by employee turnover and staffing adjustment. As professional staff, catalog librarians should be expected to possess the ability to manage or supervise others so that they may be called upon to coordinate cataloging projects, provide training, and administer support activities. In a catalog librarian, therefore, we might look for someone who holds the skills of taking instructions, serving, communicating, managing- supervising, advising-consulting, and training found in the skills with people category.

In the skills with things category may be found the fewest, although very basic, skills necessary to the catalog librarian. The first skill on this list, handling (objects), is required of almost any position and, indeed the catalog librarian must be able to move or handle books and paperwork in abundance. The ability to operate office equipment is usually necessary for the cataloger to type worksheets or catalog online using a terminal keyboard, to calculate statistics and, in today's automated environment, to access the catalog and its various files and to print hard copy. It is desirable, as well, that the catalog librarian be capable of making minor adjustments to terminals, printers, and typewriters and be self-sufficient in such routine maintenance as ribbon replacement and paper feeding.

Of the 40 skills identified by the Bolles expansion of the *D.O.T.* list, those we might seek in the catalog librarian include

15, or all, from the category of skills with information or data, 6 from the skills with people category, and 2 from the skills with things category. The total list includes: taking instructions; serving; communicating; managing, supervising; advising, consulting; training; observing; comparing; copying, storing & retrieving; computing; researching; analyzing; organizing; evaluating; visualizing; improvising, adapting; creating, synthesizing; designing; planning, developing; expediting; achieving; handling (objects); and operating (equipment). This totals 23 skills from the hierarchical structure in three categories, breaking down the skills that one should bring to a catalog librarian position in order to be satisfied and successful, efficient and productive.

The skills identified above are realistic and reasonable ones to desire in a catalog librarian. This list compares only minimally with the vision of a stereotypical catalog librarian, and compares at least as poorly with postings for cataloging positions which seek an individual who "likes to work alone and independently", and who is "detail oriented." In the past neither educators nor employers may have adequately stressed the importance of the skills with people just identified, or of skills with things, or the importance of this breadth and depth of skills with data or information. These are, however, skills that may are necessary to the performance of the job, and may legitimately be asked of a catalog librarian. As happens in recruitment for any position, it may not always be possible to recruit a candidate who holds or has the potential to develop all of these skills, but it is important to recognize that our need is for all of these abilities, and not to compromise our expectations.

In addition to being useful in the process of recruiting individuals to particular jobs, this list of skills is equally applicable, through use in course descriptions and elsewhere, to the process of recruiting students to a course of study in cataloging in library schools. Students may have no more than a vague acquaintance with the terminology of job and course descriptions which include elements such as descriptive cataloging, classification and subject analysis, and the MARC formats. The use of terminology relating to necessary or acquired skills that is at once more specific and more transparent to the uninitiated might make it clearer what type of person would be effective and would derive satisfaction from working with the complex system and rule-guided tasks that are used to provide access to a multitude of types and levels of information that are themselves produced in a variety of formats and which require multi-faceted accessibility in the catalog.

However useful it is to identify the skills exercised by catalog librarians, a simple statement of necessary skills is obviously not sufficient to describe a professional catalog librarian position. It is also necessary to specify the rules for description, classification system, subject heading type, form of catalog, automated systems used, material format(s), and language and subject knowledge required for a specific position. Rather than simply list the alphabet soup that usually fills job advertisements, however, - LC class., LCSH, USMARC, OCLC or RLIN, etc. - employers should also note the major skills that are expected of an individual who will apply knowledge or training to the standards in use. Such a statement would be especially useful for entry level positions. Articulating the need for analytical, organizational, planning, communication, supervisory and observational skills, for example, provides bottom line, clear information about what the employer is seeking in one who will get the job and who will get the job done.

The need for these skills may seem implicit to those who are familiar with what is involved in cataloging, and with the reality of what it takes to be adept and productive in the use of LC classification, LCSH, USMARC, etc., but even for such knowledgable people it is easy to fall into the trap of hiring someone who holds the appropriate credentials but lacks the skills to make use of them effectively. Conversely, stating what the most relevant skills for cataloging are might also attract candidates who do not think of themselves as matching the catalog librarian stereotype, but who enjoy using the specified skills. The need for such skills should also be covered during job interviews, and questions should be formulated to discern the presence or absence of these skills in a candidate, and the candiate's affinity for using them. That affinity or enthusiasm may be used as a measurement of interest in the work that must done.

Knowing the precise skills needed in a catalog librarian or MLS candidate, and making those necessary attributes clearly and precisely known to potential job applicants is as simple as being a wise consumer: Know what you are looking for and ask for it. Wise consumerism has a vital importance when placed in the realm of fulfillment of organizational needs.

"Obviously, the cost of improper selection of personnel can be very high. When the unsuccessful employee must be terminated, the recruiting and interviewing process must begin all over again, and the successor must first be trained before being put on the job. These costs, however, are only the more visible ones. The hidden costs are frequently even higher: low quality work performed by the unsuccessful employee while still on the job; the internal disorganization and disruption that employee may have caused; the customer ill will and alienation that may have been generated...."[5]

Knowing the full range of precise skills and interests required for successful accomplishment of the tasks we need done is the first step in filling a catalog librarian position. Making our specific skills needs known in job postings or course descriptions should aid in attracting candidates who may have or may be able to develop those skills. Only with a clear sense of skills needed firmly in mind can we assess the presence or absence of those skills in candidates. This knowledge should lead us to those who have the greatest potential for satisfaction and success in catalog librarian positions. As employers, we should be good consumers. We should be at least as thorough in our employee recruitment as are those career planners who are serious and sincere enough to assess their skills and interests, and shop for a career that will afford satisfaction and success. If we are effective in publicizing our needs accurately, we may also attract some of those career planners to the profession and to our jobs. Most of them will be individuals who would not have given the stereotypical catalog librarian position a second glance.

REFERENCES

1. Richard Nelson Bolles, *What Color Is Your Parachute?* (Berkeley, Calif.: Ten Speed Press, 1988), p. 68.
2. *Webster's Third New International Dictionary of the English Language, Unabridged,* s.v. "interest."
3. *Webster's,* s.v. "aptitude."
4. *Webster's,* s.v. "skill."
5. Erwin S. Stanton, *Successful Personnel Recruiting & Selection* (New York: AMACON, c1977), p. 3.

Recruiting Catalogers at the Louisiana State University Libraries

Marion T. Reid

There is a great hue and cry now on for catalogers. Even salaries abnormal to other functions in our library economy fail to discover these highly essential members of the library organism in numbers necessary to the health of the body bibliographic, and we are asking why.[1]

It is not surprising that we are echoing Julia Pettee's words, which first appeared in print over 60 years ago. The number of graduates of United States ALA-accredited library and information science programs declined 38% between 1976 and 1986.[2] For quite a few years now we have found it challenging to recruit librarians to fill cataloging positions at LSU, so the current national recruiting climate behooves us to approach filling our current vacancies with even more detailed gameplans than those used before.

But I want to address more than just our attracting individuals to LSU cataloging positions after they have obtained their MLS. Instead, in this paper I will address three levels at which we at LSU work to recruit catalogers. First, however, it is appropriate to describe our environment.

OUR SETTING

LSU is located in Baton Rouge, which has a greater metropolitan area population of more than 549,700. It is the state capitol, a seaport and the northernmost point for the petrochemical plants which line the Mississippi River to its mouth. We are 80 miles from the heart of New Orleans. With our Spanish and French heritage, fantastic food, strong Catholic influence, and festivals available in nearby towns nearly every week of the year, we have the opportunity to follow the Cajun tradition of "passing a good time."

Designated the flagship university for the state, LSU is a land grant, sea grant and wetlands university. It is struggling to provide quality education in spite of a depressed oil-based economy and the lowest per-capita funding for higher education provided by any state in the southeast.

The LSU Libraries is a highly centralized operation with a collection of 2 million volumes located in the main library, the special collections building, three branch libraries and one reserve room operation. The staff is small when compared to libraries of comparable collection size. Currently we have 46.6 full-time-equivalent (FTE) librarian positions, 82.25 FTE paraprofessional positions and 16 FTE graduate assistant positions. In addition, we have 398 student assistants who each work an average of 10 hours per week.

Since 1974, as a result of a university accreditation team recommendation, we have not hired librarians having an LSU MLS unless they have gained progressively responsible relevant experience elsewhere after obtaining their degree, or unless a particular position is unusually hard to fill.

Consequently, more than half of our permanent professional staff now have library degrees from other ALA-accredited schools. LSU librarians have faculty equivalency, have representation on the Faculty Senate, are eligible to serve on Faculty Senate committees, are eligible for sabbatical leave, and have a strong orientation toward professional involvement. In order to achieve the rank of "Librarian" (equivalent to full professor), an LSU librarian must have a sustained record of recognition at a state, regional and/or national level in addition to doing a fine job in the library.

At the end of October 1988 the LSU Libraries Catalog Department staff numbers 31.75 FTE positions, including 11 FTE librarians, 9.25 FTE library associates (individuals with an undergraduate degree, but no library degree), 9 FTE civil service positions (individuals with a high school diploma who meet state civil service requirements), 1.5 FTE graduate assistants (individuals working on an MLS) and 35 student assistants who each work an average of 10 hours per week. An organizational schematic of the Catalog Department is given in Figure 1.

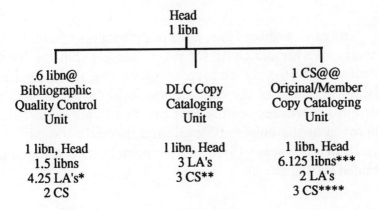

Figure 1
LSU Libraries Catalog Department
Organization Chart

Head
1 libn

.6 libn@ Bibliographic Quality Control Unit	DLC Copy Cataloging Unit	1 CS@@ Original/Member Copy Cataloging Unit
1 libn, Head 1.5 libns 4.25 LA's* 2 CS	1 libn, Head 3 LA's 3 CS**	1 libn, Head 6.125 libns*** 2 LA's 3 CS****

NOTES

Abbreviation definitions are: libn = librarian

LA = Library Associate

CS = Civil Service

A description of these categories is given in the text.

Quantities are expressed in full-time-equivalents (FTE's).

Positions are permanent and filled positions unless otherwise noted.

Information is as of 10/31/88.

@   Temporary visiting librarian. Will be filled when visa problems are solved. This individual will initially work with DLC Cataloging Copy Unit and then assist in other areas as appropriate.

@@   This vacant CS position, when filled, will either be assigned to a unit or serve as a floating position, assigned on a project basis.

*   .25 FTE is temporary.

**   One of these positions is vacant.

***   Three of these positions are vacant; one may not be reassigned to Cataloging. 6.125 FTE is temporary.

****   Two of these positions are vacant.

As of November 1988, three of the cataloger positions are vacant. We are searching for two catalogers, but the library administration may choose to place the third position elsewhere. Four of the civil service positions are vacant, but current procedures require that our justifications-to-fill be approved at the university level--and currently roughly one-fourth of the vacant Civil Service positions on campus are granted such approval.

In June 1985 the cataloging staff began implementing NOTIS. Among many other things, they have experienced being introduced to the real system on the very same day as our staff-wide barcoding project, sending off shelflist drawers for retrospective conversion, revising the recon records produced through that project, reconciling machine records with the card shelflist, linking unlinked circulation records with their appropriate bibliographic records as books are discharged, and creating machine records for those current returns which have none. In spite of the myriad additional commitments, this dedicated, hard-working staff have maintained a surprising throughput. Figure 2. outlines the technical services new title, added copy and added volume statistics for the last five fiscal years.

Figure 2.

LSU Libraries Technical Service
Cataloging Throughput: New Titles, Added Copies & Volumes
Fiscal Years 1984 - 1988

Note: In 1985 staff began work on NOTIS implementation

	1984	1985	1986	1987	1988
TOTALS	83,415	78,605	74,182	70,971	75,839
Books					
new titles	35,169	36,746	32,780	29,588	32,262
added copies/					
added vols.	21,730	18,179	19,314	20,108	24,939
Microforms					
new titles	19,979	19,038	15,741	13,770	16,287
added copies/					
added vols.	6,204	3,941	5,561	7,316	2,350
Audio/Visual					
new titles	333	701	786	189	1
Items Withdrawn	2,930	3,230	1,064	684	7,171

LSU CATALOGER RECRUITMENT EFFORTS

I mentioned earlier that we at LSU recruit catalogers at several levels. Specifically,

- We attempt to recruit promising individuals into library schools.
- We provide MLS students and librarians working on additional degrees with cataloging experiences which give them both marketable training and an opportunity to evaluate whether or not they would like to become catalogers.
- We mount concerted, flexible efforts to recruit qualified individuals for cataloger positions.

RECRUITING INDIVIDUALS FOR LIBRARY SCHOOL

With a student assistant population of 398 and a support staff of 82.25 FTE, the LSU Libraries has a large group of experienced library workers who are potential library school applicants. Since the inception of the LSU library school, which began in the 1930s under the supervision of the LSU Director of Libraries, there has been a close association between the faculties of the library and the library school. This positive relationship, in combination with the benefit for library staff to have release time from work to attend classes, and occasional opportunities for support staff to attend library conferences, or to hear visiting librarians who participate in the LSU Libraries' Ella V. Schwing Lecture Series, creates an environment which encourages some of the student assistant population and many of the library support staff to take library school courses.

I have no figures to cite as proof of the success of our recruitment efforts at this level, but I know that many former

LSU Libraries support staff are now working elsewhere as librarians, and several former student assistants are working in the book trade. Just this fall two of our library associates began taking library school courses; one of them (who wants to become a serials cataloger) as a full-time student who remains with us ten hours a week as a graduate assistant.

RECRUITING MLS STUDENTS FOR CATALOGING

Last spring the LSU School of Library and Information Science Research Center Annex for the ALA Office for Library Personnel Resources conducted a survey of master's degree students enrolled in ALA-accredited programs of library and information science education. Preliminary results of "The Library and Information Science Student Attitudes, Demographics and Aspirations Survey" (LISSADA) were presented at the ALA OLPR preconference in New Orleans in July[3] and a summary article has appeared in the November 1988 *American Libraries.*[4]

Of the 3,484 LISSADA survey respondents, only 7.6% perceive cataloging as the most desirable type of position for their first job after graduating. An additional 7.8% indicate a technical services position as the most desirable. The raw data shows that those who want to be catalogers and/or work in technical services have the same attitudes and aspirations as those who want to work with other library functions. The difference appears to be that the people who want to work as catalogers have concrete knowledge of the kind of jobs that catalogers really do--either through their own experience as student assistants, paraprofessionals or graduate students, or through knowing of someone else's experience. The Appendix provides more of a flavor of some of the LISSADA responses.

The responses of the LISSADA survey participants who hope to be catalogers suggest that the most important way to recruit people into cataloging is to provide them with a positive experience in cataloging or related work. With two or three graduate assistantships in our Catalog Department each semester, we do this on a continuing basis. Since the fall of 1969, 55 people who later obtained an MLS at LSU have worked as graduate assistants in Cataloging. Of the 45 students for which we have information, 23 (slightly more than half) have been catalogers for at least part of their careers. Two more are technical services heads, and two others are in acquisitions work. In 1979 the LSU Libraries initiated an intern program--an opportunity for individuals with MLS degrees to work half-time while pursuing an additional degree. Eight of our interns have worked in Cataloging. Three of them had worked earlier as graduate assistants in Cataloging while they were pursuing their MLSs and are included in the above statistics. Of the other five, we have been able to track four -- all of whom are now catalogers. All told, of the 49 people who have been either graduate assistants or interns in our Cataloging Department since 1969 and whom we have been able to track, 59% are working or have worked as catalogers and/or technical services heads. This method of recruitment is working!

RECRUITING LIBRARIANS FOR CATALOGING POSITIONS

Earlier I mentioned that as of November, 1988, we are down three full-time permanent catalogers from the number we had in January. In March our serials cataloger left for a job with supervisory responsibility at the University of Colorado. In June our microforms cataloger retired. And in September our science cataloger left for a job with supervisory and NOTIS implementation responsibilities at the LSU Law Library. We have clearance to fill two of these positions. We are searching for a serials cataloger and a monographs cataloger.

Actually, we have been searching for the serials cataloger for some time now. We coordinated the original search to coincide with screening interviews at the ALA annual conference in New Orleans in July. We had a very small pool with a couple of possibilities in each of two categories: experienced catalogers, and fresh MLSs. We opted to interview one or two of the experienced people and, by the time we realized that the experienced people were not even interested in coming for on-site interviews, the new MLSs already had other jobs. So in August we designed a plan for additional (mostly temporary) help in Cataloging and decided to readvertise the serials cataloger position in conjunction with the search for a monographs cataloger to replace the science cataloger position which had just become available.

In the LSU Libraries we have many people involved in the search and interview process. The primary players are:

- the assistant to the director, who handles paperwork and is the primary contact for applicants
- the search committee, an ad hoc committee of library faculty which reviews applications, may screen applicants at ALA and/or by phone, obtains references, makes recommendations to the Director of Libraries on which applicants to interview, structures and coordinates the on-site interview, and makes appointment recommendations to the Library Appointment and Promotion Committee
- the Library Appointment and Promotion Committee (tenured library faculty), which hears the recommendation of the search committee and, through written ballot, makes a recommendation to the Director of Libraries

- the Director of Libraries, who meets with the candidates during the on-site interviews, ultimately makes the hiring decisions, handles all salary negotiations, and offers the positions

In addition, the heads of the unit and department in which the position we are seeking to fill is located, and the appropriate associate or assistant director serve to varying degrees in advisory capacities if they are not members of the search committee. The search committee for the serials cataloger, which has now become the cataloger search committee, is working with both cataloging vacancies, and has consulted frequently with appropriate members of the library hierarchy.

Figure 3. graphically displays the tasks and timelines for our serials cataloger re-search and our monographs cataloger search. The narrative that follows explains key points.

Figure 3.
Contingency Plans and Hiring Timelines for
2 Cataloger Positions

Task	A	S	O	N	D	J	F	M	A	M	J
Implement Transition Plan											
develop plan	x										
revise goals											
add staff			x		x				x		
temp. ser. cat. (.125 FTE)	x	x	x	x	x	x	x	x	x	x	
temp. gen'l. cat. (.6 FTE)				x	x	x	x	x	x	x	
permanent LA (1 FTE)				x	x	x	x	x	x	x	
renew temp. micro. cat. (.5 FTE)				x	x	x	x	x	x	x	x
temp. gen'l. cat. ? (1 FTE)							x	x	x	x	x
										x	x
Advertise											
create/revise job announcements		x	x								
advertise				x							
file listing for ALA Midwinter					x						
identify and contact MLS prospects		x	x	x	x						
contact library schools				x	x						
visit library schools		x									
Interview		x						x			
screen at Midwinter					x						
interview at LSU						x	x	x			
Fill Positions									x	x	

An important factor is the transition plan to help sustain both morale and workload in the Original Cataloging/Member Copy Unit where the vacancies exist. The plan for additional staff to help with serials cataloging was developed by the unit head, the head of the Catalog Department, the search committee chair (who is also a cataloger) and the associate director for technical services. From the time the serials cataloging position became vacant in March and the time when this planning group met in August, another cataloger had been handling rush serials. More serials cataloging work needed to be done and the unit head, who had become responsible for supervising serials cataloging when the Catalog Department was reorganized in October 1987, wanted more guidance in how to handle serials. The library administration moved a vacant library associate (LA) position into the unit and one of the experienced LAs already there began to learn the basics of serials cataloging. The half-time serials cataloger who is on loan to the Louisiana Newspaper Project from the Catalog Department agreed to work an additional 5 hours per week to advise the unit head on serials cataloging policy and to assist in developing procedures.

The library administration then sought other ways to add more staff to Cataloging to help through the transition. A visiting librarian from Hebrew University in Jerusalem, who for the past year cataloged non-Hebrew materials, applied for a job. She will begin work on a part-time basis in the DLC Copy Edit Unit and the Bibliographic Quality Control Unit when visa paperwork is resolved. The university administration earlier had given permission for the microforms cataloger who retired in June to work half-time until February. We have initiated paperwork to the university system president requesting that the appointment be extended through June 1989. We are seeking permission to fill the three civil service vacancies in

Cataloging and we are seeking permission to fill another vacant civil service position from elsewhere in the library so we can put it in Cataloging as well. Next spring we may ask one of the current graduate assistants in Cataloging to work on a full- time temporary basis for several months as a General Librarian (instructor level) after receiving the MLS.

It is important for the Original/Member Copy Cataloging Unit head and the Catalog Department head to realize that the library administration recognizes the problems inherent in having fewer professional catalogers. Statistics simply cannot be as high and goals cannot be achieved as quickly as they would if we had two or three more catalogers. In October the associate director for technical services, the head of the catalog department and the unit heads carefully reviewed the fiscal 1989 cataloging goals presented in the FY1988 Catalog Department annual report. They revised them into a more realistic timeframe given current circumstances. These goals will be reviewed again in December and May during the semiannual library planning retreats conducted by the Director with members of the representative staff council, department heads and administrative staff.   The goals will be further revised by the head of the catalog department and the cataloging unit heads next January and July.

Since we believe that personal contact is a very important part of the recruitment process, we will institute three methods to identify and talk with potential applicants.

(1)   This fall we will identify former LSU MLS students who worked with us as graduate assistants and who live in the Baton Rouge area. We will contact them and ask them if they are interested in applying.

(2)   We will talk with cataloging professors in several library schools other than LSU, asking them to identify students:--who will receive their degrees by

May 1989, --who might be interested in moving and --whom they would recommend as strong candidates for a beginning cataloger position.

(3) We will contact catalogers working elsewhere who have ties to Louisiana (e.g., they went to school here, have lived here or have relatives here) and ask if they would be interested in applying.

CONCLUSION

At the LSU Libraries we recruit catalogers on several levels:

(1) We provide an opportunity for student assistants and support staff to learn about library work; as a result of this experience, some choose to go to library school. We have begun to encourage some support staff to attend library school. Perhaps it is time for us to formalize this process and actively promote library school with our student assistants as well.

(2) We provide an opportunity for graduate students in library school to experience various facets of cataloging. We are successful in recruiting catalogers at this level.

(3) We recruit individuals having MLS degrees to come work with us as catalogers. We must remember that for the Catalog Department it is important to revise goal expectations and to add temporary staff as possible while the vacancies exist. It is also important to make personal contacts with potential applicants during the recruiting process. Perhaps by March 1989 I will have some progress to report in this area!

APPENDIX:

Summary Of And Comments On "The Library and Information Science Student Attitudes, Demographics and Aspirations (LISSADA) Survey" raw data from a cataloging perspective

CAMPUS CORRESPONDENCE: LOUISIANA STATE UNIVERSITY

date: October 21, 1988

from:Barbara L. Anderson, Intern
to:Marion T. Reid, Associate Director for Technical Services
[NOTE:Barbara L. Anderson, on educational leave from her position as Head of the Cataloging Section at the Virginia Commonwealth University Library, worked 20 hours per week in the LSU Libraries as an Intern reporting to the Associate Director for Technical Services, while taking courses in the automation program of the LSU Graduate School of Library and Information Science.]

There were a number of recurring reasons offered for entering the library science profession, regardless of any specified field of interest within the profession. They are listed here in no particular order.
--love of books and information
--variety of work
--challenging and intellectually stimulating nature of the work
--service-oriented nature of the work
--good job market and job security
--opportunity to be on cutting edge of new technology
--pleasant nature of work environment
--relatively low levels of stress
--relatively short period of time to complete the MLS

Three general questions were asked at the end of the LISSADA survey: Why did you choose this profession as a field of work? How would you describe the future of this profession? What are the three reasons you would give to others to persuade them to choose this profession?

Although these open-ended questions did not ask for intended specialization within the field, reasons offered for entering the profession frequently involved a desire to go into a specific area of librarianship. Most frequently cited were school librarianship, children's librarianship, reference librarianship and special (e.g., corporate) librarianship.

Many respondents interested in these specializations indicate they are "burned out" teachers and/or persons with teaching certificates who prefer not to teach. All of these specializations are highly visible areas of librarianship -- areas in which it seems likely that non-librarians could envision what the work responsibilities might entail.

Conversely, cataloging (and other technical services positions) are virtually invisible to non-librarians, and librarians or library school students without related work experience can only imagine cataloging positions from the point of reference offered by their cataloging courses. The image is often unpleasant. Two respondents to the survey mentioned the negative aspect of cataloging in particular.

A very small number of respondents (only 18) specifically referred to cataloging as a career goal in a positive sense. For the most part, reasons offered by these 18 for entering the profession closely paralleled the reasons offered by the respondents in general. Ten of the 18 indicated prior cataloging or technical services work experiences. The most prevalent reasons for entering the profession cited by this group were:

--challenging nature of the work (5)
--variety of the work (4)
--dynamic nature of the work (4)
--service to others (3)
--congenial work environment (2)
--opportunities to keep up with current information trends (2)
The other 8 gave no indication of prior work experience.
Reasons most often offered by this group for entering the
profession were:

--service to others (5)
--job security (3)
--challenging nature of the work (2)
--exposure to information (2)
--congenial work environment (2) (interpreted by one of the
respondents as "a quiet atmosphere, conducive to
concentration.")

I have no way of knowing whether the group of 8 just
mentioned included persons with work experience that was not
described, but I think it is interesting that the group of 10 who
mentioned their previous work experience cited, in particular,
the challenging, varied and dynamic nature of the field, aspects
not mentioned or mentioned less frequently by the group of 8
indicating no work experience.

Work experience in a cataloging department is probably
the best way to obtain a true picture of catalog librarianship,
although this may depend on the nature of the tasks assigned to
a student or non-professional worker.

Obviously not everyone will have the kind of exposure to
a cataloging department (either prior to or during an MLS
program) as compared to a reference department or other more

visible aspect of the field, and not everyone can be employed as a cataloging paraprofessional or student assistant.

Alternative possibilities for attracting MLS students into cataloging positions might include:

--Bring enthusiastic cataloging librarians from the area into the cataloging course(s) to describe the nature of their work and the reasons why it is enjoyable and rewarding.

--Consider having cataloging instructors with split responsibilities (between teaching and cataloging) to better portray the practical and realistic aspects of being a cataloger.

--Encourage RTSD CCS to prepare a book (video?) portraying successful catalog librarians who are enthusiastic about their work.

From my perspective, cataloging is much more varied and stimulating than it is generally perceived. Persons who have worked in cataloging departments appear to realize this, as evidenced by the 10 respondents who cited prior cataloging/technical services work experience and by the large numbers of persons who have worked in the LSU Catalog Department while attending school and have gone on to cataloging positions.

It seems to me that more needs to be done--primarily within the MLS program--to portray the true nature of a professional catalog librarian's responsibilities.

REFERENCES

1. Julia Pettee, "Wanted--Catalogers," *Library Journal* 46 (1921): 543-545.
2. Computed from Table 1 of Kathleen M. Heim, "Librarians for the New Millennium" In *Librarians for*

the New Millennium, edited by William E. Moen and Kathleen M. Heim (American Library Association Office for Library Personnel Resources, 1988): p. 5.

3.   William E. Moen, "Library and Information Science Student Attitudes, demographics and Aspirations Survey: Who We Are and Why We Are Here." In *Librarians for the New Millennium*, pp. 93-109.

4.   William E. Moen and Kathleen M. Heim. "The Class of 1988: Librarians for the New Millenium (sic)," *American Libraries* 19 (November 1988): 858-860, 885.

5.   *Ibid*, Table 9.

PART II:
SESSION ON EDUCATING
CATALOGING LIBRARIANS

Educating Cataloging Librarians: Its Art and Craft

Jane B. Robbins

INTRODUCTION

" ... joyless, mindless, barren." "... best suited to preparing indifferent cogs for an industrial bureaucratic machine, that is, at best, to be part of yesterday." These descriptions of the American education system appeared in the early 1970's and are attributed to Charles Silberman and Amitai Etzioni.[1] Pedagogy, it appears, is not a prestigious activity. Although dictionaries give the first definition of its related term, pedagogue, as "teacher," it is with the second, "a person who is pedantic, dogmatic, and formal," that too many associate the word. To those of us for whom pedagogy is our chosen profession, it is a discomfort that an overwhelming number of others fail to proclaim the value of our work. Although many disparaging remarks are repeated about teaching, paradoxically much goodwill abounds for teachers. One reason for the paradox is that virtually everyone performs teaching roles of some sort; perhaps the most ubiquitous experience being as a parent. It is the ubiquity of teaching that on the one hand makes so many think that anyone can do it, and on the other, as they confront their teaching failures, makes so many come to see it for the challenging work it is.

For teachers of cataloging it may be that the highs and lows of the paradox are felt more intensely. The conventional wisdom is that, "The subject of cataloging and classification is perceived by all too many students as a rite of passage that must be endured in order to enter the world librarianship."[2] It may be that many of those in the field who are not catalogers, and those in library education who do not teach cataloging, incorrectly understand it as dull and routine, and that they transfer their understanding to other librarians and students.[3] It seems more likely, however, that it is the method of teaching cataloging, rather than its content, that is dull and routine. If it is the teaching method that occasions a less than enthusiastic response to cataloging as an academic subject, and subsequently as an area of work, then a remedy is available. That remedy is improving the way cataloging is taught. But first, it is important to make certain that there is nothing inherently dull or dulling in the subject matter of itself.

CATALOGERS: CHARACTERISTICS OF AN OCCUPATIONAL GROUP

While it is probable that cataloging is not inherently dull, it may be that catalogers themselves are too "orderly, role conformist, and systematic-methodical."[4] Catalog librarians (along with other librarians) have been found to lack an inclination for leadership, assertiveness, social interaction and change, as well as self-confidence; further, it is noted that they are disinclined to encourage challenges on the job."[5]

Management consultants have long maintained that there is a synergistic relationship between the influence of individuals who perform certain work requirements and the work requirements themselves. If this description of cataloging librarians is correct, then it is important to change who chooses to become catalogers. If cataloging is to become a "popular" occupational choice within librarianship positive role models need to be prevalent.

CATALOGING AS A SUBJECT TO BE TAUGHT

If there is one thing about which most librarians would agree it may be that cataloging is the subject taught in library school which is most uniquely the intellectual property of the field of librarianship. No other academic field claims bibliographic classification theory as its subject area. Saye states that the essential elements of the introductory cataloging course are:

"- descriptive cataloging (emphasis upon monographs
- access points (non-subject)
- heading work (non-subject)
- Dewey Decimal Classification
- Library of Congress Classification
- MARC format
- OCLC or equivalent (searching only)
- subject heading work
- filing
- treatment of nonbook materials"[6]

The purposes of this course he sees as:
" - preparing persons to have at least a minimal level of cataloging expertise;
- acquainting them with the basic tools of cataloging and classification; and

making them aware of where they can go to get answers to cataloging questions."[7]

While Boll's list of basic bibliographic skills[8] includes locating and using bibliographic records as well as creating them, and while the language he uses is considerably different, Boll and Saye agree that the overarching goal of the beginning course is to create professionals who can begin "... to be problem-solvers in a cataloging environment.[9]

These general descriptions of the content of a beginning cataloging course appear to allow for challenging content. It is difficult to imagine that it is the above detailed content that causes whatever the perceived difficulty is in making cataloging appealing to students. In fact, the basic cataloging course would seem to present an almost perfect opportunity to apply learning theory and to blend theory and practice into instruction.

Boll argues successfully that the learning of "bibliographic input and retrieval" easily fits into the area of learning theory called field theory in which five steps are outlined.

DIFFERENTIATION: The cognitive process by which a field changes progressively from relative homogeneity to relative heterogeneity so that the various components of the field are more readily distinguished. STRUCTURING: The cognitive process of organizing a differentiated field in some manner so as to increase the unity of the parts in identifiable patterns. INTEGRATING: The cognitive process of combining structured entities which prior to integration did not appear to be related. ABSTRACTING: The cognitive process whereby a learner incorporates the attributes of specific entities and thereby establishes a higher-order entity or whole within the context of the immediate field. GENERALIZING: A conclusion that goes beyond the data or information of the immediate context, bringing in perceptions and data from other situations.[10]   In addition, Boll points out that learning theory as an area of study within education notes the following themes:

- People have different learning styles
- Learning must have a purpose and an application
- The student must be able to participate responsibly in the learning process
- Self-initiated, experiential learning produces self-reliant learners
- Reinforcement is an important contributor to learning
- The learner's motivation is an important factor in learning.[11]

Other findings from learning theory are found in the Appendix.

Derr states that the goal of professional education in librarianship is to design an educational program which will build on the following three elements:

1. Teaching of applied theory--Generalized procedures for the performance of the primary tasks of the profession can be taught. Also, the manner in which these procedures have been developed uniting concepts and principles from various disciplines with facts pertaining to the environment within which information handling occurs can be taught.

2. Application of applied theory to analysis of specific settings--Generalized procedures and the explanatory rationale on which they are based can be united with facts pertaining to professional tasks in a specific setting to form hypothesized procedures for the performance these tasks.

3. <u>Use of applied theory in special settings</u>--
Hypothesized procedures can be united with an understanding of the salient facts in particular setting to develop skill in the performance of certain tasks.[12]

Based upon the information provided it can be claimed that:

1) catalogers are not significantly different from other librarians in terms of work values, potential, personality, etc.;

2) the subject matter of cataloging does not differ significantly from any other subject matter in terms of its being either inherently exciting or dull;

3) the findings of learning theory apply to the subject of cataloging; and,

4) cataloging can be taught through the integration of theory and practice.

It is therefore possible to return to the original premise of this paper; i.e., that improving the way cataloging is taught will result in more librarians choosing cataloging as an occupational focus.

LEARNING TO TEACH

Ideally, those who plan to enter the field of cataloging education should by their nature evidence "self-motivation, perseverance, curiosity, initiative, strong interests, and ability to work hard."[13] These are all characteristics, traits, or even skills, if you will, that are determined long before a potential faculty member becomes a doctoral student; however, evidence of these characteristics should be sought when selecting faculty. Faculty charged with the responsibility of teaching and counseling doctoral students should encourage those with the majority of the characteristics listed above to consider library education as a career, and concomitantly to dissuade those who do not possess them. Another key element is, of course, articulateness; the good teacher must be able to communicate in both verbal and written modes.

Shera says, "I submit there are three elements requisite to success in teaching--substantive knowledge, communication and experience, the last of which is particularly important in the professional school."[14] Although experience is tantamount, he also cautions against "... the great danger of excessive dependence upon it ... [for] it leads to provincialism in teaching.[15] Further he states "... the best methods in the world cannot compensate for an absence of substance to be taught."[16] It is thus becoming more clear that even though most doctoral programs do not provide opportunities for learning and/or practicing teaching methods, or for studying library education and faculty roles, they do serve the key purpose of providing the student with exposure to a substantive body of knowledge.

If one agrees that gaining substantive knowledge is the most important activity for prospective faculty to undertake during their doctoral study, then the question arises, is there time within the program to study library education, learning theory, teaching techniques, etc. and to afford an opportunity for classroom experience? This author contends that there is. Each institution offering the doctoral degree should provide one course in library education for all students contemplating library and information science teaching careers. This course should include such curriculum components as:

(1) history of library education, including the role of relevant professional organizations, accreditation, certification, international aspects, etc.

(2)   structure and organization of higher education, particularly professional education, and including such topics as tenure

(3)   structure and organization of library and information science education

(4)   the role of the faculty member

(5)   contemporary curriculum structure and content

(6)   teaching methodologies including instructional technologies

(7)   learning theory

(8)   current problems and concerns

The course should provide opportunities for participants to read widely in the field, develop a model curriculum, course, course unit and class session, and to present a class session. The presented class session should preferably be given to an actual class and should be videotaped. Performance of the participants both in terms of their grasp of content and observed ability to communicate should be taken seriously. Those unable to perform the act of teaching should be dissuaded from a teaching career. Ability in this class should be communicated to other faculty members who might be recommending the participants for faculty positions.

Those interested in teaching careers should be encouraged to visit classes given by highly-respected teachers throughout the campus. Emulation of masters of teaching, as well as learning what not to do from bad teachers, is an excellent approach to acquiring teaching skills. If it is not possible for the student interested in a career in cataloging education to have full responsibility for presenting a cataloging course, s/he should at least be given the opportunity to be a teaching assistant for a course (in any subject area) given by a "good" teacher. Aspiring faculty might be urged to take a visiting summer faculty position at an institution other than that at which they are a student so they might taste the scope of the faculty role.

It has been suggested that major universities offer new doctorates a one-year internship or residency program in teaching.[17]   It has also been suggested that new faculty join a school one term prior to the beginning of their teaching responsibilities[18] so that they might be introduced to the university, the particular library education program and its faculty and curriculum, develop courses, build confidence, etc. This latter suggestion might be feasible in the larger schools, but in most schools, each faculty member is critical, and a term without their covering classes would be impractical. Having new faculty team-teach with experienced faculty is another practical suggestion which has been offered.

CONTINUING PREPARATION OF TEACHERS OF LIBRARY AND INFORMATION SCIENCE

In reality, the early years of a faculty position are more basic than continuing preparation. After the initial introductory period of approximately three years, it is essential that in addition to espousing continuing education to their students, faculty members should also begin to look to their own continuing education. We are all aware of tenured faculty members who do not "keep up" even in their own areas of speciality. Both pressure and opportunity should be provided to faculty to increase their substantive knowledge. Participation in professional organizations is another route, but careful selection of the type of participation is essential. A return to practice for a summer or term is another method which may prove beneficial. Consulting, too, can add much to the knowledge of faculty members.

An equally important focus of continuing preparation for teaching is in the area of teaching methods, skills and technologies. Many universities offer short courses in a variety of skill areas in which faculty should be encouraged to participate. The development of course and/or instructor evaluation instruments, test/examination development, course objectives development, and use of instructional technologies such as videotaping and computer-aided instruction are but a few examples of skills that may be covered. These courses are usually conveniently offered in late afternoon hours or during intersessions. Faculty who participate should be encouraged to share highlights with their colleagues, and should be rewarded for doing so.

The continuing preparation of faculty members is one of the key responsibilities of a school's administrator. The dean should meet with each faculty member at least once each year to go over class evaluations and plans for continued development. In the absence of such plans, the dean should encourage, cajole or do whatever is necessary to ensure that each faculty member develops and attempts to adhere to a plan. The plan should include activities expected to be accomplished in each area of faculty responsibility during the academic year and summer term(s). Flexibility should be maintained in the plan to allow for unforeseen opportunities which may arise. Communication of plans among colleagues is important; a faculty meeting devoted to sharing development plans should be held each year.

The career of a library educator is a commitment to a career with unattainable responsibilities and constantly expanding areas of inquiry. While faculty members will develop specializations, and from time to time will concentrate their activities in one or another of their areas of responsibility: teaching, research and other scholarly activity, school activities, university activities, etc., the preparation is never done. This should be looked upon as one of the joys of teaching. The preparation of a teacher is continuously basic to the art.

CONCLUSION

More students would be likely to choose cataloging as a career field within librarianship if our schools had more gifted teachers of cataloging. Cataloging courses should include not only practical aspects of learning how to catalog, but courses should also deal with the challenging aspects of classification theory, technical services management, and education of support staff. (Practicing catalogers and cataloging department managers have reported that a growing part of their professional assignment entails teaching support staff about the material they themselves learned in library school.

While it may not be possible to teach the art of teaching, sundry aspects of the craft can be taught. When people think of craftspersons and artists they most often think of people who care a great deal about and gain great satisfaction from their work; they are people who enjoy the doing, the creating, as much as they enjoy the product, and they delight in quality. We must strive to be craftspersons and artists in the teaching of not just cataloging but of all the subjects covered in our schools of library and information studies.

Another, very different way to perhaps make cataloging more appealing is to embrace the idea of holistic librarianship,[19] i.e., to integrate into most professional positions responsibilities that range through the broad spectrum of professional tasks: selection, public service, technical service and management, as opposed to concentrating duties within a single responsibility area.

Whatever approaches are taken to increasing the quantity and quality of persons who select cataloging as all (or part) of their professional career focus, the field of librarianship and the service we offer our users will clearly be improved.

APPENDIX

- Learning is an active, continuous process. Purposive action is better than mere repeated motion. Humans learn many things they don't need to know.
- Learning takes place in terms of stimulus and response; conditioning is a common term to describe the process. Catching and maintaining a learner's attention provides the necessary condition for a desired stimulus to evoke a response.
- Learning is affected by the learner's set--that is, a predisposition to react to some stimuli in a particular way. Learners can be motivated in many ways to learn specific things. Conflicting motivations may get in the way of learning.
- Time and conditions affect learning greatly. Individuals vary greatly in the time they take to learn something.
- Association is an important aspect of learning. Identifying, grouping, and sequencing assist learning.
- Reinforcement is the general term for stimuli introduced to reinforce behavior that stimulates further learning
- Rewards seem to affect a wider range of learning more favorably than does punishment.
- Relearning is much easier than original learning. Recall is different from retention; given the right stimulus, learners can recall more than they commonly suspect.
- Progress in learning is not uniform, but frequently reaches plateaus where the rate of learning slows appreciably.

- Interference is a common cause of forgetting. New and similar learning can interfere with the old. Learning a thing well helps to counteract interference.
- Interfering responses may inhibit learning; therefore, they may have to be removed to foster learning.
- Transfer of learning has been too uncritically accepted in the past. success in learning some things may make it easier to learn others. It is possible to learn how to learn.

Source: Kenneth E. Eble, *The Craft of Teaching*. (San Francisco: Jossey-Bass, 1976) p. 150-151.

NOTES

1. Cited in Charles R. Martell, "Myths, Schooling, and the Practice of Librarianship," *College & Research Libraries* 45 (September 1984): 374.
2. Jerry D. Saye, "The Cataloging Experience in Library and Information Science Education: An Educator's Perspective," *Cataloging and Classification Quarterly* 7 (1987): 27.
3. Even catalogers sometimes describe their work as dull and routine, see "Letters: Remarks from a fuddy-duddy," *Library Journal* 113 (May 1, 1988): 8.
4. Suzanne O. Frankie, "Occupational Characteristics of University Librarianship." In *Options for the 80's: Proceedings of the Second National Conference of the Association of College and Research Libraries*, Minneapolis; edited by M.D. Kathman and V.F. Massman, 409. (Greenwich, CT: JAI Press, 1982).
5. Ibid. 409.
6. Saye, "The Cataloging Experience," 33.

7. Ibid. 34.

8. John J. Boll, "Should Learning Theory Play a Role in Teaching Bibliographic Information Input and Retrieval?" in *Joint meeting between the Association internationale des ecoles de sciences de l'information and the Association for Library and Information Science Education, 1st: 1988: Montreal, Canada.* pp. 170- 72.

9. Saye, "The Cataloging Experience," 34.

10. Boll, "Should Learning Theory Play a Role," 170.

11. Ibid. 174-77."

12. Richard L. Derr, "The Integration of Theory and Practice in Professional Programs," *Journal of Education for Librarianship* 23 (Winter, 1983): 197.

13. Kenneth E. Ebel, *The Craft of Teaching.* (San Francisco: Jossey-Bass, 1976), p. 138.

14. Jesse H. Shera, "... And Gladly Teach," *Journal of Education for Librarianship* 19 (Summer 1978): 60.

15. Ibid. 62.

16. Ibid. 61.

17. Christopher Jencks and David Riesman, *The Academic Revolution* (NY: Doubleday, 1968), p. 537.

18. Peter G. New, *Education for Librarianship.* (Hamden, CT: Linnet, 1978), p. 55.

19. Michael Gorman, "Reorganization at the University of Illinois, Urbana/Champaign," *Journal of Academic Librarianship,* 9 (1987): 225-7.

REFERENCES

Boll, John J. "Should Learning Theory Play a Role in Teaching Bibliographic Information Input and Retrieval?" in

Cronkhite, Bernice Brown. *Handbook for College Teachers.* Cambridge, MA: Harvard University Press, 1950.

Eble, Kenneth E. *The Craft of Teaching.* San Francisco: Jossey-Bass, 1978.

Eisner, Elliot W. "The Art and Craft of Teaching," *Educational Leadership* (January 1983), pp. 4-13.

Franzwa, Gregg. "Socrates Never Had Days Like This," *Liberal Education* 70 (1984): 203-208.

Highet, Gilbert. *The Art of Teaching.* New York: Knopf, 1950.

Jencks, Christopher, and David Riesman. *The Academic Revolution.* NY: Doubleday, 1968, p. 537.

New, Peter G. *Education for Librarianship.* Hamden, CT: Linnet, 1978, p. 55.

Shera, Jesse H. ". . . And Gladly Teach," *Journal of Education for Librarianship* 19 (Summer 1978): 60.

Saye, Jerry D. "The Cataloging Experience in Library and Information Science Education: An Educator's Perspective," *Cataloging and Classification Quarterly* 7 (1987): 27-45.

Skinner, B.F. *The Technology of Teaching.* New York: Appleton-Century-Crofts, 1968.

Making Cataloging Interesting

Michael Carpenter

Cataloging has been notoriously a dull exercise at least since the time of Panizzi. As Panizzi himself noted,

> . . . deeply impressed as I am myself with the difficulties often alluded to [in the construction of a library catalog] I am even more impressed with the difficulty of communicating to others an equal sense of these difficulties. In attempting to do so, I must enter into minutiae and details, not only apparently insignificant, but also not very easy to make plain in writing; and I must beg a more than ordinary degree of attention from those who will condescend to follow me through a narrow, rugged, uninteresting path, requiring a patience and labour which few will deem well bestowed on so vulgar a subject as an ALPHABETICAL CATALOGUE.[1]

More recently, Jerry D. Saye has stated that "The subject of cataloging and classification is perceived by all too many students as a rite of passage that must be endured to enter the world of librarianship."[2] Saye continues by noting that many have opined that the subject is uninteresting, that "A key question then to be asked is why cataloging, a topic we in the specialty field find intellectually stimulating, challenging and exciting, is perceived by so many as dull, routine and perhaps even unnecessary."[3]

That cataloging requires patience in a trip down a narrow, rugged uninteresting path seems to be a problem persisting to the present day; Panizzi and Saye are but the oldest and the most recent writers making the same complaint. Why should this be so? Why are cataloging courses uninteresting, and what can be done about the situation?

I submit that a major factor in our losing the interest of students lies in our having an inappropriate set of objectives for cataloging courses. We may well be teaching material in a way guaranteed to make the subject uninteresting.   The responsibility for changing the situation rests squarely on those who teach. In this paper, I intend to show a way, that of changing course objectives, that will make cataloging an interesting subject. What are our objectives today? Saye says the immediate objective of a beginning course is "to develop minimal level mastery of the basic operations undertaken by a cataloger."[5] A number of years ago, in considering the mixture of proper management and cataloging, Boll stated that as a first step students must be taught to "conform to currently existing standards" before learning "that current standards are not ironclad."[6] In that discussion Boll assumed that students were being taught how to catalog.

Having library science students trained in the practice of cataloging is clearly in demand by employers. Many library managers would like entry-level librarians to be well trained technicians, ready to put into production immediately upon reporting to work. Such a desire is especially keenly felt in the case of beginning catalogers.[7]

Even in the face of administrative demand, however, it must be asked whether training in cataloging techniques is indeed practical, or even wise, for an introductory course. What we want to do in an introductory course depends on the nature of our students and their needs. If the course is required, it is hard to see how training in cataloging techniques should be among its primary objectives, since very few of the class members will become practicing catalogers.[8] The ability to use, communicate directions on how to use, and manage the catalog are more likely career requirements for the majority of our students.

I believe that many of our students realize they will not become catalogers. The essays on their applications for admission to library school are impressive evidence of this contention. Further evidence is provided in the recent LISSADA (Library and Information Science Student Attitudes, Demographics, and Aspirations) Survey. Only 7.6% of the students surveyed believed that cataloging would be a desirable occupation, and it can be safely assumed that many of the respondents who thought cataloging to be desirable also considered other library jobs desirable.[9] If training in cataloging techniques is not a satisfactory objective for a cataloging course, we need to determine what such a set of objectives would be. Part of that determination can be made through a discussion of the various types of learning, a topic to which I now turn.

THE DOMAINS OF LEARNING

As early as 1948, a group of psychologists created a basic taxonomy of educational objectives through a tripartite division of the three domains of learning.[10]   Those domains are called the cognitive, affective and psychomotor. After forty years, this taxonomy, often called Bloom's Taxonomy, is still the main framework used in discussions of course objectives.[11]   The taxonomy is of student behaviors that are desired as a result of instruction. Of course, it may be that the intended behaviors specified in course objectives do not match actual student behavior, and it may also be that the instructor will not succeed in developing the desired student behaviors.[12]

Only the cognitive and affective domains will be discussed here; the third domain, the psychomotor, appears to be of little relevance to the teaching of cataloging, unless it might be thought to apply to the ability to key in entries properly, or possibly to adaptation of copy.

The cognitive domain "includes those objectives which deal with the recall or recognition of knowledge and the development of intellectual abilities and skills."[13]   This domain, like the other two, contains several levels, organized hierarchically by the "principle of increasing complexity."[14]   I shall summarize each level, including its component parts, and provide a sample objective at each level as it might be stated for a course in cataloging.[15]

1.00 Knowledge

    1.10   Knowledge of specifics.

          1.11 Knowledge of terminology. Objective: Define specific technical terms in cataloging.

1.12 Knowledge of specific facts. Objective: Reproduce key schemas such as that for a level two description in *AACR2*; Recall and reproduce the ten major classes of the Dewey Decimal Classification.

1.20 Knowledge of ways and means of dealing with specifics. Objective: Describe the differences among the three major ways of access to bibliographic records, namely author-title cataloging, application of subject headings and application of classification schemes.

1.21 Knowledge of conventions. Objective: Outline the main parts of the MARC format.

1.22 Knowledge of trends and sequences. Objective: Identify current trends in catalog code revision. Describe policy changes in the compilation of the *Library of Congress Subject Headings*.

1.23 Knowledge of classifications and categories. Objective: Describe the various kinds of descriptive practices for non-book materials.

1.24 Knowledge of criteria. Objective: State criteria by which good and bad cataloging can be distinguished, including criteria for an effective catalog.

1.25 Knowledge of methodology. Objective: State methods for evaluating effectiveness of a catalog, using the criteria articulated in 1.24 above.

1.30 Knowledge of the universals and abstraction in a field

1.31 Knowledge of principles and generalizations. Objective: Recall and describe major principles around which catalogs are constructed.

  1.32 Knowledge of theories and structures. Objective: Describe and interrelate the principles articulated in 1.31 above.

2.00 Comprehension

  2.10 Translation. Objective: State a cataloging problem in the student's own words; Translate relationships in a classification scheme into words.

  2.20 Interpretation. Objective: Distinguish between warranted and unwarranted conclusions to be drawn from cataloging data, as well as from the literature in the field.

  2.30 Extrapolation. Objective: Draw conclusions from the literature on cataloging, recognizing the limitations of the data provided by an author.

3.00 Application. Objective: Apply principles discovered in the code to new cataloging situations not yet discovered; Build new Dewey numbers.

4.00 Analysis

  4.10 Analysis of elements. Objective: Recognize unstated assumptions in the cataloging literature.

  4.20 Analyses of relationships. Objective: Detect logical fallacies in the cataloging literature.

  4.30 Analysis of organizational principles. Objective: Recognize a library's cataloging policies from particular examples.

5.00 Synthesis

  5.10 Production of a unique communication. Objective: Production of a paper on cataloging or classification.

  5.20 Production of a plan, or proposed set of

operations. Objective: Design a catalog, thesaurus, or classification to carry out predetermined objectives.

5.30 Derivation of a set of abstract relations. Objective: Formulate an appropriate set of facet-like characteristics for use in a new thesaurus.

6.00 Evaluation

6.10 Judgments in terms of internal evidence. Objective: Judge the quality of a paper in cataloging or classification on the basis of logic and consistency.

6.20 Judgments in terms of external criteria. Objective: Compare a paper in cataloging or classification, using facts known throughout the field, with material of the highest standards. Compare new theories with facts, whether or not stated by the creator of the theory.

The second domain we consider is the affective, which contains "objectives [describing] changes in interest, attitudes and values."[16] It is often assumed that if cognitive objectives are fulfilled, then students will value and appreciate the subject matter, in short that "there will be a corresponding development of affective behaviors." There is essentially no evidence to validate this assumption.[17] For this reason, it is vitally important to examine objectives in the affective domain when we seek to make cataloging an interesting subject.

Unlike the cognitive domain, the affective domain is organized in terms of increasing internalization. In my treatment of the affective domain, I follow a procedure similar to that followed for the cognitive domain.[18] Because the fifth level in the affective domain deals with whole complexes of values, however, it is impossible to assign course objectives

Values at this level are pervasive and long-term, and deal with an individual's philosophy of life. The fifth level is therefore only summarized here, included only for the sake of completeness.

1.0 Receiving (attending)
- 1.1　Awareness. Objective: The student demonstrates awareness of differences between so-called good and bad cataloging.
- 1.2　Willingness to receive. Objective: The student tolerates the validity of a number of classification schemes.
- 1.3　Controlled or selected attention. Objective: The student points out differences between important and unimportant mistakes in cataloging copy.

2.0 Responding
- 2.1　Acquiescence in responding. Objectives: The student reads and summarizes the assigned literature; Performs exercises in cataloging and classification.
- 2.2　Willingness to respond. Objective: The student voluntarily discusses in class cataloging problems discovered in laboratory session.
- 2.3　Satisfaction in response. Objective: The student finds pleasure in identifying headings from an authority file with name in statement of responsibility; Takes pleasure in building correct classification numbers and finding correct subject headings.

3.0 Valuing
- 3.1　Acceptance of a value. Objective: The student manifests a continuing desire to maintain a catalog

to current standards.

3.2 Preference for a value. Objective: The student assumes an active role in maintaining a catalog, as by reporting cataloging discrepancies to catalogers.

3.3 Commitment. Objective: The student indicates a desire to become a cataloger or demonstrates commitment to maintaining good cataloging through writing or other professional activities.

4.0 Organization.

4.1 Conceptualization of a value. Objective: The student forms a judgment as to a library's responsibility for effective bibliographic control within the context of the library's activities.

4.2 Organization of a value system. Objective: The student forms judgments about libraries and their role in the world.

5.0 Characterization by a value or value complex

5.1 Generalized set

5.2 Characterization

As the affective domain is summarized, certain trends stand out. Interest in the field being studied stands out on the first three levels, while appreciation of its values characterize levels 1.3 through 3.2.[19] These are crucial areas for the beginning cataloging student.[20] How do we achieve objectives such as those I have mentioned for those levels? As might be expected, little research has been done in this area. This may be because of the vague, but by no means synonymous, terms describing phenomena in this realm of the affective domain.[21] It presently appears that the best approach to achieving objectives found in the affective domain is through one-on-one conversations, wherein reasons are assigned for the student's

Such conversations should optimally include a discussion of how the information conveyed will affect the student's professional life.[22]

Having provided sample objectives for each of the various levels of the cognitive and affective domains, we must ask how the higher levels of the cognitive domain and the relevant levels of the affective domain can be most effectively reached. Lower-level objectives are of utility chiefly in the undergraduate environment; graduate students and their instructors may be reasonably asked to work on the higher levels; the higher levels are the natural realms of graduate education. In order to work in these higher levels, we need to know something about our students. That they are all graduate students goes without saying. But there is a new development in library education. If we examine the statistics published by the Association for Library and Information Science Education that relate to the ages of our students, we find a startling trend; in the last few years our students have become increasingly older. If we examine the figures for the 1983 through 1987, we see that there have been tremendous increases in the percentage of students who are in the 35 to 39 and 40 to 44 year old groups, while there have been concomitant dramatic decreases in the percentage of younger students who have just finished their undergraduate studies. The table below shows the distribution (by percent of the graduate library school student body) of students by age for the 1983-1988 period.

Year	20-24	25-29	30-34	35-39	40-44	45-49	50-54	55+	Unknown
1983	15.75	28.36	21.47	12.89	7.66	4.08	2.57	1.17	6.06
1984	14.42	27.57	20.92	12.92	7.84	4.45	2.47	1.14	8.27
1985	13.46	26.94	21.06	14.93	9.19	4.92	2.02	1.44	6.05
1986	12.42	26.61	21.61	17.64	10.53	5.41	2.59	1.28	1.92
1987	10.92	25.10	20.94	18.26	12.59	6.30	3.31	1.67	0.91
1988	7.1	20.3	19.4	19.9	17.3	9.3	4.5	2.1	0.1[23]

A graphic representation of these numbers is shown in the Appendix.

From these statistics, it appears that soon at least half our students will be persons who have been away from school for several years. In short, we will be dealing with classes at least half full of adult learners. The figures also make it clear that we are dealing with a student body made up of persons whose ages span a large number of years. With respect to age, we no longer have the homogeneous body of students we may once have had.

Given that our students are adult learners, there exists empirical information that their learning styles, and stages of cognitive development are quite different from those of younger graduate students. Their affective development will also be different; personal value systems are generally well-developed by the time these older students arrive at library school.[24]

We must understand the cognitive development of our students prior to deciding the level of learning to which we may expect our students to aspire. Just as the Bloom taxonomy has dominated discussion of educational objectives through the years, a model of cognitive development first enunciated by William G. Perry, Jr., some twenty years ago, now dominates discussions of the education of adult students.[25] The Perry model assumes nine different positions of cognitive and ethical development, each transcending and including the earlier ones. In what follows, I omit all transitions except of those that are strictly relevant to this discussion:

Dualism modified by multiplicity. Dualism is the division of meaning into two realms, such as good versus bad and right versus wrong. Multiplicity is the recognition that are not yet known. No judgment can yet be made among these diverse opinions.

Position 1.   Authorities know, and if read well, will give right answers.

Position 2.   True authorities are right, and other purported authorities are frauds.

Position 3.   There are some temporary uncertainties for good authorities, but they will eventually get the uncertainties right.

Transition.   There are many questions to which the authorities do not have the answers.

Position 4a.   When authorities do not have the right answers, everyone has rights to an opinion; no one is wrong.

Transition   (and/or). People ask that opinions be supported with reasons.

Relativism   (diversity of opinion and judgments from coherent sources) discovered.

Transition.   It is unclear that the faculty have the right to grade students, or even about what they grade students.

Position 4b.   In certain courses, authorities are not asking for the right answer; they want students to think a certain way about matters, and the quality of this thinking is the basis of grades.

Transition.   The way students are asked to think seems to work in most courses and even outside of courses.

Position 5.   Everything is relative, not equally valid. Theories are not truth, but metaphors with which to interpret data. Commitments to relativism developed.

Position 6.   The student sees that he or she is going to have to make decisions with no one to say that he or she is right.

Position 7.   The first commitment is made.

Position 8.   Now that several commitments have been made, they have to be balanced one against the other.

Position 9.   Life will have to be wholehearted and tentative. The journey will be retraced, hopefully with increasing wisdom.[26]

(Positions 4a and 4b are alternate routes to Position 5)

The importance of the above scheme is that Perry's followers, such as Daloz, note that most adults returning to college "arrive carrying some degree of dualism and a great deal of multiplicity."[27] In essence, these students are at the transition between points 4 and 5 on Perry's continuum, the place where two alternative routes to position 5 are available.[28] In Position 4a, a student is likely to rely on intuitive experience and devalue hard work. Once the student passes to Position 5, the student sees Position 4a as having been self-indulgent. On the other hand, at Position 4b, a route more frequently traveled than 4a, the student wishes to give the authorities what it is perceived that they want, namely the use of evidence in testing hypotheses and the weighing of both sides of an argument. Daloz refers to this phenomenon as the Trojan Horse effect; authority assists in its own overthrow.

It is difficult not to see the stage just described, that of Position 4b, as the ideal position to achieve cognitive learning on the highest of levels, that of evaluation, or in the very least, on the levels of analysis and synthesis. The fact that our student body is of increasing age gives us an excellent opportunity to change attitudes about cataloging. The actual doing of cataloging is not among the objectives outined above, cognitive objectives. We make cataloging interesting just by our achievement of the affective domain objectives.

Near the beginning of his career as a teacher of cataloging, Lubetzky noted that cataloging as a subject for library schools should not have as its objective the practice of techniques outlined in rules, but rather the appreciation of the role a catalog plays in the library.

"In a library school whose objective, as that of a professional school, is to cultivate not only practitioners but also thinkers and critics of the art, not only followers but also leaders of the profession -- librarians who will not only carry on but also advance the art of the profession -- in such a school it is proper to treat the subject of cataloging not as a how-to-do-it routine outlined in so many rules, but rather as a problem in the methodological system to facilitate the exploitation of the library's resources by its users."[29]

In summary, the advantage we can take of the transition in the cognitive development among our adult students is to be teaching at the most important affective and highest cognitive levels. All we need to do is select out objectives wisely and assign good reasons for them. What an opportunity we have!

REFERENCES

1.   Sir Anthony Panizzi, "Mr. Panizzi to the Right Hon. the Earl of Ellesmere.--British Museum, January 29, 1848," in Commissioners Appointed to Inquire in the Constitution and Government of the British Museum, *Appendix to the Report of the Commissioners Appointed to Inquire into the Constitution and Management [sic] of the British Museum* (London: 1850), pp. 378-95. Reprinted in Michael Carpenter and Elaine Svenonius (eds.) *Foundations of Cataloging: A Sourcebook*

(Littleton, Colo.: Libraries Unlimited, 1985), pp. 18-47. The quotation is from page 378 of the original and page 18 of the reprint.

2. Jerry D. Saye, "The Cataloging Experience in Library and Information Science Education: an Educator's Perspective," *Cataloging & Classification Quarterly* 7 (Summer 1987): 27.

3. Saye, p. 28.

4. Jon G. Penner, *Why Many College Teachers Cannot Lecture: How to Avoid Communication Breakdown in the Classroom* (Springfield, Ill.: Charles C. Thomas, Publisher, 1984), see especially pages 114-131.

5. Saye, p. 32. Later on the same page, Saye states that the immediate objective is the presentation of the basic principles of information organization. I am not sure how he meshes this version of the immediate objective with the one just quoted.

6. John J. Boll, "Teaching 'Efficient and Economical' Cataloging," *Journal of Education for Librarianship* 2 (Spring 1962): 154-157.

7. Conversations with many library administrators at state and national library association meetings often start with this kind of request.

8. Many students will eventually have to catalog as part of their jobs. Those who become librarians at institutions whose libraries are not part of a network, some few special librarians, and those who eventually have to produce "finder" records on a rush basis are virtually the only librarians outside of full-time catalogers that will have to do original work.

9. William E. Moen and Kathleen M. Heim, "The Class of 1988: Librarians for the New Millenium [sic]," *American Libraries* 19 (November 1988): 858-860, 885.

10. Benjamin S. Bloom (ed.) *Taxonomy of Educational Objectives: the Classification of Educational Goals. Handbook 1: Cognitive Domain,* by a committee of college and university examiners. (New York: David McKay Company, 1956, reprinted 1965), p. 4.

11. See Richard Carter, "A Taxonomy of Objectives for Professional Education," *Studies in Higher Education,* 10 (1985): 135-149. On p. 137, Carter notes that the Bloom scheme has been criticized for not distinguishing between knowledge and skill, i.e. the fundamental difference between knowing how to do something and being able to do it.

12. Bloom, *Taxonomy, Handbook 1,* pp. 11-12.

13. Bloom, *Taxonomy, Handbook 1,* p. 7.

14. David R. Krathwohl, Benjamin S. Bloom [and] Bertram B. Masia, *Taxonomy of Educational Objectives: the Classification of Educational Goals. Handbook II: Affective Domain.* (New York: David McKay Company, 1964, reprinted 1974), p. 10.

15. In what follows, I use Bloom, *Taxonomy, Handbook 1,* pp. 201-207. The examples are my own.

16. Bloom, *Taxonomy, Handbook 1,* p. 7.

17. Krathwohl, et al., *Taxonomy, Handbook II,* p. 20.

18. Krathwohl, et al., *Taxonomy, Handbook II,* pp. 176-185.

19. Krathwohl, et al., *Taxonomy, Handbook II,* p. 37.b.

20. It is to Prof. Orvin Lee Shiflett that I owe the crucial insight that it is often best to treat introductory cataloging courses as courses in cataloging appreciation.

21. Krathwohl, et al., *Taxonomy, Handbook II,* p. 35-38, discuss the problem of ambiguity of terms like 'interest', 'appreciation', 'attitudes', etc.

22. Personal communications with Professor Gary Moore, Louisiana State University, September - October, 1988.

23. The figures for 1983-1987 are drawn from Association for Library and Information Science Education, *Library and Information Science Education Statistical Report* (State College, Pennsylvania, 1983-1987). The 1988 figures are taken from William E. Moen, "Library and Information Science Student Attitudes, Demographics and Aspirations Survey: Who We Are and Why We Are Here," in William E. Moen and Kathleen M. Heim, eds., *Librarians for the New Millennium* (American Library Association, Office for Library Personnel Resources, 1988), pp. 93-109. As noted on page 95 the 1988 numbers reflect a 40% response rate to the survey. The same 1988 numbers are presented in Moen and Heim, "The Class of 1988."

24. Krathwohl, et al., *Taxonomy, Handbook II*, point out that "In the adult, changes [in internal values] are made with much greater effort and difficulty than in the child; the organization becomes more rigid with age and less ready to accept to accept a value inconsistent with those already embraced." As we shall see, this may be an overly pessimistic view of the nature of value systems in adult students.

25. Perry's most recent representation of his model is found in William G. Perry, Jr. "Cognitive and Ethical Growth: the Making of Meaning," in Arthur W. Chickering and Associates, eds. *The Modern American College* (San Francisco: Jossey-Bass, 1981). The present representation is drawn from this source.

26. Paraphrased from Perry, p. 79.

27. Laurent A. Daloz, *Effective Teaching and Mentoring.* (San Francisco: Jossey-Bass, 1986), p. 81.

28. Daloz, p. 18.

29. Seymour Lubetzky, "On Teaching Cataloging," *Journal of Education for Librarianship* 5 (Spring 1985): 257.

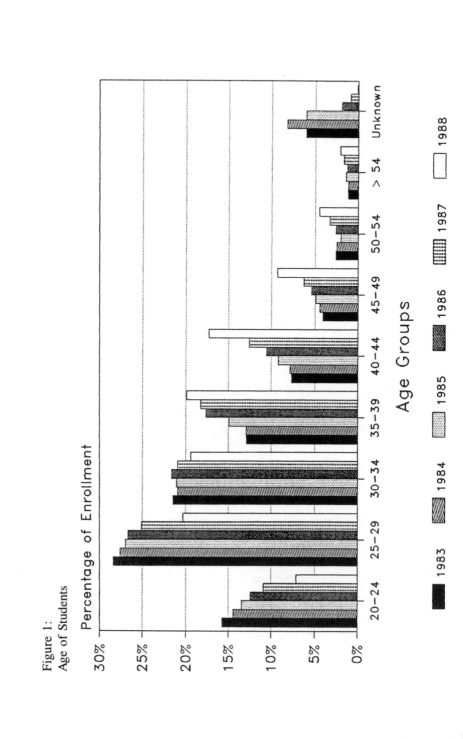

Figure 1:
Age of Students

Preaching to the Unconverted: The Cataloging Educator's Challenge

Carolyn O. Frost

Is the library profession experiencing difficulty in attracting students to cataloging careers? Is this hypothetical recruiting problem unique to a specialization in cataloging? Is the problem embedded in a true perception of cataloging as it is practiced today, or is it a mis-perception based on cataloging practices which have faded into the past? Is the actuality of the professional role of catalogers so new that is has not yet penetrated the professional consciousness? These interlocking issues deserve serious examination, not through speculative self-examination but through verifiable data collection and careful analysis. As background for this discussion, the charge by Janet Swan Hill is offered.

"Library schools are somehow conveying the impression that cataloging is an undesirable occupation; that cataloging is a dead end; that catalogers are shy, retiring, and organizationally invisible; that cataloging is a dry, picky, mechanical, menial process involving the exercise of neither thought nor imagination; and that cataloging has nothing to do with service. I am confident that this message is not consciously delivered, but it appears to be delivered nonetheless."[1]

This criticism was echoed by the ALA CCS [Cataloging and Classification Section] Task Force on Education and Recruitment for Cataloging (of which Hill was a member).[2] In turn, library educator Herbert White counters that the major source of students' negative perceptions is librarians in general, not library schools. He charges that "today's library school students opt not to become catalogers not because of any faculty plot to divert them to other areas of the profession, but because students have the opportunity to see how cataloging is done in the libraries in which they work and have worked, and to a large extent they don't like what they see."[3]

Which, if either, of these two views is based in fact? A major premise of this paper is that we need to learn more about the factors that underlie an individual's consideration of cataloging as a career choice. In particular, we need to hear from one key source of prospective catalogers--students in library studies programs. The present study will present results from a questionnaire survey of students in the University of Michigan School of Information and Library Studies program (UM SILS). The paper will also consider the following questions:

- How can library practitioners and educators attract more people to the cataloging profession?
- What is the place of cataloging-related courses within the library and information studies curriculum?

- How can courses reflect the actuality of cataloging as it is practiced in progressive libraries today, particularly those which combine advanced information technology with a creative philosophy of organizational behavior?

To determine students' perceptions of cataloging as a career, a questionnaire was distributed to students in the School of Information and Library Studies at the University of Michigan. One hundred eighty-two students (of a total of 287) responded to the survey, which addressed the following questions:

- What percentage of students have identified a specialization in cataloging as a career choice?
- What influences have determined this decision?
- What perception do students have of a specialization in cataloging?
- What perceptions of this subset of the profession have led students to select or reject cataloging as a career option?

A large majority (82%) of the students in the sample had some work experience in a library. Some had experience in more than one area. Over a quarter (27%) had previous work experience in a cataloging department, while about a third (31%) had work experience in another branch of technical services. Over half (53%) had work experience in public services, and 26% had other library work experience. (Multiple responses were allowed for this and most other questions reported).

The majority of students with work experience (59%) had worked in libraries for three or more years. Twenty-nine percent had one to two years of experience, and only 12% had less than a year of library work experience. At the time of the survey, 41% of the students were beginning their library studies program. Thirteen percent were in their second term of the program, 8% in their third term, and 39% had completed three or more terms. The UM SILS curriculum includes one required cataloging course and four elective cataloging-related courses. Most (86%) students in the survey sample had taken or were presently enrolled in the required cataloging course ("Organization of Information Resources I"), while 14% had not taken any cataloging courses. About 20% had taken one of the four cataloging-related elective courses.

As expected, the findings revealed that cataloging is the first career choice for a small minority of students. A mere 2% stated that cataloging was their first career choice within the library profession, while a larger minority (13%) indicated that they were considering cataloging as one of their options. Some encouragement can be taken from the finding that almost a third (31%) would consider a position with partial cataloging duties (e.g., half-time cataloging and reference). Forty-one per cent said they were not considering cataloging as a career choice, while 13% indicated that they were undecided at this point.

The situation appears less bleak if we consider that the survey findings show that less than half of the respondents had definitely ruled out cataloging as a career choice, and that there is recruitment potential for the remaining students. Past experience has also shown that, even among those students who have definitely ruled out cataloging at this stage, there are still some who will eventually assume cataloging positions.

Since the data suggest that even among undecided students there is still potential for persuasion and recruitment, it is crucial to determine what influences are most important in making career decisions among specializations in the library and information profession. The survey findings showed that work experience, and particularly contacts with practicing librarians, were the key influences. For almost three fourths of the respondents (72%), a primary influence was library work experience. Over half (57%) felt that practicing librarians had been a prime influence. Over a third (38%) indicated that they were influenced by courses in the UM SILS program, and 32% said that a primary influence was professors. About a quarter (24%) were influenced by the professional literature, and 17% by fellow students. As shown earlier, the work experience of the students in the sample was almost evenly divided between public services and technical services.

Another key factor in determining the potential for recruiting students lies in students' general perceptions of the cataloging profession. The findings, while not exactly encouraging, still offered room for optimism. Most students' perceptions of the cataloging profession were neutral to positive. Twelve percent had a "very favorable" perception of the cataloging profession, a third (34%) were "somewhat favorable", and a quarter (26%) were "neutral". Students with negative perceptions were in the minority: 26% were "somewhat negative", and only 3% "very negative". Students were next presented with a list of statements reflecting perceptions and stereotypes and asked to circle the statements reflecting their own views. Once again, the findings offered grounds for encouragement. Most students did not agree with the statements that could be considered as reflecting a negative stereotype, while many of the positive views were held by a majority of students.

About three-fourths (75%) of the students felt that "cataloging positions provide opportunity for work with automated systems". A sizeable majority viewed the cataloger's work as "requiring problem-solving skills" (80%) and "involving independent decision-making and judgment" (72%), and a similar percentage (75%) felt that cataloging work requires analytical abilities. However, only a third (36%) of the students felt that "management skills are important to cataloging work," a rather small percentage in view of the supervisory or management functions that most catalogers perform. The apparent "invisibility" of these management functions may hold lessons for job definition and organizational structure in technical services units. All of the views that could be regarded as negative were held by only a minority of the students. The most widely-held negative views were that "cataloging work is repetitive and routine" (46%), and that "most decisions that catalogers make are strictly prescribed by rules" (42%). A third of the students (34%) felt that "catalogers are isolated from the mainstream of library work." (This might explain the similar percentage (31%) who expressed an interest in joint cataloging/reference positions.) No more than a quarter of the students held the negative views that "most cataloging work can be performed by paraprofessionals" (21%), and that "catalogers are not outgoing, people-oriented individuals" (17%). Only 6% felt that "with the growth of bibliographic networks and automated systems, cataloging is becoming an obsolete profession".

Most students had already formed some opinion of the cataloging profession. Only 14% responded that they had "little knowledge of what catalogers do, or of cataloging as a career."

In considering their own aptitudes or qualifications for the cataloging profession, 59% of the students felt that they "[did] not have the mindset to become a cataloger", but only 15% felt that they "lacked the necessary skills and qualifications to become a cataloger (e.g., foreign language skills)."

Distinctly negative perceptions were not widely held. Twenty-eight per cent of those rejecting cataloging as a career felt that cataloging work lacked sufficient potential for career advancement, and a similar percentage (29%) had a largely negative perception of the type of work that catalogers do. Twelve per cent felt that catalogers have low prestige in the library profession. Only 5% thought that catalogers are not as well paid as other librarians, and the same percentage indicated having a largely negative perception of catalogers.

Similarly, students who had decided in favor of, or were considering cataloging as a possible career option, were asked to indicate statements reflecting considerations which had influenced their career preference. In response to this question, 73% indicated that they had "a largely positive perception of the type of work that catalogers do". Almost three-fourths (71%) said that they "enjoyed the kind of intellectual challenge that cataloging work offers". Over half (52%) felt that their "skills and qualifications are well suited to the requirements for cataloging positions", and forty-eight per cent attributed their career choice to "a large number of job openings for catalogers". Almost a third (30%) indicated that "cataloging offers good opportunities for career advancement". For 73% of these respondents, an important influence was "a largely positive perception of catalogers." Only 21% felt that "cataloging work is less stressful than working in public services." In a concluding question, only 22% of the students considering cataloging as a career indicated that they see cataloging as a long-term career choice, while 78% viewed cataloging as a first step in their career ladder.

The survey showed that a large majority of students in library school have had previous library work experience, and that this work experience and the librarians with whom they have come in contact have had a substantial influence on career decisions within the library profession. Thus a potential area for recruitment lies in the library work environment, and librarians are in a key position to encourage paraprofessional workers to consider cataloging as a career option.

While the majority of students in the survey do not have a negative impression of catalogers and of the work that catalogers perform, a substantial percentage of students are still reluctant to consider cataloging as a full-time career option. To counter this reluctance, libraries should consider structuring catalogers' work (as many have already done) to expand the role of catalogers to include a range of activities and responsibilities involving other departments.

What can library educators do to encourage students to consider a cataloging career? The findings indicate that, if cataloging-related courses focus on the minority of students with an interest in cataloging as a career, the audience for potential recruitment will be small indeed. One strategy for recruitment is to develop broad-based courses which have relevance for both cataloging and non-cataloging specialists. Providing a broad-based curriculum for both required as well as elective courses can provide an opportunity to inform and to persuade large audiences. At the same time, a broad-based approach of value to a large audience of students ensures the continuance of cataloging content in the total curriculum--an important survival strategy for courses which otherwise suffer from dwindling enrollments.

The findings suggest that students are interested in work responsibilities which transcend individual departments. In the teaching of cataloging-related courses, it can be stressed that many of the skills essential to effective cataloging are also transferable to other library environments. Instructors can relate cataloging content to skills and knowledge which will be needed by the cataloger in a variety of library environments. Such "generic" skills and knowledge include decision-making, problem solving, management, and communication.

The findings also suggest that both practicing librarians and educators need to project a stronger and more positive image of the cataloging profession. While this image is not as negative as some have suggested, there is still a need to foster the development of a stronger professional image, with which prospective catalogers can identify. Cataloging curricula can include a "professional socialization" component to instill attitudes and provide information about the cataloging profession.

In the remainder of this paper, the recommendations outlined above will be discussed in further detail.

Library school curricula have been criticized for offering too few cataloging courses, and for including information that is "cataloging-related" rather than "cataloging content per se".[4] In large part, recent developments in library curriculum development can be attributed to an expanding knowledge base and a broadening spectrum of specialized roles for information professionals. In this environment, the number of cataloging courses has diminished to allow room for other areas of content within the standard one-year program. Those cataloging courses which continue to be offered must now address the needs of librarians in a greater variety of settings. Library studies programs have expanded to include increased attention to areas such as the design and evaluation of information systems, the analysis of information needs and information seeking activity, and information policy and management. Information and library studies curricula have additionally expanded to include other information environments such as corporate settings, information brokering and other entrepreneurial ventures, publishing, and the development of commercially-available information systems, resources, and services. Furthermore, schools of information and library studies are beginning to attract students who do not plan to work in library settings but will offer their skills to other information constituencies. These students will not be practicing cataloging in the traditional sense, but many will apply what they have learned in cataloging classes as they design classification systems, describe and organize information products, and provide access to information.

While a number of schools of information and library studies have dropped cataloging as a requirement, most still retain such a course as part of their core curriculum.[5] In this context, cataloging courses or modules must necessarily be directed to the large majority of students who do not plan to make cataloging their career specialization. The purpose of the required cataloging course therefore is not to prepare students to become catalogers, but to introduce concepts, standards and models, issues, and developments, with which all librarians must be familiar. With this goal in mind, the required course or module should enable students:

- become more effective users or consumers of the catalog;
- to understand the place of the cataloging or technical services functions within the library;
- to understand how concepts of bibliographic description, organization, and access underlie the structure of automated systems, and
- to understand technical-service issues which have an impact on the library community in general.
  This same knowledge base can serve as a building block for students who plan to specialize in cataloging.

Even the elective cataloging-related courses cannot serve exclusively the student who plans to make cataloging a career, or who plans to work in a library setting. Simply put, library schools cannot afford to offer classes with only a few participants. With increasing and persistent pressure from university administrations to increase class size, it is difficult to justify a class with a narrow and specialized audience. Much as we would like to see classes with large numbers of students who have chosen cataloging as a career, the present realities often require us to offer large classes appealing to broad audiences.

In their 1986 survey of the teaching of cataloging, the CCS Task Force on Education and Recruitment for Cataloging made the following observation: "As librarianship and cataloging have become more complex, library schools have striven to provide students with background in principles and issues, and in the context in which operations are performed. In the case of cataloging, background, and context (bibliographic control, structure and history of the catalog, syndetic structures, access, automation developments, national projects, cooperative ventures, etc.) are perhaps being taught at the expense of the function itself. Cataloging courses include so much cataloging-related information, that cataloging content per se is sometimes meager".[6] In response, library educators should argue that "cataloging related information" such as syndetic structures and bibliographic control are essential on a practical as well as theoretical level. This is true not only for the cataloger, but also for other librarians who use these concepts outside a cataloging setting. For example, the public services librarian designing a subject heading system for an information and referral system, the bibliographic instruction librarian explaining the *Library of Congress Subject Headings*, and the database searcher seeking subject access must have a knowledge of syndetic structures for practical application. The same principles can, of course, be applied to the use of subject heading tools for a specifically cataloging application.

Library educators need make no apology for including such "cataloging-related" content in their introductory classes, and for designing the introductory courses to address the needs of a broader clientele. By arguing for the general value and application of this "cataloging-related" content, and the need to include this content as part of the core curriculum, cataloging educators are in a better position to recruit students who might otherwise not have considered cataloging as a specialization.

SKILLS NEEDED FOR CATALOGERS IN EXPANDED ROLES

The expanding scope of the responsibilities of catalogers brings about the need to educate students in areas which extend beyond the cataloging process itself. As Lizbeth Bishoff points out, the increased use of paraprofessional staff to perform copy and even original cataloging has resulted in the need for catalogers to provide training for paraprofessionals, as well as direction and supervision.[7] In this instructional role, catalogers must be able to explain the principles and practices of cataloging to nonprofessional staff. Catalogers must thus become skilled in developing training programs, and in using communication skills to convey instructions. The widespread implementation of integrated library systems, and the increased complexity of interrelationships among all units within the library, also creates the need for catalogers both to communicate effectively with other library units and to participate actively in library-wide planning.

Additional opportunities for cooperative ventures with the staff of other library units occur as libraries begin to design local information systems, such as information and referral systems in public libraries, and end-user systems for specialized areas in academic libraries. It has already become apparent that catalogers can play a key role in developing bibliographic instruction programs for users of the library's online catalog. With their knowledge of subject access, authority control, bibliographic description, and their familiarity with standards which can serve as models for new systems, catalogers can provide a unique perspective. To do this sucessfully, catalogers must be able to think beyond the mere implementation of existing rules. They must have a sound grasp of theoretical concepts which would allow them to extend and adjust existing standards and models to new applications. Robert Hayes points out that "cataloging not only still is the heart of library operations, but is fully as important to the broader range of information professions". He goes on to urge that cataloging courses "focus on problems rather than rules, [and] clearly identify the significance of database issues in contexts broader than just the library catalog".[8]

As libraries become involved in the selection, implementation, maintenance, and evaluation of automated systems, it becomes imperative for catalogers and other librarians to communicate effectively with vendors. Catalogers must be able to assess needs, understand and critically evaluate capabilities of available systems, and communicate their positions forcefully and effectively. The increasing utilization of clerical staff in most catalog departments requires catalogers to assume supervisory responsibilities, and to possess communication skills needed to convey goals and objectives, to communicate procedures and policies, and values, and to motivate staff. From another perspective, catalogers must also be able to communicate their department's needs effectively to their own supervisor.

In addition to learning specific areas of cataloging content, cataloging courses should also introduce students to the application of decision-making skills to cataloging problems. For example, the instructor can stress that cataloging rules and standards still leave a great deal to the cataloger's discretion, and that the application of these rules requires considerable decision-making and judgement. In teaching the use of cataloging and classification tools, the instructor has ample opportunity to emphasize that there is seldom only one correct answer to a problem.

There are a number of strategies that can be employed to encourage decision-making in the cataloging process. The instructor can place as much emphasis on students' thought processes and on the justification of their answers as on the answer itself. Assignments and examinations can include an essay component which allows the instructor to evaluate students on the strength of their arguments and the effectiveness of their presentations. The instructor can provide the students with an opportunity to present and defend a point of view. For example, an exam question can ask students to identify which rule options, subject headings, etc., are appropriate in a particular library setting or for a given library clientele.

Since for many students the image of the catalog librarian is that of a shy, reserved, and isolated individual, it is especially important that catalogers be given the opportunity to display attitudes and skills which will make them more assertive, articulate, forthright, and outspoken in presenting their views and ideas (or to develop those qualities, if they are in fact lacking). Students should be required to develop a point of view in situations where decision-making and creativity is appropriate.

PROFESSIONAL SOCIALIZATION AND THE DEVELOPMENT OF A PROFESSIONAL IDENTITY

Catalogers-in-the-making need to acquire a sense of the profession that they are about to enter. As with library students in general, a professional socialization forms an important part of the library education program and a component that is not easily acquired on the job. For this reason, cataloging courses should serve the purpose not only of introducing cataloging content, but of introducing students to the profession as well. Areas of content can include:

1) An introduction to organizations with a cataloging focus: What are the organizations, who are the key people in these groups, and what are the primary issues and contributions associated with these groups?

2) Current research in the field:
   What types of questions are being addressed by the research? Who are the key researchers? What areas need further exploration? How have research results been implemented by practising catalogers? How can the practitioner play a role in the research process? What types of projects have been initiated by cataloging practitioners? What are the journals which regularly report research, developments, and issues in the field? What areas might be addressed in grant proposals?

3) Professional development, continuing education: What opportunities are offered in continuing education? What are the primary groups and vehicles? What knowledge areas are rapidly changing and will require continuing development? What informal mechanisms are available to the cataloger?

4) An introduction to the job market:
   It is helpful to students to examine the current job

postings for catalogers, to identify the qualifications, credentials, and attributes listed, and then to determine which of these can be acquired in class, which through previous job experience, which through reading the professional literature. It is also important to stress that many skills can only be acquired through professional experience. Many students are daunted by the belief that they will be expected, in an entry level position, to have a complete command of the cataloging rules. The instructor can stress the concept of open-ended learning, and the need for continual development of professional skills. Students who have undergone job interviews can be encouraged to share the experience with other class members. Questions asked in job interviews can be solicited from practicing catalogers and used in class as discussion topics.

5)　Guest speakers who reflect positive attributes:
By carefully selecting guest speakers who convey the attitudes, skills, and knowledge we would like to instill in students, the library educator has considerable opportunity to provide role models for aspiring catalogers. These role models should include leaders at all levels--relative newcomers (for example, recent graduates) to the field, middle managers, as well as top-level administrators.

CONCLUSIONS

A survey of students at the University of Michigan's School of Information and Library Studies suggests that:
1)　students' overall perceptions of the cataloging profession are predominantly neutral to positive

2) most students' perceptions are shaped primarily by library work experience and by contact with practicing librarians

3) while relatively few students express interest in cataloging as a full-time career, almost half of the students show a willingness to consider cataloging as at least a part-time responsibility.

4) while negative perceptions of cataloging work are not widely held, students still indicate a strong preference for other areas of librarianship, and in working more directly with library patrons.

This survey represents the views of a single school, and further studies are needed to determine the views of students on a nation-wide basis. If Michigan's students are representative of their peers in other library schools, neither Hill nor White is correct in assuming that students have a distinctly negative perception of the cataloging profession, and Hill is also incorrect in her assertion that students' (negative) views are molded by library educators.

Few students are interested in cataloging as a career specialization. Even among those students who express an interest in beginning their professional careers as catalogers, most are interested in cataloging as a stepping-stone to positions with broader responsibilities. Some argue that fewer students become interested in cataloging since fewer classes are offered. This is not necessarily the case. The UM SILS program offers one required and four elective cataloging-related courses, and the elective courses are well attended. Still, relatively few students take the skills they have acquired in school and apply them in a cataloging setting. Since few students are willing to commit to full-time cataloging responsibilities, libraries will need to consider the development of multi-dimensional cataloging work which allows the cataloger the opportunity to interact with other library personnel and with patrons.

A recruitment strategy is needed on three fronts. An aggressive effort must be made to communicate a more knowledgable, more visible, and more positive image of cataloging work: 1) in the paraprofessional work environment, which can serve as a rich source of potential catalogers; 2) within the profession-at-large, and 3) in schools of library and information studies.

REFERENCES

I would like to acknowledge the assistance of Robin N. Downes and Dana Rooks in the preparation of this manuscript.

1. Janet Swan Hill, "Wanted: Good Catalogers," *American Libraries* 16 (November 1985): 730.
2. American Library Association, Resources and Technical Services Division, Cataloging and Classification Section. "CCS Task Force on Education and Recruitment for Cataloging Report, June 1986," *RTSD Newsletter* 11 (1986): 71-78.
3. Herbert White, "Catalogers - Yesterday, Today, Tomorrow," *Library Journal* 112 (April 1, 1987): 48.
4. "CCS Task Force", p. 74.
5. Roxanne Sellberg, "The Teaching of Cataloging in U.S. Library Schools," *Library Resources & Technical Services* 32 (January 1988):30-41.
6. "CCS Task Force", p. 74.
7. Lizbeth J. Bishoff, "Who Says We Don't Need Catalogers?" *American Libraries* 18 (Sept. 1987):694-696.

8. Robert M. Hayes, "Education of the Information Professional: A Library School Perspective," *Journal of the American Society for Information Science* 39 (Sept. 1988):312-317.

The Crisis in Cataloging:
A Feminist Hypothesis

Suzanne Hildenbrand

The central thesis of this paper is that the crisis in cataloging today is linked to a largely unexplored aspect of sexual stratification within librarianship. It will be argued that many of the problems faced by cataloging reflect the fact that it is an even more female-intensive occupation than librarianship as a whole. According to this perspective, since research on female-intensive professions indicates that those professions are characterized by low earnings and low status, relative to education and responsibility, then cataloging will also be characterized by lower earnings and status than librarianship in general.

Two lines of investigation are suggested by this thesis. First, data must be collected to determine if cataloging is more female intensive than the rest of librarianship. Second, if women are overrepresented in cataloging, data are needed to determine if working conditions and careers are worse in cataloging than elsewhere in librarianship as the literature on female-intensive professions would suggest. Finally, if the hypothesis is supported, the data collected will provide evidence to use to bring an improvement of conditions within cataloging that should ease the crisis.

WOMEN'S WORK, SO-CALLED

The world of work has been and continues to be segregated by sex, and a growing list of facts about sex segregated work has emerged.[1] Focusing on the female-intensive professions such as librarianship, elementary school teaching and nursing, the most striking fact is that the work of the entire profession is devalued or perceived to involve less skill and intellectual effort than it actually does. The widespread belief that teaching is a natural gift, for example, devalues the effort that goes into good teaching. A recent study shows that most library users underestimate the education and skill of librarians.[2] Of particular importance to this paper is the fact that not only are individual professions sex-typed, but within professions certain activities or specialities are sex-typed. Men are overrepresented in the higher status activities and women are overrepresented in the lower status ones. In elementary education women are underrepresented in school administration. Women are still underrepresented in library management and other prestigious areas.[3]

Most members of female-intensive professions, male or female, work in public or not-for-profit agencies. Few have individual practices. Other major characteristics of female-intensive professions include low pay relative to training and responsibility for both the men and women in them, although in general the men continue to earn more than their female colleagues. Women in these fields experience short career ladders, and relatively less upward mobility than men. Low autonomy or heavy supervision are frequently found in female intensive professions. Isolation and ambiguity about roles and credentialing are also prevalent in "women's work."

Some of the characteristics of female-intensive professions--isolation, lack of autonomy, limited opportunities for promotion or mobility and role ambiguitiy--may foster eccentric or tyrannical behavior. Sociologist Rosabeth Moss Kanter found such behavior typical of the powerless within organizations and of those "stuck" with little hope for advancement.[4]

Gender ideologies, or myths that support the sexual status quo, surround the female-intensive professions. For example, it is widely assumed that the presence of women is the cause and not the symptom of the low status of these occupations.[5] This is reinforced by the phrase "female dominant" which is often used to describe these occupations and suggests control by women.[6] Failures associated with these professions are often seen as stemming from the presence of so many woman. Several researchers, for example, have claimed that the disappointing achievement in reading among American school children stems from the "feminization" of teaching.[7] Another myth, more common in an earlier time, was the link between women's supposed attributes and the large number of women in these fields. Thus "maternal instinct" was often used to explain the numbers of women in nursing and elementary school teaching.

Not surprisingly, as employment opportunities for women have expanded in recent years it has been increasingly difficult to attract the well-educated, middle-class women who were formerly the traditional recruits in female intensive occupations. It was these women, denied the opportunities to enter the "real" professions enjoyed by their brothers, who supplied a highly skilled pool of recruits available at low wages. Now that these women can seek careers more like those of their brothers, the female-intensive professions may be left with fewer recruits and less able ones.[8]

While many today recognize that librarianship is a female-intensive profession within the world of professional occupations, the dimensions of sex typing within librarianship are less widely recognized.

"WOMEN'S WORK" WITHIN LIBRARIANSHIP?

The literature on sexual stratification within librarianship has focused largely on the areas where women traditionally have been underrepresented: management and academic librarianship. Far less literature is available on the areas, such as children's work, which are more female-intensive than the profession as a whole. Yet patterns of sex differentiation cannot be understood without also studying these activities.

Library literature has been reviewed for evidence of sex distribution, working conditions, and career development in cataloging. Informal interviews with librarians, catalogers, and others have also been utilized. It will not surprise feminists to learn that little hard data exists that would test the hypothesis that cataloging is an especially female intensive-activity within librarianship. This is a familiar pattern in librarianship, as collection of data on sex ratios was a hard won struggle of early feminist librarians. Most of what is available is highly impressionistic. Information uncovered through this survey has been grouped below in categories suggested by the literature on female-intensive professions: sex ratio and distribution; salaries; ideological arguments; status of the activity; and working conditions, including career development.

It is impossible to know whether cataloging is more female intensive than librarianship as a whole, or how men and women are distributed in cataloging. Historical evidence indicates that the first woman employed in an American library was employed as a cataloger.[9] Scattered references seem to indicate that, excluding children's work, cataloging was more female-intensive than other library work. In a 1904 review of library attitudes towards women librarians, Salome Fairchild Cutler reported that women were preferred for cataloging.[10] Norwegian librarian Wilhelm Munthe, who visited numerous American libraries in the 1930s, reported that he had seldom seen a male cataloger.[11] Contemporary historian Dee Garrison concluded that cataloging was a female speciality for the period 1876-1920.[12]

Statistical data on cataloging are often restricted to small groups. A 1985 study established that the teaching of cataloging and classification is predictably more female-intensive than library education as a whole. For example, in 1983, subject cataloging was listed as a teaching speciality by 12 percent of the female faculty in ALA accredited schools, but by only 5 percent of the male faculty. Researchers found that while some specialities had fluctuated over time in terms of male or female predominance, cataloging and classification (along with children's and youth services librarianship) remained a female speciality.[13]

In a 1986 study that drew upon this work, a trio of researchers assessed the work and attitudes of the graduates of one ALA accredited program in Canada. Female graduates reported more time spent in cataloging on both their first and currently held positions than did male graduates. The differences were, for first job: males approximately 13 percent, females, approximately 17 percent; and for current job, males 9 percent and females, just over 10 percent.[14]

The most recent ALA survey of librarian salaries shows catalogers' salaries to trail those of reference librarians by approximately $550. The study reports data from 1,133 randomly selected academic and public libraries from 20 groups of libraries formed by stratifying five library types and the four major geographic regions of the U.S.[15]

The rhetoric linking women to cataloging by some supposed characteristic of women is historical. For example, Cutler found that libraries believed women were suited to cataloging because of their "greater conscientiousness, patience and accuracy in details." [16]   Similarly, Herbert Putnam noted in 1916 that "qualities such as those of patience, of enthusiasm and of loyalty" meant that women were largely responsible for the "vast mass of detail incidental to the organization of rapidly growing collections into an effective mass..." [17]

But if women's qualities suited them to cataloging, it was not necessarily a good thing for cataloging. Wilhelm Munthe deplored the absence of men, indicating that it hindered the development of adequate classification schemes, especially in technical subjects.[18]

In the study of Canadian graduates referred to above, participants were asked to rank by prestige twenty professional library activities. Cataloging and classification was ranked in the bottom half by both sets of respondents. It was eleventh in the ranking of those having received an undergraduate Bachelor of Arts degree, and sixteenth among those having received a Bachelor of Science degree.[19]

In a 1986 study based on extensive interviews, San Jose State University library director Ruth Hafter posited a decline in the status of catalogers since the introduction of network cataloging. Those doing original cataloging have been left with the least desirable materials and there is widespread skepticism among library administrators and others, "about the real value of catalogers' work."[20] Hafter also reported that catalogers questioned the value of their own work, including the records they created. [21]

Much of the material on this topic is impressionistic and even anecdotal, yet, given the shortage of higher quality data, it cannot be ignored. Surveys of job satisfaction that compare catalogers and other librarians are also included.

As one reviews the negative reports and attitudes toward working conditions in cataloging, two questions arise. First, is the work environment in cataloging really worse than in other library departments? Second, if these reports are not true, why do such myths persist about cataloging and not reference or circulation?

Munthe observed that physical conditions in cataloging workrooms were overcrowded, noisy and much in need of "humanizing."[22] Everyone is familiar with descriptions of contemporary cataloging departments that sound like institutional backwaters where outdated modes of management prevail in a kind of white collar sweatshop. Reports of idiosyncratic practices such as keeping new professional catalogers at copy cataloging for long periods of time (six months or a year) suggest methods of discipline or socialization designed to establish hierarchies, not professional behavior. Persistent rumors of the use of cataloging departments as warehouses for personnel with problems that make their retention in a public service capacity no longer feasible are also prevalent. Many agree with Dean Herbert White that library school students reject cataloging careers because they are familiar with cataloging departments and don't care to work in them.[23]

Hafter offers some observations on role ambiguity: she found that the role of the clerical assistant in cataloging became much more powerful after the introduction of network cataloging and this caused "dismay" among many professional catalogers.[24]

In an indictment of library educators for deterring students from cataloging careers, Janet Swan Hill lists characterizations of cataloging that she indicates may be fostered, albeit unconsciously, by some educators. These include lack of opportunity for career advancement, menial or clerical nature of the work, and isolation.[25]

One research tradition that provides data of peripheral relevance on this question is the study of job satisfaction.[26] A 1983 study compared librarians in different specialities, and found that reference and circulation librarians were significantly more satisfied with their jobs than catalogers.[27] An earlier study found reference librarians with slightly higher levels of overall satisfaction than catalogers, although the difference was not statistically significant. Catalogers, however, were significantly less satisfied on measures of creativity, social service, and variety.[28] Yet another study reporting on job satisfaction by speciality found no significant difference between catalogers and reference librarians.[29]

It is especially painful to review this material, since recent research finds that the nonmonetary aspects of work may reflect even greater inequities between men and women, and blacks and whites, than do salaries. That is, efforts to end salary inequities between gender or racial groups, even if successful, would still not end workplace injustice since the very experience of work can be so different for men and women, blacks and whites.[30] Catalogers working in highly structured settings may be among the most victimized of supposedly professional workers.

The evidence, while inadequate to determine whether women are overrepresented in cataloging, indicates that cataloging may indeed be trailing librarianship in general in salaries and status of the activity. What role does library education play in this process?

EDUCATOR v. PRACTITIONER

While the relationship between practitioner and educator in any profession is problematic, the situation in the female-intensive professions appears to be worse. A recent study of elite university schools of education illustrates the "stigma of sex" associated with schools that educate practitioners for the female-intensive professions and has been adapted for a discussion of library education.[31]

Suffering from status anxiety, brought on by a sense of marginality, library educators have sought to identify with higher status or more successful campus colleagues.[32] This involves a pull toward the interests and styles of departments with heavy enrollments, outside sources of funding and other elements of success, including higher faculty salaries.[33] Such departments also have a lower percent of women students. There is also a push away from the practitioners. This may be fostered by the fact that library educators are predominantly men, while practitioners are predominantly women.[34] The generally higher levels of income and education of library educators may also help to distance them from library practitioners.[35] Certainly identification with the campus community is encouraged by the fact that individuals from that community, and not from the library world, evaluate library educators for tenure and promotion.

While this situation undoubtedly has been exacerbated in recent years as library educators have faced closings and mergers of schools, it is not clear that the problem began with bad economic times on campus.[36]

Given this background, it is not surprising that subjects considered to be of utmost importance to practitioners are sometimes overshadowed in library education. In the study of education schools it was found that teacher education, given top priority by actual teachers, was shunned by university education faculty.

In library education, cataloging has been pushed to the periphery of the library program even though demand for catalogers has been strong for years. To some it seems that "cataloging no longer represents a basic professional concern."[37] Other "more exciting elective subjects"[38] identified with successful areas such as business and computer science receive high priority. While no one denies the need for library education to evolve, and for new methods and issues to be included, the basic needs of the profession must continue to be met.

There have been too many instances in recent years of cataloging courses being taught by part-time, marginal (non-tenure track) faculty. Clearly there is considerable loss when cataloging is not represented by a full-time faculty member, and practitioners teaching as adjuncts "cover." Under these circumstances, no one representing cataloging speaks up at committees where decisions are made concerning the curriculum, new faculty, and so on; nor are time, support and money needed for research in the area provided.

In some ways, however, it may be better to have knowledgeable part-timers teaching courses without according the speciality full representation on the faculty than, to have it assigned to a full-time faculty member whose interests and training lie elsewhere, but who takes on this burden as job protection or for another questionable motive.

It will be argued, of course, that their cataloging is taught by adjunct faculty because there are no qualified candidates for full-time, tenure-track positions to teach the subject. But what is cause and what is effect? It could as well be argued that library schools have not developed candidates in these fields as assiduously as they have in other areas.

One could fill a whole volume with anecdotes illustrating negative attitudes of library educators toward cataloging. ("You wanna be a WHAT...?") Yet cataloging is central to librarianship and, judging from the job ads, what libraries most need in terms of professional skills.

CONFRONTING THE ISSUE

On the basis of the available evidence, it can be reasonably hypothesized that the current crisis in cataloging is linked to the identification of cataloging as "women's work" within librarianship. This hypothesis can be tested by data collection to determine sex ratios and distribution in cataloging. If women are overrepresented in cataloging, further data are needed to determine whether, as predicted from the literature on the female-intensive professions, working conditions and careers are worse in cataloging departments than in other library settings. If they are, it is clear that precedent exists within librarianship for the use of data demonstrating sex inequities to promote equalization. Similar data have been used to promote the movement of women into management positions. Publicity or promotion of an awareness of the issue has facilitated the entry of women into management, and should be the first step for cataloging. Beyond publicity there are legal measures which may be appropriate. Where union contracts are negotiated funds for equalization are often a bargaining issue. State legislatures have provided funds for some types of equalization measures.

First priority must be the collection of accurate data adequate to assess the problem. While it will not be easy to collect data for the entire profession, individual institutions and systems can begin. Library schools should encourage research in this area.

Specifically, statistics are needed to illuminate who does what, under what conditions, and what they get paid for doing it in various library and information center settings. Promotion rates and opportunity for career development should also be assessed for different specialities.

Data collection must also include the nonmonetary aspects of employment for catalogers. Among elements to be considered here are type of supervision, scheduling patterns, and workspace considerations (e.g. privacy, telephone access). In academic libraries where library staff have to publish, catalogers must receive treatment equal to that given other librarians, including time and support for research.

Statistics on library school course offerings and personnel utilized in library education are also important data to collect. Promotion or time-in-rank figures and added duties of cataloging instructors (laboratory hours, network liaison, and so on) in comparison with other faculty must be included.

Since a major reason offered to explain the reduction of time given to cataloging in library education is the need to educate students for nonlibrary positions, the placement of graduates needs to be more carefully tracked: What are these positions? Where are they? What tasks are involved? How much do they pay? Who fills these positions?

Finally, perceptions of catalogers and cataloging need to be assessed. Is the cataloging department perceived as more female than other departments? How do catalogers perceive the issue? Library directors? Library educators?

CONCLUSION

In an address entitled "Woman As Cataloger" given in 1898, Celia Hayward of the San Francisco Public Library listed the many qualities needed by a good cataloger and concluded, "so it is, after all, if looked upon without prejudice, a question of the individual and not of sex."[38] While we may all agree with Hayward, the nagging question remains, has cataloging become a kind of female ghetto within librarianship?

REFERENCES

1. Some basic works on the female labor force that include data on women professionals are:
Martha Blaxall and Barbara Reagan, eds., *Women and the Workplace: The Implications of Occupational Segregation* (Chicago: University of Chicago Press, 1986).
Rudolph C. Blitz, "Women in the Professions, 1870-1970," *Monthly Labor Review* 97 (May 1974): 34-39.
Cynthia Fuchs Epstein, *Woman's Place: Options and Limits in Professional Careers* (Berkeley: University of California Press, 1970).
Amitai Etzioni, ed.,*The Semiprofessions and Their Organization: Teachers, Nurses and Social Workers* (New York: Free Press, 1969).

Patricia A.Roos, *Gender and Work: A Comparative Analysis of Industrial Societies* (Albany: State University of New York Press, 1985).

Nancy Rytina, "Earnings of Men and Women: A Look at Specific Occupations," *Monthly Labor Review* 105 (April 1982): 25-31.

Ann Helton Stromberg and Shirley Harkess, eds., *Women Working: Theories and Facts in Perspective* (Mountain View, Ca.: Mayfield Publishing, 1988).

U.S. Labor Dept. Women's Bureau. *Time of Change: 1983 Handbook on Women Workers* (Washington D.C.: Superintendent of Documents, 1983).

2.   Roma M. Harris and Christina Sue Chan, "Cataloging and Reference, Circulation and Shelving: Public Library Users and University Students' Perception of Librarianship," *Library and Information Science Research* 10 (January-March 1988): 95-107.

3.   The latest Association of Research Libraries salary survey reports that men still outnumber women as directors of ARL libraries, 75 to 28. For the first time, however, women directors were reported as earning higher salaries than their male counterparts. Another study of ARL managment librarians showed a dramatic increase, from 27.6 percent women to 45 percent women during a seven year period, but with higher salaries continuing to go to men. Kay Jones, "Women in Librarianship," *ALA Yearbook* (Chicago: American Library Association, 1988), p. 329-331. A study of perceptions of prestige for various library tasks, and the percent of time that men and women librarians spent at these tasks revealed that men spent more time on the more prestiguous tasks than did women. Men reported spending 7.6 percent of their time on policy making and planning while women reported

spending only 4.7 percent of their time at it; men reported spending 5.1 percent of their time at budget preparation, women, 2.3 percent. Roma M. Harris, Susan Monk and Jill T. Austin, "MLS Graduates Survey: Sex Differences in Prestige and Salary Found," *Canadian Library Journal* 43 (June 1986): 151.

4. Rosabeth Moss Kanter, *Men and Women of the Corporation* (New York: Basic Books, 1977), pp. 189-95. For what happens to people with limited opportunity for advancement see her "Impact of Organizational Structure: Models and Methods for Change," in Ronnie S. Ratner, ed., *Equal Employment Opportunity Policy for Women: Strategies for Implementation in the United States, Canada and Western Europe* (Philadelphia: Temple University Press, 1980), p. 313.

5. This promotes the view that women must be kept out of occupations in order to protect those occupations from a devaluation. The historical evidence on librarianship and elementary school teaching, both of which were primarily male activities that became female ones, fails to support the view that they were once higher status occupations that were degraded by feminization. For librarianship, see Anita Schiller, "Women in Librarianship," in Kathleen Weibel and Kathleen Heim, *The Role of Women in Librarianship 1876-1976: The Entry, Advancement and Struggle for Equalization in One Profession* (Phoenix: Oryx Press, 1979), p. 222.

6. Vocabulary problems plague this topic. Because women have numerical superiority in these occupations does not mean that they dominate or have control. No one thinks that privates control the army, although they outnumber generals. The term semi-profession is also often used to describe these occupations, but rarely -- if ever -- to

describe occupations in which men are the majority.

7.   For example, Reddings S. Sugg, *Motherteacher: The Feminization of American Education* (Charlottesville: University of Virginia Press, 1978).

8.   On the "creaming off" of women students, see Geraldine Joncich Clifford and James W. Guthrie, *Ed School: A Brief for Professional Education* (Chicago: University of Chicago Press, 1988), p. 256, and footnote, p. 101. 9. William Landram Williamson, *William Frederick Poole and the Modern Library Movement* (New York: Columbia, 1963), p. 28.

10. Salome Fairchild Cutler, "Women in American Libraries," in Weibel and Heim, *The Role of Women in Librarianship, 1876-1976: The Entry, Advancement and Struggle for Equalization in One Profession* (Phoenix: Oryx Press, 1979), p. 54.

11. Wilhelm Munthe, *American Librarianship from a European Angle* (Chicago: American Library Association, 1939), p. 157.

12. Dee Garrison, *Apostles of Culture: The Public Librarian and American Society, 1876-1920.* (New York: Free press, 1979), p. 179.

13. Roma M. Harris, B. Gilliam Michell and Carol Conley, "The Gender Gap in Library Education," *Journal of Education for Library and Information Science* 25 (Winter 1985): 167-76. A revision of the conclusions of this article, but still supporting the findings, can be found in Claire Beghtol, "The Gender Gap in Library Education and Publication," *Journal of Education for Library and Information Science* 27 (Summer 1986): 23.

14. Harris, "MLS Graduates Survey," p. 151-52.

15. *ALA Survey of Librarians Salaries, 1988* (Chicago: American Library Association, 1988), p. 30.

16. Cutler, "Women in American Libraries," p. 54.
17. Herbert Putnam, "The Woman in the Library," *Library Journal* 41 (December 1916): 880.
18. Munthe, *American Librarianship*, p. 157.
19. Harris, "MLS Graduates Survey," pp. 151-52.
20. Ruth Hafter, *Academic Librarians and Cataloging Networks: Visibility, Quality Control and Professional Status* (Westport, Conn: Greenwood, 1986), p. 69.
21. *Ibid.,* p. 77.
22. Munthe, *American Libraries,* p. 168.
23. Herbert White, "Catalogers--Yesterday, Today, Tomorrow," *Library Journal* 112 (April 1, 1987): 48.
24. Hafter, *Academic Librarians and Cataloging Networks*, p. 74.
25. Janet Swan Hill, "Wanted: Good Catalogers," *American Libraries* 16 (November 1985): 728-730.
26. It is impossible to know whether respondents in job satisfaction research are framing their answers with reference to their own circumstances or to the characteristics of the jobs. A person may report him or herself very satisfied if he or she thinks that is realistically the only job available to them.
27. Beverly Lynch and Jo Ann Verdin, "Job Satisfaction in Libraries: Relationships of the Work Itself, Age, Sex, Occupational group, Tenure, Supervisory Level, Career Commitment and Library Development," *Library Quarterly* 53 (October 1983): 434-47.
28. Steven Seokho Chwe, "A Comparative Study of Job Satisfaction: Catalogers and Reference Librarians in University Libraries," *Journal of Academic Librarianship* 4 (July 1978): 139-43.
29. George P. D'Elia, "The Determinants of Job Satisfaction Among Beginning Librarians," *Library Quarterly* 49

(July 1979): 283- 302.

30.   Christopher Jencks, Lauri Perman and Lee Rainwater, "What Is a Good Job? A New Measure of Labor-Market Success," *American Journal of Sociology* 93 (May 1988): 1322.

31.   They wrote about elite schools since they incorporated their experience as faculty members at one, the University of California at Berkeley, and also because these schools, for better or for worse, exert considerable influence on education schools nationwide. Clifford and Guthrie, *E d School*, especially chapter one, "Education, Educators and Education Schools" and chapter eight, "Places of Action and Places of Analysis: Advice for Schools of Education."

32.   Factors contributing to this sense of marginality among education faculty included the belief that their work was either not known or respected by the campus community and that the school was vulnerable, having few sources of outside funds. Schools of education also often suffer from unclear mission and from identification with an institution, the public school, which is widely attacked or denigrated. Many of these factors appear relevant to library education. The small size of library schools further contributes to their marginality.

33.   The average new assistant professor in a publicly supported school of library science earns $25,084. but the average salary for all new assistant professors in these institutions is $27,792. Looking only at newly appointed professors in computer and information science, and in business administration and management, new assistant professors in these discipline earn an average of $33,589 and $35,800 respectively. Differences diminish at higher ranks, but full professors in library science still trail the

average of all full professors by about $200. They trail computer science professors by about $5,000 and those in business administration by $4,000. "Average Faculty Salaries by Rank and Selected Fields, 1987-88," *Chronicle of Higher Education* (July 6, 1988): A10.

34. The percent of males employed full-time in ALA accredited schools in 1988 was 54.6, and females, 45.3. *Library and Information Science Education Statistical Report, 1988* (State College, Pennsylvania: Association for Library and Information Science Education, 1988), p. 4. In 1985, the percent of the professional library work force in randomly selected public and academic libraries, that was male was 24.9, and female, 75.1. *Academic and Public Librarians: data by Race, Ethnicity and Sex* (Chicago: American Library Association, 1986), p. 3.

35. The average salary reported for beginning librarians in all regions and types of institutions participating in the survey was $20,346. Directors averaged $40,076. *ALA Salary Survey, 1988*, pp. 26-7. New assistant professors in library science earned on average $25,084. and full professors earned $42,370. "Average Faculty Salaries," *Chronicle of Higher Education*, (July 6, 1988): A10.

36. Clifford and Guthrie provide brief histories of several university schools of education and it seems that such problems have existed in good times and bad. Clifford and Guthrie, *Ed School*, chapter four, "Tensions: Relations on the Campus."

37. Roxanne Sellberg, "The Teaching of Cataloging in U.S. Library Schools," *Library Resources and Technical Services* 32 (January 1988): 33.

38. Celia Hayward, "Woman as Cataloger," *Public Libraries* 3 (April 1898): 123.

Responding to Change:
New Goals and Strategies for
Core Cataloging Courses

Sheila S. Intner

INTRODUCTION

Last year, I conducted two quite different cataloging studies: The first examined the accuracy and fullness of original cataloging records in OCLC (Online Computer Library Center) and RLIN (Research Libraries Information Network) contributed by member catalogers (i.e., catalogers other than those at the Library of Congress or national libraries);[1] the second asked selected educators and practitioners to define "theory" and "practice" in cataloging as well as to indicate which curriculum elements from a list of 29 suggested topics they thought should be taught in a core cataloging course.[2] The results of these studies, although performed at different times for different purposes, if interpreted together in the context of problems of educating cataloging librarians, expose a disturbing problem that this paper attempts to address.

The study of cataloging quality in national bibliographic networks found that virtually all the records examined contained errors, although most of the errors did not affect retrieval (there were more than two errors per record, on average; fewer than one percent of the 430 records examined were error free), and that certain kinds of errors appeared with greater frequency: application of the cataloging rules according to the Library of Congress rule interpretations (called, officially, LCRIs); encoding of the MARC format fixed fields; and punctuation of the entries.

The study of cataloging practice and theory found that those queried disagreed about what constituted practice and theory. This lack of agreement over what constituted theory included a few respondents who did not accept even generically-worded "Theory of - - -" topics as cataloging theory; further, respondents split almost evenly over the placement of "History of - - -" topics in the theory or practice categories. Asked to identify curriculum elements that should be taught in basic cataloging courses, some of them, including the Library of Congress rule interpretations and MARC formats used by the networks to enter and communicate bibliographic data in computerized systems, were selected by very few respondents, whether educators or practitioners, as appropriate to a core cataloging course.[3]

It appears that the librarians who cataloged the records examined in the first study did not do a high quality job. It also appears that what they did least well coincides with what a good many cataloging educators and practitioners who participated in the second study felt was inappropriate for a beginning course in cataloging: applying the cataloging rules according to LC policies and practices, and encoding the resulting entries properly for the MARC communications format.

Problems of time and space for advanced and specialized cataloging courses in library/information science curricula have been documented in several excellent studies, both recent and historical.[4]   Attending to them assumes, however, that we focus primarily on students who know they wish to specialize in cataloging from the start of their professional training. These, I submit, are not a real problem. They are few in number and, we can be sure, they will take all the advanced level courses available to them. The more critical issue, I believe, is teaching students who *might* become cataloging librarians even though they do not intend to and do not prepare for it (which includes almost everyone enrolled in master's degree programs) what they must know to begin doing a high quality professional job in the one course they are likely to take: the core cataloging course. (Beginning to do a high quality job is not the same as doing it, but being armed to absorb the lessons taught by experience should be part of every degree-holder's academic preparation.)

The changes to which we must respond, I believe, are the following: (1) the belief that only students who prepare for cataloging careers are likely to take cataloging jobs; (2) the idea that cataloging is a relatively simple, repetitious, and stable type of work. For a variety of reasons the explanation of which lies outside the scope of this paper, jobs abound in cataloging and bibliographic activities. Many former students return to tell me that they looked for work in reference or administration, but the jobs they were offered were in cataloging. Naturally, they took them, even though they had not prepared for them. This fact, while mildly disturbing itself, points to a need to respond to the situation and to do more for the would-be reference librarian or would-be middle manager who might wind up being a cataloging librarian or a retrospective conversion supervisor. Moreoever, cataloging today, in the highly technical, computer-based environment of library bibliographic operations, is relatively complex and dynamic. The repetitious nature of cataloging activities has always been a myth and will remain so, at least until publishers and producers eschew any creativity in the presentation of bibliographic data and authors and artists eschew any creativity in their works.

In suggesting solutions to these problems, I beg the reader's indulgence. Library/information scientists stand accused of debasing their professional discourse with an endless stream of acronyms unintelligible to any but their cohorts. In the spirit of fighting fire with fire, however, I suggest the adoption of two more acronyms to set new goals and objectives for coursework in cataloging and to help educate the unintentional cataloging librarians: SERA and WYTIWYG. SERA, or Stimulation, Experimentation, Resolution, Analysis, represents a teaching process particularly well-suited to cataloging issues; WYTIWYG, or What You Teach Is What You Get, defines the substance of the curriculum to be covered in a beginning course.

QUE SERA, SERA

Authors of articles in the literature, speakers at meetings, and faculty and students in library schools all seem to agree on three things about cataloging coursework: there is an enormous amount of material to be covered; it is difficult and it is dull. Nothing is clearer than the compelling need to make cataloging issues manageable for students learning about them and to make the learning process interesting.

I find that cataloging involves making a series of decisions, from the choice of titles and other elements of identification and access, to the choice of classification numbers for shelving items with other works on the same subject. Decision-making is interesting--a great deal more interesting than cataloging might appear to be on the surface-- so I teach cataloging as a decision-making process. Cataloging decisions are no more cut-and-dried than other sorts of decisions, and a necessary step in making them is considering alternative solutions. To stimulate students to consider and discuss potential choices, I put them together in teams, provide them with real books to catalog, and allow them to argue each point among themselves, knowing they will have to defend their choices during a review period in which they argue their choices with one another and with me. I call the quasi-Socratic dialog that results SERA--Stimulation, Experimentation, Resolution, and Analysis.

Stimulation occurs in two ways: first, students work in small teams--three persons to a team is ideal, but two or four will do--in which they find themselves arguing about the interpretation of rules and decision alternatives; and, second, they work with attractive, current, real materials, always including some quirky items I think they might enjoy, e.g., a book of trivia questions to be used for games of *Trivial Pursuit;* a book (actually a musical score) of Tom Lehrer parodies with outrageous illustrations; a book of Charles Addams' cartoons, a tiny nutshell edition of *The Night Before Christmas*, a libretto of a musical comedy or the book version of a *Star Trek* episode. This is superior, I believe, to using traditional textbook exercises or even duplicates of title pages.

Student catalogers in the teams quite naturally experiment with various methods of finding answers to their questions. They read and explain rules to one another. Enterprising teammates peruse the compilations of LCRIs provided for them or run to an OCLC or BiblioFile terminal for previously cataloged entries. A few ask me questions, since I act as a resource person for everyone, and I try diligently to answer them with reference to documentation of some sort.

After a short time--15 or 20 minutes--the teams must complete their entries. The time factor intensifies the need to make choices. Then, team by team, a review is conducted in which the student teams must explain the decision points they encountered, the alternatives considered, the choices they made and why they made them. The review is open, and often elicits vigorous attacks or defenses of the team's positions by other students in the class (not just those on the defending team). Everyone in the class participates, asking questions, contributing information, taking positions, and helping to confirm or overturn a particular choice. Although I retain the right of final veto over something I know is not correct, a curious phenomenon tends to occur in which someone other than me, as the teacher--either a member of the defending team or a classmate outside the team--finds sufficient documentation for a resolution to the problem.

Then, I do a retrospective analysis of the problem, alternative solutions, information gathered from rules and references, and final resolution, in the form of a short summary to conclude the effort.

A camaraderie among the teammates springs up, even when they disagree violently on what should be done. Frequently a dissident member does separate entries on her/his own, making different choices than those of the team. If the team is found to be incorrect, however, it is rare that this person will say, publicly, "I told you so!" Usually a knowing look passes from one to another, or I will overhear them discussing it in the hallways after class. Students hate to put down an unresolved problem, even at the end of the session, and they will remain in their seats working on it after the class is officially dismissed.

Occasionally, a SERA session will end leaving one or more items undiscussed. It is surprising how many times people in the class will work on the problems during the week, looking up questionable pieces of information or searching databases for precedent, bringing their findings triumphantly to the next class. These successful searchers are not necessarily the same persons responsible for the problem, i.e., the team doing the cataloging. It seems that these problems have an appeal of their own, perhaps akin to the appeal of television game shows.

SERA simulates what occurs in real-life cataloging departments where there are peer groups of cataloging librarians. Collegial discussions among peers in cataloging are fun, just as they are among any group of professionals (talking "shop" is a bore only to outsiders) and they are an extremely powerful educational strategy. The caution is that the resolution and analysis phases must provide an informational base for sound decisions. Classroom decisions, at any rate, cannot be justified in ignorance, even though in a real-life situation, we might believe something merely because it comes from a peer we deem knowledgeable or authoritative.

An important part of SERA is gathering documentary evidence. Accepting things on faith is to be avoided at all costs. Nothing highlights the value of a skeptical attitude better than for a student to find a flaw in the teacher's reasoning. Rather than embarrass the teacher, it provides an opportunity to reiterate that facts should be verified and nothing should be taken entirely on faith. It also gives dramatic evidence of the fallibility of authority. In cataloging, Library of Congress (LC) records are the standard against which every other library's cataloging is measured, yet LC records are not without error. One study of LC cataloging beginning as Cataloging-In-Publication (CIP--it is the program that provides publishers with the preliminary catalog entries they print in books on the back of title pages) found that 40% or more of the entries contained errors.[5] Thus, it is imperative that students be taught to rely on what they see in the items they have in hand and what they know to be the latest information in rules and interpretations, not on what someone else has put in a catalog entry.

Students must also learn flexibility in cataloging and SERA enables a teacher to distinguish between correct and incorrect judgments and multiple correct judgments, i.e., two or more possible choices both or all of which are correct, deliberately left to the discretion of individual catalogers. It may come as a shock to some traditionalists among us, but there might be no "one right way" to catalog something. The reason cataloging cannot be straightforwardly right or wrong in every element is that individual libraries have different clients with differing needs. Permitting a measure of variation enables these differing needs to be served. Generally, the variance in cataloging is in the amount of information included in the record. Sometimes, however, it affects the placement of information or the form in which it appears. Students should be able to recognize the alternatives and the difference in rules between "thou shalt" and "thou may, if desired."

WYTIWYG IN THEORY AND PRACTICE

SERA is an acronym that represents a process of teaching cataloging with high interest and involvement in a collegial, colloquial, problem-solving approach, while WYTIWYG addresses the content of the course curriculum. Imitative of that favorite computing acronym, WYSIWYG--What You See Is What You Get--the acronym stands for What You Teach Is What You Get. If we do not teach our students something, we cannot expect them to know it, at least not immediately upon graduation. Obviously, students cannot learn in library school absolutely everything they will ever have to know in their careers. They should be *and are* learning more all the time--on the job, in personal professional reading, participating in professional associations and other related activities.

A professional, by definition, takes on a career-long obligation to keep up with the chosen field and to continue developing his or her expertise. The question for us is, what knowledge base should be common to all library and information science professionals, even (or, especially) new graduates? The answer, at least for programs in which such a core curriculum has been identified, usually includes basic skills in reference and cataloging, along with a varying list of other important fundamentals: management, research methods, history, information production, societal issues, etc.

If we want to prepare catalogers who can do themselves and/or supervise others in doing original cataloging according to current standard practices, we must teach it to them in the basic course. We need to examine the relationships between our theories and our practices and view these as harmonious and reinforcing to one another, not as two poles at opposite ends of the universe. The functions of entry-level jobs should not depart so far from either the theories underlying professional practice or the fundamentals of that practice that newly graduated librarians cannot understand and use those relationships.

Just as form follows function, practice should follow theory. If, in analyzing a particular practice, one discovers that it negates the underlying principles it is supposed to serve, it is time to blow the whistle and reevaluate the practice. If, in the course of research, a particular theory is negated, a reevaluation of the entire context in which that theory figures must be undertaken.

Explaining the principles and reasoning behind cataloging rules and rule interpretations as part of teaching those rules, etc., enables a teacher to relate underlying theories to the context of concrete practice. It also makes for greater understanding of the principles than would teaching them entirely in the abstract. To prepare cataloging librarians who understand more than isolated principles, i.e., who understand the standard applications of those principles in the form of cataloging rules, LCRIs, subject heading lists, classifications, and the MARC formats, and can use them easily and well, we must teach this material to them in the basic course.

Standard cataloging tools should be taught in the core cataloging course as well as the principles they serve. Standard applications and manuals must accompany teaching of the tools, not just the rule books without the applications that are accepted in the field as authoritative. Thus, it is not enough to teach the *Anglo-American Cataloguing Rules*; one must also teach the LCRIs and use of the LC Name Authority File as their standard applications. It is not enough to teach the *Library of Congress Subject Headings*; one must also teach the *Subject Cataloging Manual: Subject Headings* as their standard application. It is not enough to teach the Dewey Decimal or Library of Congress classification schedules. Methods of assigning numbers from them as well as the balance of the codes and symbols that comprise complete call numbers (including *Subject Cataloging Manual: Shelflisting* and the

Cutter-Sanborn tables) must be taught, too. Above all, one must teach the MARC formats for computer-based communication of bibliographic information, since in a computerized environment, cataloging information must be translated into that standard language.

A good many of the students in my classes hold jobs in catalog departments and their responsibilities include original cataloging (a few are the only catalogers in their libraries). Some of them have never heard of LC's quarterly periodical, *Cataloging Service Bulletin*, in which the Library's decisions about application of the cataloging rules, subject headings, and classifications are published. Others have never seen *Subject Cataloging Manual* or heard of an LCRI. They are unaware of the LC Name Authority File and adhere to no substitute, local or otherwise, for the systematic establishment of name headings in their catalogs. These people are not equipped to conform to national network bibliographic input standards-- they have not yet had the training and even if they did, they are not being given the tools to do the job right. Thus, it is not surprising that my study of original cataloging in OCLC and RLIN revealed a startling number of errors. It is not that these paraprofessional cataloging librarians are unwilling or recalcitrant. They--and their supervisors--must be made aware of the requirements involved in producing new data in standard format, exposed to the processes and the tools, and furnished with the rationale for observing the standards as well as the trade-offs to be made in departing from them.[6] Only then can a librarian think critically about bibliographic standards and decide how to implement them given the parameters of the local environment, budget, client base, and collections.

Even when all of these elements are included in a core cataloging course, library schools cannot graduate world-class cataloging librarians with just one course under their belts.

That lofty level can only be reached after gaining experience in hands-on work, preferably with continuing guidance from master cataloging librarians or others with bibliographic expertise. But, we could expect that the knowledge of what constitutes standard practice and why it is important would keep these neophytes from thinking that just following whatever local procedures were already in place in an institution was the same as meeting national and international standards, constituting acceptable input into any database or network union catalog.

Is this too much for a core course in cataloging? No doubt it is taxing to incorporate so much into one term of 13 to 15 weeks. There is no question that a much more thorough treatment of both the theory and the practice of cataloging could be accomplished if we had twice that time. Sellberg and several of the colleagues who answered the "Practical and Theoretical Knowledge in Cataloging" survey called for longer master's degree programs. In an ideal world, we might just lengthen the basic cataloging requirement. But this is not an ideal world and, as Miksa points out, cataloging courses must compete for the limited space allotted to the total curricula. Nonetheless, I disagree with those who believe that *AACR*2R can be taught without LCRIs or that any kind of practical cataloging can be taught without MARC. I suspect that overlaying the aspect of computer-based cataloging on the traditional fundamentals of cataloging (i.e., descriptive cataloging codes, subject cataloging lists, and classifications) is what has caused some educators to throw up their hands and call for curriculum reform.

While MARC is merely a set of codes applied in a mechanical way to cataloging data, it requires knowledge and understanding of the codes and their operation so that local workflow and decision-making about local system design can be done intelligently. It is unfortunate that students lacking general knowledge of computing find the MARC format extremely difficult to fathom. One solution to this problem is for them to acquire some general computing knowledge *before* taking the core cataloging course. Another is to track people into the course according to their knowledge of computing (and also, perhaps, their knowledge of cataloging jargon--something that makes cataloging easier for people who already work in a library environment, but difficult for those new to the entire field).

Ignoring the variation in students' pre-existing prerequisite knowledge--not untypical in schools that assign people to cataloging sections according to the initial letter of their surnames, the relative convenience of the daily schedule or some other arbitrary division of the troops--is a major obstacle to success for teachers. Explaining MARC format tags, indicators, delimiters and subfield codes to the informed is tough enough. Doing so in a class where some students have never encountered computing is almost impossible. The answer, however, is not to put networking and the MARC formats off for other courses at advanced levels. The answer is to teach the traditional subjects in the modern mode, emphasizing those elements of *AACR*2R that harmonize with MARC or that translate into coded data. Once these elements are understood and in place, the rest are less formidable to contemplate.

If students are well-grounded in standard practice, decisions to depart from that practice can be evaluated in terms of the potential benefits vs. losses in individual cases. If they do not know what consitutes standard practice, cataloging is an eternal game of chance and the odds are not in favor of having it come out right.

CONCLUSIONS

In conclusion, this solution rests on the belief that newly-graduated librarians become cataloging librarians even though they might not anticipate this as the goal of their professional school careers. (In some instances, these neophytes remain cataloging librarians throughout their careers and in others, they move on to other types of responsibilities after devoting some period of time to cataloging work. Either way, they have an impact on the national pool of bibliographic resources.) Its thrust is to prepare all graduate librarians to be able to make cataloging decisions that conform to standards as implemented by mainstream originators of bibliographic data: the Library of Congress and national bibliographic utilities. In order to insure that libraries can continue to reap the rewards of upholding standards, i.e., sharing the burden of generating bibliographic data and sharing the resources those data represent, we must teach them to our students. If what appears in our national network databases is what we have been teaching (and, clearly, I think it is), we must try to do better. What we teach is what we get.

This achievement involves conscious decisions on the part of faculty teaching core cataloging courses to focus on including these elements, at a minimum:

1. Bibliographic descriptions made according to *AACR2R* and associated LCRIs, found in *Cataloging Service Bulletin* or other compilations;

2. Assignment of subject descriptors according to *Library of Congress Subject Headings* and the practices of the Library of Congress as explained in *Subject Cataloging Manual: Subject Headings;*

3. Assignment of classification numbers according to the Dewey Decimal and Library of Congress

classification schemes, as well as commonly employed methods of shelflisting, including Library of Congress practices explained in *Subject Cataloging Manual: Shelflisting*, and the *Cutter-Sanborn* tables; and

4. Encoding of the resulting data into the MARC format.

Since this last element is based to some degree on knowledge of computing in general, it is suggested that students be tracked into the beginning cataloging course according to their pre-existing knowledge in this area. Students with no knowledge of computing might be expected to acquire familiarity with basic concepts of computing before entering the library/information science program, or they might be asked to take such a course as an added requirement, prerequisite to courses that presume such knowledge, including beginning cataloging, reference, collection development, research methods, etc. Library schools might offer a brief preparatory course for no credit, to be taken before registering for the first term.

A strategy well-suited to teaching cataloging concepts is SERA: Stimulation, Experimentation, Resolution, and Analysis. It involves presenting intellectually challenging problem-solving tasks to student-catalogers, allowing them to discuss potential solutions, choose alternatives, and defend them before a jury of their peers, under the guidance of a knowledgeable teacher who helps them analyze the solution(s). Naturally, the attitude toward such exercises is most important. One cannot promote a questioning atmosphere without acknowledging that students have something to contribute as well as to receive from the process. SERA must operate in a rather free-wheeling fashion, in which the professor might not always be right and in which there is more than one right way to view things. What should be emphasized are the principles underlying rules, and the assumptions made about bibliographic services.

Conferring the master's degree upon a student who has taken one cataloging course does not make that student a cataloging librarian; yet, in many libraries across the nation, such students are hired for the job. Even if this entry level job does not involve making many original contributions to a national database, after a year or two, the no-longer-neophyte cataloging librarian can move on to one that does. Given the need expressed by many library administrators, it is a likely supposition, if only the librarian is willing.

If knowledge is power, then it is within the scope and purpose of our professional school programs to empower graduates with knowledge of the tools of their practice as well as the theoretical structures underlying bibliographic services.

REFERENCES

1.   Dorothy McGarry and Sheila S. Intner, "Quality in Bibliographic Databases: An Analysis of Member-Contributed Cataloging in OCLC and RLIN: Final Report." (Unpublished document submitted to the Council on Library Resources, Washington, D.C., 1988).

2.   Sheila S. Intner, "Practical and Theoretical Knowledge in Cataloging: What We Should Teach and Why," in *Theorie et Pratique dans l'Enseignment des Sciences de l'Information: Comptes rendus du premier Colloque conjoint entre l'Association Internationale des Ecoles de Sciences de l'Information (AIESI) et l'Association for Library and Information Science Education (ALISE) = Bridging the Gap Between Theory and Practice:*

Proceedings of the First Joint Meeting Between the Association Internationale des Ecoles de Sciences de l'Information (AIESI) and the Association for Library and Information Science Education (ALISE), Montreal, Canada, 25-26-27 Mai/May 1988, ed. by Rejean Savard (Montreal: the Meeting, 1988), p. 259-73.

3. According to network policies, members are required to input cataloging conforming to these codes and guidelines.

4. Publications covering a span of more than 50 years include: Roxanne Sellberg, "The Teaching of Cataloging in U.S. Library Schools," *Library Resources & Technical Services* 32 (Jan. 1988): 30-42; Maurice F. Tauber, "Training of Catalogers and Classifiers," *Library Trends* 2 (Oct. 1953): 330-41; and Margaret Mann, "The Teaching of Cataloging and Classification," *Bulletin of the American Library Association* 31 (May 1937): 285-90+.

5. Arlene G. Taylor and Charles W. Simpson, "Accuracy of LC Copy: A Comparison between Copy That Began As CIP and Other LC Cataloging," *Library Resources & Technical Services* 30 (Oct./Dec. 1986): 375-87.

6. Carol A. Mandel, "Trade-Offs: Quantifying Quality in Library Technical Services," *Journal of Academic Librarianship* 14 (Sept. 1988): 214-20. In this article, Mandel explores the application of cost-benefit analysis to library cataloging operations. This thoughtfully-written and eminently practical article encompasses a great deal of theoretical territory as well as essential practical ground. It should be required reading for every cataloging librarian and cataloging manager.

Alternatives for Educating Catalogers: A Small Library School Perspective

Beatrice Kovacs and Beth A. Reichardt

INTRODUCTION

It is difficult to recruit and educate individuals as cataloging librarians today. If it were not, this colloquium would not be of such interest and value. If cataloging were an attractive career path for entry-level librarians, the literature would not have had so many articles in the past few years about the shortage of catalogers and the problems of training quality catalogers.

In a small library school, such as the University of North Carolina at Greensboro (UNCG), Department of Library and Information Studies, only one brief cataloging survey course can be offered. In such a situation, students who express an interest in cataloging as a career may occasionally be discouraged by the rules and details they must learn for all types of libraries, instead of being able to focus on the type of library in which they are specifically interested. Those students may be frustrated in their desire to learn the intricacies of cataloging and classification because there is not enough time in one semester to discover the challenging and complicated theories and practices involved. Other students, however, have little interest in discussing rules and theories of cataloging and classification because, as they express it, they will "either buy the service or let the computer do it in the future." Therefore, the course must be designed to provide the optimum learning situation for both groups, and all students in-between. Alternative inducements toward cataloging and classification as a course of study and as a career option, must be offered by small library science programs. Most small programs do not have the resources and personnel available to counsel, mentor, and develop cataloging professionals. There is also likely to be insufficient faculty to develop the technical expertise and provide the amount of detail and experiential opportunities that are needed to identify the quality of the individuals and their appropriateness for a career in cataloging and classification.

How can educators in such programs excite and entice sharp, imaginative, people-oriented individuals into careers in cataloging?   This article summarizes the efforts at UNCG to develop an educational environment that presents cataloging and classification as an attractive and challenging career opportunity.

THE SETTING

UNCG's Department of Library and Information Studies (LIS) is one of five departments in the School of Education. The program offers an ALA-accredited Master of Library Science as well as post-master's courses for individuals wishing to pursue state certification as system-wide school media supervisors.

During any semester, the student body is composed of a variety of persons interested in one or more of the following library studies: school, academic, public, or special librarianship combined with reference, reader's services, and technical services specializations. Some students have no library experience, while others are (or were, prior to enrollment) employed in a variety of library settings. In addition, local librarians occasionally return for courses to update their knowledge or to pursue additional certificates offered by the state of North Carolina.

All students must complete the basic course requirements including: Foundations of Librarianship, Reference Sources and Services, Administration of Library Programs, Problems in Library and Information Studies (a research methods course), and Organizing Library Collections. Added requirements include one bibliography/materials course, one "type of library" course, and any offerings that are needed to meet certification standards in certain "tracks" for professional positions. Elective courses, taught by both regular and adjunct faculty, provide instruction in most areas of library and information studies.

Regarding "Organizing Library Collections" (LST 640), few generalizations can be made about the composition of the class during any particular semester. Some students are familiar with the concepts of cataloging and classification and may have been copy-catalogers. Some have no knowledge of what is involved in getting the materials on the shelf and into the catalog.

THE SOLUTION

Students in LST 640 are presented with a variety of aspects of organizing collections. Included on the course schedule are discussions about *AACR2* and descriptive cataloging, subject cataloging and subject classification, access points, and MARC records. The basics are presented, along with the major philosophies concerned with organization and access. There is a strong effort to describe cataloging and classification within the context of librarianship and information studies. Cataloging is presented as a user-oriented discipline that is not inherently tedious or boring, which requires accuracy without punctiliousness, and for which imagination and awareness of user needs are essential.

A balance between theory and practice is attempted each semester. After students have practiced descriptive cataloging of monographic, serial, and non-print materials, they are introduced to microcomputer-based cataloging software programs. This is accomplished by the provision of a study module that a student must complete outside of class time. Beyond the minimum completion requirements, the module is designed to enable students to have as much hands-on experience with microcomputers and cataloging software as they wish. It should be noted that prior experience with computers, as well as an awareness of cataloging software and the OCLC bibliographic database, varies among students.

DEVELOPMENT OF THE CATALOGING LABORATORY

The cataloging laboratory was developed primarily through grant funds received from a variety of sources. The initial impetus for such a facility began with a Library Services and Construction Act grant from the Division of State Library,

North Carolina Department of Cultural Resources, in the Fall of 1985. This grant enabled UNCG to purchase an M300 workstation and begin offering OCLC training through a tutorial and limited online access.

The next opportunity to purchase additional equipment and supplies came from the Computer Technology Education Program (CTEP), sponsored by the R. J. Reynolds Foundation and administered through UNCG. The purpose of this grant program is to provide faculty with financial resources to develop effective uses of microcomputers in educational offerings. CTEP awarded $2,500 for the purchase of six cataloging software programs, paper supplies (including card stock and labels), and a printer that would accept card stock.

During 1987-1988, a number of software producers were generous in donating copies of their programs to UNCG. Other producers provided demonstration diskettes that offer a simulation of their product's operation. The H. W. Wilson Company donated a Wilsonline workstation that expanded the computer capabilities to include CD-ROM products. Also in 1988, the State Library awarded another grant for equipment and software that enabled the Department to purchase an IBM-compatible computer (with a hard disk, color monitor, CD-ROM drive, and printer), an Apple IIGS, and additional cataloging software and supplies.

As the collection of hardware and software increased, available space to use them decreased. A crisis developed as tutorial sessions were conducted in office hallways and other inconvenient places. At this point, UNCG's Academic Computing Center (ACC) was contacted and, through a series of negotiations, agreed to provide space in a computer laboratory located near the LIS offices and classrooms. ACC also guaranteed maintenance, service, and regular supplies in exchange for use of the equipment when not needed by LIS students.

USE OF THE CATALOGING LABORATORY

During the fall and spring semesters of 1987-1988, each student in LST 640 was required to schedule a time, outside of class, with the Laboratory Assistant for a hands-on session with at least one Apple-based and one IBM-based cataloging software program and with the OCLC tutorial program. The student response to these sessions was generally enthusiastic, although some individuals complained that they did not have enough time to experiment with the equipment. (Time constraints were a problem when there was a large number of students to schedule during the Laboratory Assistant's workday.)

Individual appointments could not be scheduled for students in LST 640 during the summer of 1988 because of the structure of the summer session. Therefore, a decision was made to provide an in-class demonstration session showing two of the microcomputer-based cataloging software programs, one on an Apple and one on an IBM. Time was allotted for students to input a record for an item of their choice. They were instructed to try both programs, and were given the option to look at two other software programs on other computers. Students were free to discuss problems with classmates or to ask technical questions of the Laboratory Assistant. The programs used for demonstration were in *AACR2* format, while the optional programs were not. In addition, students were required to reserve time outside of class for individual instruction with the OCLC tutorial program on the Department's only OCLC workstation. The students do not go online in the session, and there is no budget at present for any online work as part of LST 640. Any persons wishing to experience online searching must pay any charges that might accrue. (Most of the students went through the OCLC tutorial in pairs during the summer session, again because of the limited amount of time and the size of the class.)

ADVANTAGES OF THE LABORATORY

A number of advantages to this laboratory have been observed. For example, students actually input records in both IBM-compatible and Apple computers. This enables them to have hands-on experience with both types of hardware and to recognize the good and not-so-good aspects of the equipment and the operating languages. The terminology and the concepts taught in the classroom are reinforced by the programs, demonstrating to the students the importance of understanding the language of cataloging and classification. The students practice the new descriptive cataloging skills they develop, while they learn the various features of the software programs which might influence purchasing decisions for their library settings in the future. They see the difference between *AACR2* and non-*AACR2* description in action, and they learn that with many turnkey programs concessions must be made to the capabilities of the programs. As examples: one program will only enable the cataloger to view the entire record by printing it--onscreen formatting is not supported. Errors and omissions can therefore only be seen when the record is test-printed. Another program automatically erases a record upon printing: test-printing is not supported, but onscreen formatting is.

As students have been trained individually and in pairs, a number of advantages have been noted for training in pairs. The obvious advantages include a savings in work time for the Laboratory Assistant, since half as many hours are needed for scheduled training sessions. Pairs training also offers the opportunity for students in carpools to train together, and make joint transportation arrangements. A less obvious, but perhaps more important, advantage is that a pair of students may engage in discussion and clarification of concepts, particularly if the individuals have the ability to communicate with one another. Two participants can ask questions, discuss ideas, and explain concepts to each other, when one or the other of them experiences difficulty understanding the information. This works well when the students in question are either friends, or are working at the same pace, or are on the same interest level. This last advantage seems to occur more often with pairs that request time together, than with pairs that happen to have the same scheduled time.

Using the OCLC tutorial also has a number of advantages. The tutorial demonstrates, more than class lectures can, a basic overview of characteristics and capabilities of the OCLC systems. Many of the students have been made aware of the database through a variety of classes and readings, but few have had any personal exposure to the system. In the OCLC tutorial, terminology and concepts presented in the classroom are once again reinforced. In addition, students can experience the various aspects of the MARC format with examples of data entry and retrieval. The screens provide examples of the MARC format that can be correlated to the cataloging textbook, since it lists the MARC fields related to each area of a cataloging record. The tutorial also assists students in completing one or two class assignments. Some students begin to overcome their fear of computers, and many remark on how useful the system seems to be and how much it can do. Even those who have worked with OCLC as copy catalogers learn at least one or two new things about the system through the tutorial.

Some of the students will one day be working, and some are already working, in situations where they are the only 'librarian'. These laboratory sessions help them identify which software program features may be best for their present (or future) jobs. The experiences may help them make more informed decisions about which software they might need, based on knowledge and experience rather than on producers' literature or demonstration diskettes. Many students see the importance of having first-hand knowledge with a program whenever possible before making a decision, so they might explore the differences in options, formats, memory capacities, additional features, etc.

DISADVANTAGES OF THE LABORATORY

The major disadvantage of the laboratory is the limited amount of time available for students to use the equipment and software. This is a problem because so many of the students commute, sometimes more than an hour each way, and need the assistance of the Laboratory Assistant in the initial stages of work with the programs or the OCLC tutorial. The Laboratory Assistant has the flexibility to provide training whenever it is convenient with the students, as long as the building is open and available for general student use.

A disadvantage with the use of some of the programs is the fact that they are only simulations. Simulations provide only limited experiences with the capabilities and drawbacks of the programs. They do not provide complete reflections of the speed, accuracy, or strength of the software. With the limited sources of funding, however, and with the objective of providing as many options and opportunities as possible, it is necessary to rely on simulations of some programs rather than on fully operational versions of the programs. It is hoped that most of these demonstration programs and simulations will be replaced with actual programs in the future.

Another disadvantage noted is that the beginning cataloging students cannot use the laboratory without the aid of the Laboratory Assistant. This is a result of the non-*AACR2* programs and the confusion that results when the record created does not look like the records developed in the classroom. Some explanation beyond the software manual is consistently needed. Although the cataloging laboratory was originally envisioned as a self-study facility, experience so far indicates that such independent use of the equipment is not feasible at the present time.

Working in pairs, although in general a satisfactory arrangment, does have some disadvantages. Many individuals have dissimilar interests: one student may be fascinated with the computer while the other may be bored with the enthusiasm of the partner. Partners have had problems with the "keyboard hog" who refuses to relinquish control of the computer terminal, as well as with the "no-touch" person who is afraid that s/he will break the machine and destroy all the data. Also, partners with different pace and learning levels do not seem to gain as much benefit from the exercises as do others who are better matched.

Disadvantages of using the OCLC tutorial include the facts that it is a simulation, and that it requires a good deal of time to complete. A shortened version has been developed by the Laboratory Assistants over the past two years, which enables students to test the major features of the database in just over three-quarters of an hour. Those students who wish to take more time can then arrange to follow the entire tutorial by themselves whenever the M300 is available. The first time the student uses the longer tutorial, however, the Laboratory Assistant must be careful to explain differences between the tutorial and the online system. Two examples of such explanation include:

- When a MARC record is displayed, the part of the record that was searched is highlighted,
- Unsuccessful searchers are given hints regarding what was wrong with their strategies.

While there are some disadvantages, as noted, it seems clear that the pluses outweigh the minuses. To date, students have been unanimous in their evaluation of the laboratory experience as beneficial and worthwhile.

IMPLICATIONS OF THE CATALOGING LABORATORY

There are a number of implications of this aspect of the cataloging course. Of primary importance is the face that students presently enrolled in the course can have additional time and practice with cataloging programs whenever the computers are available, thus enabling them to develop a better foundation for and understanding of descriptive cataloging.

Implications that extend beyond the semester in which a student is registered for the class are also evident. For example, individuals who have obtained jobs after completing the MLS degree have occasionally returned to ask questions about the cataloging programs owned by the Department, and to schedule demonstrations. At least two students who finished the LST 640 course prior to the development of these computer exercises have requested demonstrations of the software packages, and they have been accommodated as schedules permit. The Department's Alumni Association sponsored a workshop on the advantages and disadvantages of the School's currently owned software packages for the creation of catalog records during their annual meeting in 1988.

To date, two outside agencies have requested demonstrations of the cataloging software in order to make a purchasing decision for creation of their library's catalogs. These agencies do not librarians on staff, and were not aware of what was involved in providing access to their collections until they viewed some of the cataloging software.

Word is spreading about the availability of this service. Recently, one student described how a "cataloger's eyes lit up" when the student told her about the existence of the cataloging software laboratory, and the appropriateness of one package to her particular library. The cataloger was excited to discover that she would no longer have to type a card several times, and immediately went to tell her Director about the programs and where they could be seen.

CONCLUSION

The cataloging laboratory is still in the initial stages of its evolution. As additional software and hardware is purchased, tested, and used, it will be easier to evaluate the effectiveness of this educational tool. As current students graduate and begin to apply the skills and knowledge they have gained, it will be apparent whether this particular methodology has a positive impact on their work. Until that time, evaluation of the experience is dependent on the immediate impressions of the students and on the few cases when their new knowledge could be used immediately in a work situation. No formal evaluative surveys have so far been conducted, but an attitudinal survey is planned for the Spring of 1989. This survey will attempt to identify the effect of the cataloging laboratory experience on the knowledge-base of the students.

Another survey is planned for a point farther in the future. This will assess the impact of the laboratory experience on individuals who have graduated and worked for a period of time in a professional position. Unfortunately, it is too early to be able to determine whether there is such an impact.

Will this laboratory help this small library school recruit and educate individuals as cataloging librarians? For that, too, it is too soon to tell. Judging by the comments that are occasionally heard in the halls, students are beginning to see that there is more to the process of cataloging and classification than memorizing rules and dabbling in details. Persons who are interested in technological applications appear to find the concept of cataloging software and its uses appealing. Others indicate discovering that cataloging and classification are not boring, contrary to what they had been led to expect. Still others find challenge in trying to determine what is the best place and the best way to identify something for the patron.

Every effort is made to make the cataloging materials and the laboratory available to anyone in the community who may wish to use them, and the public relations benefit is growing. Librarians who never considered participating in cataloging are now interested in at least trying some of the software programs. Perhaps they too may become interested in being catalogers someday.

APPENDIX

The following software programs are currently available in the cataloging laboratory:

IBM-compatible programs:
1. Bib-Base/Cat (Small Library Computing)
2. Catalog Carder (Right On Programs)
3. Librarian's Helper (Scarecrow Press)
4. Online Catalog (Right On Programs)

5.   Subject List (Right On Programs)
6.   Subscription Control (Right On Programs)

Apple-compatible programs:

7.   Catalog Card and Label Wrtier - K-12 MicroMedia (Wehner Educational Software)
8.   Catalog Card Assembler III (Microtech Software Company)
9.   Catalog Carder (Right On Programs)
10.   Librarian's Helper (Scarecrow Press)
11.   Quick Card (Follett Library Software)

Simulations or demonstration diskettes:

12.   The Assistant (Library Automation Products)
13.   Bibliofile (Library Corporation)
14.   Books In Print Plus (Bowker Electronic Publishing)
15.   Winnebago Cat (Winnebago Software Company)

Using Computers to Enhance Cataloging Productivity

Joseph R. Matthews

Cataloging, the raison d'etre of librarianship in the minds of many, has been a subject that is either loved and embraced or hated and rejected by librarians since the time of Melvil Dewey. In recent years, cataloging and the MARC record[1] have become almost inexorably entwined. It is rare, indeed, that a cataloging class is not taught today without the use of terminals linked to one or more of the bibliographic utilities, e.g., OCLC, RLIN, UTLAS and WLN. Yet, while the students are probably taught more about the MARC record structures than they would ever care to learn, much confusion abounds about the MARC record.

For example, many librarians continue to believe the myth of the universal MARC record. There is no widespread recognition that the Library of Congress' MARC (or USMARC) is not identical to OCLC MARC or RLIN MARC or UTLAS MARC or WLN MARC or Brodart MARC or any other version. In addition, the amount of data contained within a MARC record is often confused with the fact that the data found within the machine readable record conforms to the MARC format. For example, full, brief or augmented records are often interchanged, when in fact, the data may or may not actually be in the MARC format.

But, perhaps most important, it is often forgotten that the MARC record is actually designed to "transport" bibliographic and authority records via magnetic tape (see Exhibit 1). That is why there are leaders and fixed fields. Yet, if we were to ask a random sample of cataloging and/or reference librarians what a MARC record looked like, most would respond with the OCLC MARC record representation, which was arbitrarily decided upon by the early pioneers at OCLC (see Exhibit 2).

Before we examine how the computer might aid in the teaching of cataloging, it might be prudent to enumerate the problems faced by catalogers on a daily basis.

PROBLEMS

1.   Unfamiliarity with different MARC formats. Staff might be asked to shift from one MARC format to another, e.g., from the MARC format for serials to the MARC format for audiovisual materials.[2] If the MARC format and the concepts driving the MARC format are not that familiar to the cataloger, then it may take some time to "get up to speed" before the cataloger becomes productive.

2.   Problems with International Standard Bibliographic Description (ISBD) conventions. ISBD, established to identify and organize elements of bibliographic description into a consistent, uniform structure, can be a problem generator as much as it is a problem solver.

Some catalogers have difficulty understanding and applying the ISBD punctuation rules in a consistent manner.

3. Inability to remember all of the valid MARC codes. There are many codes available within any MARC format and, unfortunately, they are not always consistently applied. Thus, relying on memory is rarely the best choice, but checking the appropriate documentation can take time, particularly if the format itself needs to be tracked down. Given a particular cataloger dealing with a material format not usually encountered, what code should be used in a particular situation can, indeed, be puzzling.

4. Needing to consult a large number of sources to complete a single record. Catalogers need to consult a wide variety of reference materials, e.g., the MARC format, *Anglo-American Cataloguing Rules, Library of Congress Subject Headings* (LSCH, also called "Big Red"), etc., along with manuals interpreting or applying the rules, in order to produce quality cataloging.

5. Lack of consistency in data placement. Data in the leader, fixed fields, variable length data fields and indicators must be applied in a consistent manner in a wide variety of situations.

6. Ordinary human errors. Typographical errors and spelling mistakes do occur. According to Richard DeGennaro, then director at the University of Pennsylvania and now at the New York Public Library, cataloging librarians have developed a "perfectionist" mentality now that their peers are able to see (and comment upon) the quality of their cataloging.[3] This results in very expensive cataloging records. In the view of some decision-makers, especially those in libraries

with declining budgets, "perfect" records may not be necessary.

7.   Inconsistent forms of entries. In the absence of authority control, author, series, uniform title and subject headings may not be consistently entered. The result, according to Lucia Rather, is a "catalog where bibliographic records get lost alphabetically."[4]

8.   Difficulty in assigning subject headings. Applying useful subject headings on a consistent basis is a challenging intellectual task for any professional.

9.   Inability to assign subject headings from multiple sources. While the MARC record allows a librarian to enter subject headings using LCSH as well as from one other source, in some situations it would be desirable to assign subject headings from multiple sources, e.g., LCSH, *Sears List of Subject Headings, Medical Subject Headings*, Department of Transportation subject headings, headings from the *Art and Architecture Thesaurus,* locally generated headings, and others.

10.   Knowing and applying descriptive cataloging rules consistently. Knowing the intricacies of *AACR* 2 and the interpretations of those rules applied by the Library of Congress is a challenge for any professional cataloger.

11.   Following a rigid sequence for data entry. Most catalogers must enter original cataloging data in the MARC format, i.e., leader, fixed fields, and variable length fields.

12.   Difficulties determining the appropriate classification number. Clearly, it is important to group related materials together to facilitate browsing and improve the patron's efficiency while in the library. Assigning classification numbers from the Dewey or Library of Congress classifications consistently is a challenge similar to that of

assigning subject headings. Also, the importance of good classification numbers must be balanced with the reality that for a good many patrons the call number is only an "address" where the item is "parked."

13. Difficulties determining the rest of the call number. The challenge of determining the appropriate book number(s) to add to the classification number to round out the call number without access to the past history of local practice with regard to assigning book numbers, (which usually includes Cutter numbers, dates, collection designations, etc.), may result in a high error rate. These errors usually are not discovered until the time the item is placed on the shelf.

14. Poor record keeping quality. Record keeping quality in local catalogs ranges from marginally acceptable to terrible! The number of filing errors and negative results from questionable record keeping practices--attributable, perhaps, to policies that changed over time and constantly changing personnel filing in the public and library's shelflist--detract from the value of these essential tools.

While all of the problems enumerated above should and must be addressed, the professional cataloger must not lose sight of the real objective: Namely, that cataloging is done to provide the library's patrons--especially those who are not present in the building, but who gain access to the catalog via a terminal or microcomputer located at the home, office or dorm room, or even at another library--the means to determine, easily and efficiently, what is and is not in the library's collection.

COMPUTER-BASED SOLUTIONS TO THE PROBLEMS

The problem with "problems" is that, while they may be recognized, there is seldom sufficient internal encouragement within the organization to resolve them. One opportunity for spotlighting a majority, if not all, of a library's pre-existing problem practices occurs when a local computer-based cataloging system is implemented. Then, there is a real possibility that there will be incentives to find solutions.

The speed and ease with which computers could solve some of the problems experienced by catalogers, either wholly or in part, might result in positive influences on the overall quality of the cataloging done in any library. There is also the possibility that, if a computer-based tool was employed as part of the teaching process for cataloging in library school, students would be more likely to focus on the products of cataloging than on the nitty-gritty details of the process.

Some ways in which a computer could provide solutions to the above problems include the following:

1. Unfamiliarity with different MARC formats: A "smart" computer-based cataloging system could store the various MARC record formats. Then, as a cataloger proceeded through the cataloging process with an unfamiliar record format, the available codes and options could be displayed from which the cataloger could choose those representing the item being cataloged. Should the definition of a code be unfamiliar, then additional definitions and help screens could be accessed by the cataloger, as needed.
2. Problems with ISBD: A computer-based cataloging system could have the ISBD rules embedded within the system. ISBD punctuation would be inserted

automatically at the appropriate places, all without cataloger forethought or direct action.

3. Inability to remember all of the valid codes: Having all of the codes and definitions for each code instantly available online would certainly help improve the accuracy and productivity of the cataloger, especially if they could be called up simultaneously with the workform. In addition, the computer could go the extra mile by performing a series of consistency checks when a record is filed to ensure that appropriate rules have been followed and correct codes have been used, included as a part of the system.

4. Needing to consult a large number of sources: Unfortunately, important sources for information about cataloging, i.e., the MARC formats *AACR 2, LCSH,* classification schedules, and rules for interpreting and applying them take considerable shelf space. Through the cataloger's terminal, much of this information could be immediately accessible as part of an integrated system's cataloging module. Considerable improvements in cataloger productivity could result.

5. Inconsistency in data placement: Larry Osborne, Assistant Professor at the Graduate School of Library and Information Studies at the University of Hawaii, tells cataloging students, "It is more important to be consistent than to be correct when cataloging." If data is not placed consistently within the MARC record, automatic correction and editing to clean up the mess can be nearly impossible to program. It also might be very costly for the library to correct manually. The computer, through a series of consistency checks, could be programmed to check for the correct type of data within a particular field

or subfield as well as to check for the consistency of data between fields.

6. Misspelled words: The computer, through the use of a dictionary of significant size, could check the spelling of words in free text data fields. The computer would at least alert the terminal operator about words not found in the dictionary or words that might be misspelled.

7. Inconsistent form of entries: The value of an authority file cannot be over-emphasized in a library's local catalog. In addition to containing the relevant cross references and scope notes, the authority file by definition will remove or at least alert the cataloger when inconsistent forms of entries are found. Through the use of an authority control file, headings could be examined by the computer to ensure consistency. This can be done by matching and/or retrieving an "authorized" heading from the appropriate file. New headings for which there are no existing matches can be reported to provide an opportunity for a second review and authorization by another cataloger before the heading is accepted into the catalog.

8. Assigning subject headings: Assigning subject headings is still more of an art than a science. A computer might be used to assist the cataloger in the choice of appropriate subject headings with a keyword search for all the words contained in the title. The word or combination of words retrieving various subsets of the database would be displayed, optionally, to the cataloger. The cataloger could select that subset(s) retrieving a manageable set of records, e.g., between 100 and 500, or within limits set by the cataloger. The computer would then retrieve each of these records, identify and count each of the subject headings used on them, and then display the subject headings. They even could be arranged from the most

frequent appearing to least frequent appearing. The cataloger then would be able to select and insert desired subject headings into the new cataloging record.

9.   Inability to assign subject headings from multiple sources: A sophisticated cataloging module might be able to link subject headings from multiple sources to a single bibliographic record. In addition, the system could be designed to allow the cataloger to change a subject heading that happens to be identical with a subject heading from another source, without affecting the other subject authority control files.

10.   Knowing and applying cataloging rules: It is possible for a computer system to contain a file of the cataloging rules so that they can be made accessible online to the cataloger, as needed. Combining each rule with the related LC rule interpretations would make it easier to choose the correct options from the rules, too. It would be possible for the local library to add examples and illustrations of its local practices, especially important if they happen to be at variance with the national standards (not that anyone would be encouraged to depart from standards often.)

11.   A rigid sequence for data entry: Most computer systems, including those of the various bibliographic utilities, prescribe an orderly sequence for entering the data elements, i.e., in numeric order (with some exceptions). Alternatively, the MARC record format shell is displayed in numerical order and the terminal operator is allowed to move the cursor to the appropriate field so that data entry may proceed. In my view, a cataloging system that allowed the cataloger to specify the sequence of data elements to be displayed would improve the productivity of the cataloger and lower the overall error rate of the

records input. The computer could sort the record elements, once data entry is completed, so that it matched the required MARC format prior to filing the record in the database. (This kind of automatic reformatting is available for dial-access systems in OCLC that require line-editing and applies to all fields except the 5xx fields.)

12. Excessive time to determine the appropriate call number: If the cataloger could have immediate online access to the library's shelflist within the cataloging module, then assigning the appropriate call number should be easier, quicker, and, we might hope, have fewer inconsistencies.

13. The challenge of determining the appropriate book number: The quality of Cutter number assignments and other shelf marks should be improved through online access to the shelflist. This will improve the overall quality of book numbers and identify potential errors during the assignment process.

14. Poor record quality: The great virtue of the computer catalog, both for the public and for library staff, is that the computer follows the assigned rules in a very precise manner very rapidly. Any exceptions will be brought to the attention of the cataloger for resolution. Thus, the consistency and accuracy of filing will increase significantly with a computer-based library catalog.

CONCLUSION

In all, a computer based cataloging module that has even a modicum of "smarts" will help improve the accuracy and productivity of the cataloger, and in turn, the teaching of cataloging can focus on the broader and more important fundamental questions of patron access and success in searching the library catalog.

NOTES

1. The term MARC refers to the MAchine Readable Cataloging format developed by the Library of Congress for the identification and transmission of bibliographic data in its computer systems. It has since become a familiar, library-wide standard for such data.

2. This format, originally named the Films format and broadened to include other kinds of audiovisual materials and renamed the Audiovisual format, was revised again to accommodate a still wider variety of nonprint materials and renamed the Visual materials format. However, OCLC opted to retain its former name, the Audiovisual format. Thus, depending on the network into which a cataloger inputs data, they will know it as Visual materials or Audiovisual format.

3. Richard DeGennaro, "Libraries and Networks in Transition: Problems and Prospects for the 1980's," *Library Journal* 106 (May 15, 1981):1045-49.

4. Lucia Rather, "Authority Systems at The Library of Congress," in *Authority Control: The Key to Tomorrow's Catalog. Proceedings of the 1979 Library and Information Technology Association Institutes*, edited by Mary W. Ghikas (Phoenix, Ariz.: Oryx Press, 1982), p. 158-65.

Exhibit 1:
Sample MARC Record Format

Leader **Record Directory**

00515 | n | a | m | ￠￠ | 2 | 2 | 00145 | ￠￠￠4560 | 001001300000 | 008004100013 | 050001800054 ￠
                                          24   36   48

082001600072 | 100002300088 | 245006300111 | 260006100174 | 300003900235
       72   84   96   108

LC Card Number **Fixed Fields**

500003700274 | 650005900311 ￐ ￠￠￠75010118 ￐ ￐ 700319 ▪ 1969 ￠￠￠￠ xx￠ ab￠￠ ￐
       132   145   13
                            ￠

LC Call Number **DDC Number**

￐￐￐￠￠￠￠￠0 0 0 0 1 0 ￐ eng ￐ ￐ ￐ 0￠ $aHD9560.5$b.S8 ￐ ￠￠ $a338.2/7/282 ￐
                                        54   72

Main Entry **Title**

10 | $aSugarman,￠Stephen. ￐ 10 | $aPetroleum￠industry￠handbook.$c[Edited￠by￠
88   111

Imprint

Stephen￠Sugarman. ￐ 0￠ $an.p.|$bPublished￠by￠J.￠M.￠Weiner￠for￠D.￠H.￠Blair￠
                  174

Collation **General Note**

$c[1969] ￐ ￠￠ $axxi,￠794￠p.$billus,￠maps.$c29￠cm. ￐ ￠￠ $a"For￠limited￠ ￐
                    235   274

Subject Heading

distribution￠only." ￐ ￠0 $aPetroleum￠industry￠and￠trade$xHandbooks, ￠
                       311

manuals,￠etc. ￐

￠ = blank   ￐ = field terminator   ￐ = record terminator

270

Exhibit 2:
Sample OCLC MARC Record

```
▶NO HOLDINGS IN XXX - FOR HOLDINGS ENTER dh DEPRESS  DISPLAY RECD SEND
  OCLC: 801273        Rec stat: c Entrd: 740111        Used: 781021 ¶
▶Type: a Bib lvl: m Govt pub:  Lang:  eng Source:  Illus:
  Repr:    Enc lvl:    Conf pub: 0 Ctry:  nyu Dat tp: s M/F/B: 10
  Indx: 0 Mod rec:    Festschr: 0 Cont: b
  Desc:    Int lvl:    Dates: 1973,      ¶
▶ 1 010      73-180875//r77 ¶
▶ 2 040      DLC ‡c DLC ¶
▶ 3 020      0061361224 ‡a 0061317880 (pbk.) ¶
▶ 4 050 0    HB171 ‡b .S384 ¶
▶ 5 082      330 ¶
▶ 6 090       ‡b  ¶
▶ 7 049      XXXM ¶
▶ 8 100 10   Schumacher, Ernst Friedrich. ¶
▶ 9 245 10   Small is beautiful; ‡b economics as if people mattered ‡c
[by] E. F. Schumacher. ¶
▶10 260 0    New York, ‡b Harper & Row ‡c [1973] ¶
▶11 300      290 p. ‡c 21 cm. ¶
▶12 350      $3.75 ¶
▶13 490 0    Harper torchbooks, TB 1778 ¶
▶14 504      Includes bibliographical references. ¶
▶15 650  0   Economics. ¶
```

Cataloging Education in the Library and Information Science Curriculum

Francis Miksa

INTRODUCTION

Recent comments about cataloging education and recruitment suggest that cataloging has suffered a decline in status in the Library and Information Science (LIS) profession in general and within LIS curriculum in particular and that this has led in turn to a serious shortage of new, well-qualified catalogers to fill open positions.[1] Although a precise chronological sequence has not been affixed to the idea of the decline, there can be little doubt that it is implied as having taken place since the 1970s because it has only been during the 1980s that the recruiting difficulties mentioned have taken place.

One of the several assumptions underlying the foregoing scenario is that cataloging is in competition with other occupational roles in the field and that at least in the context of LIS curriculums the success (or failure) of cataloging can be measured by how much curicular space is controlled by cataloging. Curricular space means in this regard the number of courses wholly or mostly on the subject of cataloging. Another assumption underlying the scenario is that there is a direct correspondence between cataloging education viewed as courses on cataloging and cataloging work as an occupational position so that a decline in the first will affect the size and quality of the candidate pool for the second.

Common sense suggests that each of these assumptions bears some validity. However, a full investigation of the initial claims about cataloging education and recruitment would first necessitate testing the assumptions in some useful way so as to determine more precisely what is valid in them and what is not. Such a thorough course of investigation is beyond the scope of the present paper. But, as a useful substitute, comments will be offered on two questions raised by the assumptions. First, quite apart from the validity of the idea of curricular competition, what is known from general developments in LIS education about the position of cataloging courses (named as such or by some reasonable synonym) in the LIS curriculum? Second, and without struggling with the validity of the idea that courses do or should correspond directly to specific occupational roles, how is the definition one affixes to cataloging reflected in course offerings? Hopefully, answers to each of these questions will provide insights into how further investigation of the status of cataloging might be conducted.

The first question to be addressed asks what is known from general developments in LIS education about cataloging courses in the curriculum. More specifically it focuses on the extent to which cataloging courses (named as such) have been represented as a proportion of the total curriculum. This question is deemed important not only to see if the general perception that the proportion of such courses has declined is true but also to provide a general or gross estimate of the positon of cataloging courses in the curriculum over the history of LIS education. The findings of this brief survey, based as it is on LIS curricular trends as reported and summarized in the field's literature, suggests an interesting and, at least to this writer, unexpected picture. LIS educational developments are viewed here in terms of three approximate periods: 1887 to the mid-1920s; the mid-1920s to the mid-1960s; and the mid-1960s to the present.[2]

CURRICULAR TRENDS AND CATALOGING

During the first period, most of the more substantial library educational ventures followed the pattern set by Melvil Dewey in his work at Columbia College and the New York State Library in dividing the curriculum into two parts. The first consisted of library operational matters (i.e., "Library Economy") and occupied the lion's share of the curriculum-- practically two-thirds in Dewey's first educational venture.[3] Within that sector of the curriculum, cataloging occupied the largest single proportion of space. The second consisted of bibliography (over time, renamed "Reference work") and occupied the diminutive proportion of the total curriculum. In short, cataloging, especially as represented in programs heavily laden with an emphasis on library operations, occupied a large proportion of the larger sector of the curriculum. Of course, schools and their curricula were barely organized in any modern sense so that any measurement of the curriculum at all is at best only very general. Still, this sense of the primacy of cataloging seems firm even if it is fuzzy in detail.

The second period of LIS education covers the years from the mid-1920s to the mid-1960s. Notable general features of this period include C.C. Williamson's Carnegie report of 1923, the eventual emigration of library education into academic settings by the 1930s, the fixing of library education's academic position at the master's level by the 1950s, and the rise of substantive research in the field.

In curriculum development, the most important feature consisted of the general standardization of curriculum across the field. The most distinct feature of that standardization was the establishment of two different levels within library educational programs. The first consisted of a general curriculum and came to be called its core studies. The second consisted of specialized studies and came to be called the program's electives. Within this framework a general consensus developed as to the content of the core. It most common expression was in the form of separate courses on selection, cataloging, reference, administration and, sometimes, the history of libraries (or, alternatively, the "library and society").

With respect to amount of curricular space allocated to cataloging, the most significant matter is that the very effort to rationalize curriculum more fully during this period automatically ensured that cataloging would have a much more diminutive position than it had had during the first period when curriculum was not so closely scrutinized. In short, the very effort to structure the curriculum carefully removed cataloging from being more or less the queen bee of the strong side of the standard curriculum to being only one of four or five basic subjects in the core. Further, there was almost no corresponding development of it among the electives. At best one will find an "advanced" form of the core course or one or two elective courses that provided more intensive practice on parts of the basic course-- for example, one special course that emphasized further work in descriptive cataloging, a second on further work in subject cataloging. This contrasts sharply with the proliferation of other electives by the 1940s and 1950s on types of libraries or types of user populations.

The third period of educational development, that which began in the mid-1960s and continues today, has had for its most notable landmarks the adoption of the one year master's level program as a de facto standard in the field (with only a few exceptions), the enormous expansion of the field's educational structure in terms of the number of accredited programs, a period of enormous infusion of government monies directly into educational programs, and, most importantly, the rise of information science or study as an essential component of the educational landscape.

With respect to curriculum development, the two-level program consisting of core and electives has persisted, although not without vicissitudes in the extent and importance of the core for at least some schools. Most important, the content of both levels of the curriculum has changed dramatically as the full impact of information science has come to be felt.

The core topics, established only by the 1940s and 1950s, have had to make place for an increasing number of information science topics or themes, especially in the form of new technologies. Consequently, the proportion of space given over to the previous topics has been reduced particularly by compaction. However, the position of cataloging in the core compaction process appears not to have suffered as greatly as other older standard topics of the core, at least not over the period between Thomas' study published in 1976 and the more recent CCS Task Force study. All things being considered, the proportion of cataloging courses in the core across the field as reported in those two studies has remained relatively constant although there has been some shifting in how the courses are named.[4]

On the elective side of the curriculum and in comparison to the second period, electives directed at a huge variety of specialties have continued to proliferate. Here, the absolute curricular space of cataloging among the electives has actually risen, if anything, not in terms of basic cataloging procedure, but rather in terms of the control of specialized materials and in terms of technology useful to cataloging. However, much of the expansion of cataloging's absolute space appears not to have been under the aegis of unique courses with names using the term "cataloging" but rather as parts of other courses that first stress the materials or technological environment to be coped with in specialization. In contrast, the relative or proportionate space occupied by cataloging courses in the elective curriculum has fallen, or so it would seem, with even more proliferation of specializations.

IMPLICATIONS OF CURRICULAR TRENDS

Given the foregoing very general rendition of educational and curricular developments, the most obvious conclusion with respect to cataloging courses (named as such) in the curriculum is that, indeed, as current comment suggests, cataloging education has suffered an overall decline in curriculum space. Its decline did not begin in the 1970s, however, but rather in the 1920s, at exactly the same time that the field began seriously to rationalize LIS educational curricula. Cataloging's absolute curricular space might be said to have at least held its own during the more recent period, at least in comparison with the period before the mid-1960s. But as a proportion of the entire curriculum, cataloging education per se--that is, cataloging in the form of courses specifically called or focused on "cataloging"--has not simply gone from good to bad in the near past but rather, from bad to worse.

CONCEPTUAL DIMENSIONS OF CATALOGING

The foregoing survey of the position of cataloging courses in the LIS curriculum over the latter's longer history provides a seemingly useful, though very general, estimate of how cataloging education in the form of curricular space has fared over time. On the surface, it would appear to be a valid way to proceed in estimating the position of cataloging, although it is obvious that the results could be greatly improved by using more complete historical evidence.

Upon closer scrutiny, however, the entire procedure betrays a more trenchant difficulty that casts its findings in question. That difficulty lies in the assumption that what is meant by "cataloging" is established and that the curriculum in general and cataloging in particular plainly have or have not covered whatever that established sense of what the term refers to. If the meaning of the term is not established, however, even the very best historical accounting of cataloging courses will not show whether cataloging education has done well or poorly.

We are forced to ask, consequently, what is meant by the term cataloging? What, in fact, does the term cover conceptually? And how do variations in its meaning affect the way one assesses its health in the curriculum? In order to deal with these issues, a range of meanings will be suggested. Afterward, they will be applied to the historical picture already drawn to see how they might affect the way cataloging education has been represented in the LIS curriculum.

DEFINITIONS OF CATALOGING

Over the one hundred years or so of LIS education under scrutiny here, cataloging has been spoken of in at least three different but interrelated ways. When framed in terms of the object in question--that is, in terms of a "catalog"--the three senses of the term may be listed as follows. First, the term has sometimes been used to refer to the entire process of making a catalog. Second, it has sometimes been used to refer to preparing the entries for a catalog that is in the process of being made. Third, it has sometimes been used to refer to managing the personnel and other logistical features that make the first two tasks possible.[5]

A closer look at these uses of the term will show more adequately what each implies and how they are interrelated. Making a catalog is actually a shorthand way of talking about the overall task of engineering a system of bibliographic entries for items called knowledge records. This overall task includes planning and designing such a system (or, of carefully adopting a design already in existence) with a given set of technologies, implementing the design or, at least, directing its implementation by others, and maintaining the system once it has been set up. Maintaining a system refers to monitoring the system, changing its structural features and implementation procedures when necessary, and, especially, augmenting the system once complete either by making supplements for it if the original system is fixed in form as in the case of a published catalog, or by continuously adding new entries to the system if it is designed to grow as in the case of card or online catalogs. The overall task also implies other managerial concerns, including controlling costs associated with the task.[6]

A moment's reflection will show that the second and third senses of the term here actually fall within the purview of the first. The first is an all-encompassing definition that includes all parts of the process of making such a system. The other two definitions cover only parts of that overall range of activities. For example, the second definition, preparing entries for a catalog system, is part of the first definition's process of original implementation as a system and part of its process of supplementation. The third definition, managing personnel and other logistical features of the process, were it to include planning and design, would for all practical purposes be synonymous with the first definition. But, more often than not it more specifically means dealing with a design already established and focuses on the oversight of costs and processes necessary for achieving all or at least parts of the more specific stages of implementation, supplementation, monitoring and making changes in the system.

The foregoing might seem to cover the entire range of what is meant by cataloging, but in two further respects it does not. First, by common parlance cataloging ordinarily includes the process of classification. Classification at its simplest level means assigning call numbers to items included in the catalog and, as such, would seem to be only part of the catalog implementation operation. But, these call numbers are more than merely one feature of a catalog. They are by themselves the access points of an entirely separate system of control for the same items. The latter may usefully be called an item file-- an organized system of items themselves--in contrast to a catalog which is an organized system of surrogates of items. Handling the materials of an agency ordinarily requires both kinds of files--item and surrogate--with links between them if the materials are to be adequately identified and accessed. Thus, when we speak of cataloging, we ordinarily include the entire range of meanings already discussed above not simply in relationship to one kind of file but rather in relationship to two different kinds of files--that is, to both item and surrogate files.

Second, the range of meanings that the term cataloging covers also includes still another set of variations that are related to what is controlled by the file systems under considerations, how that control is to be accomplished, and in what kind of environment the control is exercised.

At one extreme, cataloging is typically tied very specifically to a particular agency or group of cooperating agencies, to a very specific set of files within the agency or agencies, to a very specific range of materials treated in a certain way and entered into the files, and to a very explicit set of procedural conventions that provide structure to the files being made. In this respect, the term typically refers to organizing books, serials, and a limited range of other materials treated chiefly as single published items and entering them title-by-title in the main catalog and item file systems of a particular library or information agency or group of such agencies joined in some cooperative bibliographic system such as OCLC, RLIN, or WLN. It also typically implies the use of such particular standardized procedural conventions as the *Anglo-American Cataloguing Rules,* second edition (*AACR* 2-- with or without Library of Congress Rule Interpretations), the *Library of Congress Subject Headings,* the particular coding conventions and other data structure parameters of the particular cooperative and local automated systems, and the Library of Congress or the Dewey Decimal classification (or both if conversion is taking place). This particular scenario is not the only one, of course. One may infer in the term a limitation to, say, business records in a particular agency and the use of some standard conventions in making a bibliographic file related to those records. Or one may refer to controlling a defined range of audiovisual materials and make use of some specific code for making both surrogate and item files for them. The important thing to recognize is that cataloging at this extreme is, for all practical purposes, agency, file, material, and system specific.

At the other extreme the three original meanings of cataloging as applied to two kinds of files refers to a generic approach to the process. At this level of generality a vast range of kinds of materials, kinds of systems and their operating parameters, and kinds of agency situations serve chiefly as concrete manifestations or exemplars useful to grasp fundamental principles and procedural ideas. In short, this extreme stresses generic aspects of the entire process and uses specific systems, materials, and agency situation to illustrate those generic aspects.

In between these two extremes there is, potentially at least, a vast array of mixed cases where differing degrees of specificity in systems, agencies, and materials, are involved, although there would appear to be a more explicit dividing line between the two extremes than might be apparent at first. That dividing line has to do with whether, in speaking of making a system of entries or of creating entries in their own right or of managing a system, one begins with a more or less specifically denoted system and then speaks of generic principles as they affect that system; or whether one begins with the generic issues involved and uses a specifically denoted system (or, perhaps, several specific systems) to illustrate those generic issues.

Some may well object to including this broad array of meanings in cataloging, claiming that in doing so the very idea of cataloging becomes too indefinite or general to provide an explicit method of estimating how well cataloging education is doing in preparing catalogers and too indefinite or general to provide a basis for teaching cataloging as an explicit task. In short, this broad approach to cataloging turns it into something akin to generalized bibliographic control or generalized information or document retrieval that includes everything from regular book cataloging to periodical article indexing, to records management, to archival procedures--in other words, everything from soup to nuts.

This objection is precisely the point at issue in describing and evaluating cataloging education in terms of its curricular space, however. If cataloging may, potentially, mean all of these things, and I do not see how this breadth in meaning can be avoided, then apart from agreeing that cataloging is to be restricted to only one or another of the meanings identified and to only one or another specific kinds of materials, agency situations, and systems, the entire range of meanings must be taken into account if an accurate accounting of cataloging education in the LIS curriculum is to be made. In fact, when one reviews cataloging education over its history with even some of this broader range of meanings in mind, a significantly different view of the matter results.

CATALOGING IN THE LIS CURRICULUM--AGAIN

On the face of it, a re-survey of cataloging education on the basis of the range of meanings of cataloging suggested above is by its nature much more difficult than surveying merely on the basis of course names, because one would need to have access to the particular contents of a wide range of individual courses. This is information that is not, frankly, readily available except in occasional instances. Some additional help is provided, however, when one includes the occurrence of landmark events in cataloging in general and also whatever can be gleaned from catalog instructional tools such as codes, system tools and textbooks.

The most remarkable feature in cataloging education during the first period in LIS educational development (1887 to the mid-1920s) is the context in which it began. At its start there were almost no agreed-upon standards for making surrogate and item file systems. There were no widely accepted codes for description and access points and no lists of subject headings. And classification systems of the kinds now accepted as standard, with their detailed specification of the subject contents of items, were still in a primitive state and not yet fully accepted.

In this light, it is understandable that cataloging education began with an emphasis on the entire process of making such systems, including their planning and design. Cataloging lecture content during the initial years of Dewey's school, for example, took few things for granted and presented pros and cons about a great variety of such basic things as the best way to display bibliographic data, how thoroughly names should be established and written, the relative merits of different sizes and thicknesses of cards, the design and arrangement of card catalog furniture, problems in handwriting (or typing) bibliographic data, and, with respect to item files, the merits of closely classified, relative position systems.

By the end of this period, extraordinary changes had already taken place in cataloging methods and technology in general. Lists of subject headings had been published. Usable shelf classification schemes had been completed enough to be reasonably dependable (with the *Dewey Decimal Classification* available in two different versions, full and abridged, and enforcing a policy of class number integrity). In descriptive cataloging a standard cooperative code had been published with supplementary rules available from the Library of Congress. Most important, beginning in 1901, the Library of Congress had begun to distribute its cards. This not only provided a ready source of catalog copy, but began the general process of establishing the unit entry system on cards as a system standard.

If one can legitimately use textbooks such as those by Hitchler, Fellows, and Akers as indicators of what was being taught in cataloging education, one may easily observe a steady progression toward the adoption of such standards. The effect was a general diminution of discussions of planning and designing bibliographic systems and a growing emphasis both on preparing catalog entries from a given code and a given subject heading list and on devising classification numbers (i.e., preparing class number entries) from a given classification scheme--in short, on cataloging more narrowly conceived as simply preparing entries rather than as the entire process of making a system.

The foregoing developments set the stage for the second period (mid-1920s to mid-1960s), in which three significant developments took place. The first consisted of the extension of the main theme of the first period. Cataloging instruction did not merely become more thoroughly involved with teaching entry preparation rather than system making. It became entry preparation for catalogs with very specific parameters--that is, for card catalogs which were based on the unit entry system and which, for all practical purposes, followed Library of Congress conventions with respect to description and access points (often based on catalog copy).

This movement to even greater specificity did not take place all at once, but appeared to have been completed by the 1940s and 1950s. The latter is suggested, for example, in the differences between the two editions of Margaret Mann's classic textbook, *Introduction to Cataloging and the*

Classification of Books, far and away the chief training manual for cataloging instruction for at least the 1930s and 1940s.[7] It is also evident, however, in newer version cataloging textbooks that began to appear in the 1950s and 1960s.[8] Finally, the change was also greatly reinforced by the increasingly prominent role of the Library of Congress in cataloging during the 1940s and 1950s, when it resumed the kind of leadership in cataloging discussion that it had exercised prior to World War I. When one adds to that the significant increase in the number and dependability of the Library's cataloging products taking place during the same period, the Library's role in tieing cataloging even more firmly to the parameters of its own systems is understandable.[9]

A second development during this period was the appearance of an administrative perspective of cataloging, i.e., of cataloging as the management of the process of catalog supplementation and maintenance. An early striking expression of this concern will be found in the published papers of the 1924 American Library Association Cataloger's Round Table discussion.[10] Thereafter, the theme was repeated not only in the striking conference held at the University of Chicago Graduate Library School in 1940 on acquistion and cataloging,[11] but also increasingly in cataloging publications throughout the 1940s and afterward. The issue that prompted this concern is simple enough to discern. Cataloging, when narrowed in scope primarily to the preparation of entries and, particularly, when faced with rapidly increasing acquistions, had a pronounced tendency to disregard the costs involved in accomplishing the task. Thus, the concern in this theme was to control costs by adopting a rational approach to cataloging management.

The third development in this period consisted of the rise of widely disseminated research and discussion on cataloging. Research first arose in the form of catalog use studies, especially during the 1940s and 1950s, at the University of Chicago Graduate Library School and at the Columbia University School of Library Service. During the 1950s, it also ranged over into issues related to subject access and, especially, principles underlying the determination of access points in the descriptive cataloging code.

The latter two themes, cataloging management and cataloging research, represented countercurrents to the triumph of cataloging education as the preparation of entries. Their growth in prominence set up a tension in cataloging education that expressed more general LIS educational themes. One such theme was the need for more explicit attention to administration and management of library agencies and less to the details of simply operating a library and maintaining its processes. Another was the belief, carried along by the movement of LIS education in general into the post-baccaleaureate realm, that education at that level should be directed more toward principles and less toward explicit operational details.

The response of cataloging education to these two themes appears to have been mixed and not a little resistant. For the most part, regular courses on cataloging remained oriented to the preparation of entries. In some schools, additional courses were sometimes included that stressed management, although these appear to have been more broadly pointed towards technical services concerns in general rather than toward cataloging operations in particular. And in some schools, one can detect a growth in emphasis on cataloging principles as well as on cataloging as the preparation of entries.

The most recent period in LIS education (mid-1960s to the present) has seen the further extension of the three developments of the second period. In each case, however, they have been made enormously more complicated by two further factors.

The first complicating factor has been a concern, especially since the late 1960s when audiovisual materials became a topic of wide interest, to accommodate in regular library catalogs a wider array of types of materials than ever before handled on a systematic and standardized basis. This factor has not only become a regular issue in the ongoing development of our standardized catalog systems as based on *AACR* 2, but also a theme stressed by the concurrent international interest in universal bibliographic control. Its end does not appear to be in sight, however, because the more recent expansion of a number of LIS schools to accommodate such boundary fields as records management, archival enterprise, and even, to some extent, museology, has driven the range of types of materials now spoken of as necessary to LIS agencies conceived as informaton resource centers far beyond any boundaries previously imagined.

A second complicating factor and one that needs no extensive repetition of its details here has been the appearance of new electronic technologies in seemingly endless waves of innovation. These two factors together have placed an inordinate burden on cataloging education, especially where the latter is viewed either as preparing catalog entries or as catalog system management. In cataloging as entry preparation, educators have had to cope not only with ever new layers of detail associated with specific electronic systems and with new types of materials, but also with determining an appropriate basic selection of materials and set of experiences to focus on that will do justice to this meaning of the term. One response has been to pack courses with incredible amounts of detail. Another has been to bury elements of catalog entry preparation as well as other matters associated with it in a variety of other courses, field experiences, and independent studies that are primarily focused on special types of materials, special types of agencies, and specific technologies, the latter often under such labels as automation, or microcomputers, or some such thing.

In the case of cataloging as management, the situation has taken an even more decided turn away from specifically named cataloging courses. Insofar as coursework that emphasizes this realm is plainly of a management cast, this meaning of the term has become resident in such courses as systems analysis, management of automation, and a raft of other more specific curricular innovations.

Apart from the foregoing complicating factors, the most striking development to have taken place since the mid-1960s has been the development of information retrieval techniques and theory (broadly conceived), combined more recently with microcomputer technology and the growing emphasis on database creation. The essential genius of information retrieval thinking since its beginning in the 1950s, at least in the mind of this writer, has not been its emphasis on handling large files with ever increasing amounts of sophistication nor its emphasis on doing repetitious operations with great speed, though both of these emphases are important to it. Rather it has been the infusion throughout the LIS field of the ideal that information retrieval can only become truly significant when it has a beginning focus on the more explicit needs of particular users or groups of users. As this ideal has encountered new, more powerful, and cheaper computing power and an increasing emphasis on database creation, the stage has plainly become set for the creation of a new generation of system makers who are able, especially, to plan, design, implement, monitor, supplement, etc. special systems of bibliographic files of materials of particular interest to specific users or groups of users. This combination of an information retrieval ideal with new technology has set the stage, in other words, for a return to cataloging education conceived of in its broadest sense--that is, as learning the principles of creating bibliographic systems or parts of them from scratch, a process that necessarily begins without being system-, agency-, or materials-specific.

The latter development has been growing in forcefulness throughout the 1980s. It has begun to appear in LIS curriculums under any one of a number of guises, sometimes with the weight of traditional information retrieval theory behind it and at other times in plainly unsophisticated versions. Regardless of its tone and regardless of what it is called or how it is placed in the curriculum, however, to the extent that it represents the engineering of bibliographic systems of entries, it is cataloging. But, it is cataloging in the initial and broadest sense of the term where the entire process of creation is involved and where education in the matter is not specific to any particular materials, agencies or systems.

CONCLUSION

In response to the question about what LIS educational development in general reveals about the proportions of curricular space allocated to cataloging courses per se in the LIS curriculum, the picture drawn here is one of decline since the 1920s. However, when one takes into account a broad range of meanings of the idea of cataloging, an entirely different picture of the status of cataloging education emerges.

Cataloging education began with a focus on bibliographic system making as a total concept. Over the decades, however, this sense of cataloging has been narrowed in regularly named cataloging courses to the idea of cataloging as the preparation of entries. With that narrowing, however, new emphases have arisen, specifically, cataloging as management and cataloging theory. More recently, the combination of information retrieval thinking and new powerful technologies has brought back the notion of cataloging as the entire process of making bibliographic systems.

Evidence of the foregoing changes in the LIS curriculum has not readily taken the form of courses specifically on cataloging but rather has taken the form of a variety of other curricular expressions. Regardless of how these developments have appeared, however, they suggest that the status of cataloging is greater than ever. Its power does not reside in either a narrower sense of the term (i.e., cataloging as entry creation) nor in cataloging as a system-specific operation. It resides in the broadest sense of the term--in short, in cataloging as the planning, designing, implementation, supplementation, monitoring and changing of systems that are not system specific at first blush.

The latter puts one to mind of the oft-repeated remark by Cutter made at the end of his life that "the golden age of cataloging is over and that the difficulties and discussions which have furnished an innocent pleasure to so many will interest them no more."[12]. Cutter made that remark in the light of the beginning of catalog card production and distribution by the Library of Congress. Reflecting on what that event might have represented to him leaves little doubt that it referred to the loss of the need to create catalog systems in the manner that had given him so much creative pleasure since his earliest days in librarianship. The present situation of cataloging in the LIS curriculum and in the LIS field in general suggests the opposite situation. For the first time in decades, cataloging has gained the capability of once again creating bibliographic systems in a way Cutter considered lost. In that respect, one would be justified in now asserting that the golden age of cataloging has reappeared.

NOTES

1. "CCS Task Force on Education and Recruitment for Cataloging Report, June 1986." *RTSD Newsletter* 11 (1986):71-8; Janet Swan Hill, "Wanted: Good Catalogers." *American Libraries* 16 (1985):581-606; Smith, Laurie E., "Where Are the Entry Level Catalogers." *Journal of Library Administration* 6 (1985):33-6.

2. Established general educational surveys upon which this paper is based are:
Lester Asheim, ed., *The Core of Education for Librarianship: A Report of a Workshop Held Under the Auspices of the Graduate Library School of the University of Chicago, August 10-15, 1959.* (Chicago: ALA, 1954).
--------, "New Trends in the Curriculum of Library Schools." *Education for Librarianship: The Design of the Curriculum of Library Schools*, ed. by H. Goldhor (Urbana: University of Illinois, Graduate School of Library Science, 1971).
E. Edward Carroll, *The Professionalization of Education for Librarianship with Special Reference to the Years 1940-1960.* (Metuchen, NJ: Scarecrow Press, 1970).
Charles D. Churchwell, *The Shaping of American Library Education.* (Chicago: ALA Association of College and Research Librarians, 1975). ACRL Publications in Librarianship, no. 36.

Carl M. White, *A Historical Introduction to Library Education: Problems and Progress to 1951*. (Metuchen, NJ: Scarecrow, 1976).

Charles C. Williamson, *Training for Library Service: Report Prepared for the Carnegie Corporation of New York*. (New York: Carnegie Corporation, 1923.

All of these except Williamson in turn make heavy use of specific contemporary surveys and comments. Of the latter, the most notable not specifically cited here are those by Tse-Chien Tai in 1925, Ernest J. Reece in 1936, Keyes D. Metcalf, et al. in 1943, Edward A. Wight in 1943, J. Periam Danton in 1946, Joseph L. Wheeler in 1946, the University of Chicago Graduate Library School conference of 1948, edited by Bernard Berelson, and Robert D. Leigh in 1954. Additional insights come from Robbins-Carter and Seavey, and Heim (see ADDITIONAL SOURCES, following). Additional information on the development of cataloging comes from Henderson (see ADDITIONAL SOURCES) and, for the earliest period, from transcribed notes of lectures given at Melvil Dewey's Columbia College School of Library Economy for the years 1887-1888. A substantial selection of the notes, including many on cataloging, are being prepared for publication. Preliminary findings will be found in:

Francis L. Miksa, "Melvil Dewey: The Professional Educator and His Heirs." *Library Trends* 34 (1986):359-81.

--------, "The Columbia School of Library Economy, 1887- 1888." *Libraries and Culture* 23 (1988):249-80.

3.   Miksa, "The Columbia School."

4.   In terms of straightforward percentages of required cataloging courses across the field in the two studies, it

would appear that LIS schools are actually doing better today than ten years ago. For example, the percentage of schools requiring either one-half course on cataloging or one full course on cataloging has actually risen from 77 to 87 percent during the decade. Those requiring one full course or two full courses have risen from 70 to 80 percent. And, those requiring one-half or one or two courses has risen from 91 to 93 percent. However, when one realizes that Thomas (see ADDITIONAL SOURCES) received responses from only 47 of the 62 accredited programs for 1975, i.e., a 75 percent return--in contrast to the CCS Task Force's examination of 100 percent of the schools' catalogs in 1986--and that some of the schools that did not respond to him are known to have had strong cataloging requirements (e.g., UCLA and the University of Texas at Austin, etc.), it seems likely that Thomas' figures are low; that, in fact, there has not really been much significant change in the figures over the decade.

5. The three definitions here represent my own synthesis of trends in the history of cataloging and classification over several years. In many respects, however, the definitions are time-bound, i.e., they are readily associated with particular periods in modern cataloging development. The idea of a catalog or index as a system of bibliographic entries based on definite planning and design, including an estimate of the specific information needs of users is especially characteristic of the period before 1900, particularly in the work of Charles A. Cutter (see ADDITIONAL SOURCES) and after 1950 or so among persons who generally style themselves as information scientists rather than as catalogers per se.

Two unusually "strong" recent representations of this view are Soergel and Taylor (see ADDITIONAL SOURCES). The other two definitions come shiefly from the intervening period as the discussion that follows will show.

6. An excellent information systems expression of this holistic view of the total process can be found in Taylor's "user-driven model." See, Robert S. Taylor, *Value-Added Processes in Information Systems.* (Norwood, NJ: Ablex, 1986).

7. Margaret Mann, *Introduction to Cataloging and the Classification of Books.* (Chicago: ALA, 1930) and the second edition, 1943.

8. Margaret Egan's text, for example, first appeared in the 1950s, that of Bohdan Wynar in the 1960s.

9. The Library of Congress' original leadership in this realm was prompted by its librarian, Herbert Putnam. After the beginning of World War I, however, Putnam's interests appeared to turn toward such other matters as reference services, collection building, and promoting the role of the Library as a cultural agency. The result was that by the 1930s, the Library's processing work was close to a disaster. After 1940, strong divisional chiefs such as Richard Angell, David Haykin and the notable work of Seymour Lubetzky helped the Library to recoup its former position of technical prominence in the broader library cataloging community.

10. Henry B. Van Hoesen, ed., *Selective Cataloging: Cataloger's Round Table, American Library Association, July 3, 1924.* (New York: H.W. Wilson, 1928).

11. William M. Randall, ed., *The Acquisition and Cataloging of Books: Papers Presented Before the Library Institute at the University of Chicago, July 29 to*

August 9, 1940. (Chicago: The University of Chicago Press, 1940).

12.   Charles A. Cutter, *Rules for a Dictionary Catalog*, 4th ed., rewritten. (Washington: Government Printing Office, 1904), p. 5.

ADDITIONAL SOURCES

Akers, Susan G. *Simple Library Cataloging.* Chicago: ALA, 1927.

Cutter, Charles A. "Library Catalogues." *Public Libraries in the United States of America: Their History, Condition and Management. Special Report.* Washington: U.S. Bureau of Education, 1876, Volume I, p. 526-622.

Fellows, Dorcas. *Cataloging Rules, with Explanations and Illustrations*, 2nd ed., rev. and enl. New York: H.W. Wilson, 1922.

Heim, Kathleen M. "The Changing Faculty Mandate." *Library Trends* 34 (1986):581-606.

Henderson, Kathryn L. "Some Persistent Issues in the Education of Catalogers and Classifiers." *Cataloging & Classification Quarterly* 7 (1987):5-26.

Hitchler, Theresa. *Cataloging for Small Libraries.* Boston: ALA Publishing Board, 1905. ALA Publishing Board, Library Handbook no. 2.

Robbins-Carter, Jane and Charles A. Seavey. "The Master's Degree: Basic Preparation for Professional Practice." *Library Trends* 34 (1986):561-80.

Soergel, Dagobert. *Organizing Information: Principles of Data Base and Retrieval Systems.* Orlando, FL: Academic Press, 1985.

Thomas, Alan R. *The Library Cataloging Curriculum, USA: A Survey of the Contemporary Compulsory Instruction.* London: The Panizzi Press, 1976.

PART III:
SESSION ON TRAINING
CATALOGING LIBRARIANS

Developing Catalogers for the Nation: Problems and Issues in Training Cataloging Librarians for the Future

Henriette D. Avram

INTRODUCTION

The task before us during this two-day symposium--to put forward viable solutions to the problems of recruiting, educating, and training cataloging librarians--is a gargantuan one indeed. Automated bibliographic systems are coming to dominate access to information in our libraries. If these systems are to serve us well, they must be based on accurate bibliographic data. In this climate, I find it paradoxical that library and information science students show so little interest in technical services in general and in formulating bibliographic data in particular. If our future systems are to succeed, it is imperative that we fire the enthusiasm of those needed to provide this essential service. We must re-examine how we teach technical services. We must find exciting and enticing ways of showing how the various tools that underpin bibliographic control--authority files, bibliographic files, and holdings files--are logically integrated. (I have long felt that an effective method is to make the MARC format an integral part of the teaching of cataloging.) We must further rethink and restructure how best to present this material in our library schools and then reinforce it in our on-the-job training.

As the session leader for the training component, I begin with certain assumptions. Apart from focusing on cataloging librarians, a premise is that education for these specialists will remain what it presently is for the foreseeable future. (I am assuming this to hold true even if my colleagues who are addressing the education component come up with innovative ideas for educating catalogers, since implementation of changes is likely to be slow.) As it stands, employers of potential catalogers can expect to welcome beginners who will bring to the job only one year of formal education in library science, and only a portion of that will have been devoted to cataloging. Education is critical because a further assumption is that the training catalogers receive on the job will build on the prior education that they have had in library school.

EDUCATION VERSUS TRAINING

As the structure of this symposium reflects, education and training are two different processes with different results as their goal. Education should impart a body of knowledge and theory; training on the other hand, should result in the mastery of specific routines. When training occurs, emphasis shifts from theory to practice--the focus turns to "do." A person is taught to do a particular thing, be it a new task or learning to do an existing one better. The trainee's proper response is to show that he or she has mastered the technique and can now perform that which has been taught.

An element of excitement needs to be reintroduced into the education of cataloging librarians. Through imaginative presentations, education should produce librarians who are capable of being trained to perform cataloging tasks in any environment, because they will have been imbued with the theoretical precepts enabling them to adapt to changing needs. The education process should provide catalogers with a solid grounding in what bibliographic control purports to do. It has been my experience in the twenty-odd years I have been involved in the technical services side of the profession, that many of our library school graduates have little sense of the significance of bibliographic control. That bibliographic control is fundamental to all library operations has to be stressed in library schools. When a cataloger arrives on the job, what remains to be done is training in the mechanics of cataloging. the hiring institution will not have a full-fledged, functioning cataloger on Day One, but, if appropriate education has taken place, an adaptable one who is ready for training to meet the current demands of cataloging because he or she fully understands what bibliographic control entails.

The training of catalogers has taken on added importance in today's climate of quotas and performance standards. Because of the accountability factor introduced by performance standards, training is needed not only by newly hired catalogers, but also by staff already on board. Libraries are forced into the position of training seasoned staff in new techniques and new staff in both old and new procedures, compounding the difficulties of efficient training. Libraries have been compelled to seek ways to produce more and reduce backlogs, feats that are increasingly difficult to achieve with budgets reduced by rising inflation. The library community will benefit by having catalogers who are properly trained so that quality work is produced from the start, obviating the need for protracted revision and review of their output once the training period ends.

CATALOGERS FOR THE NATION

I have chosen as the theme of my presentation on training, " Developing Catalogers for the Nation: Problems and Issues in Training Cataloging Librarians for the Future." This is where I see the profession heading in regard to preparing catalogers in the future. We have reached a point where bibliographic and information networking is such that cataloging data created by any professional cataloger is likely to be shared at the national level. This sharing is facilitated through established channels such as uploading to and downloading from the bibliographic utilities and through the loading of tapes and CD-ROM disks into local systems, which more libraries are installing as micro- and mini-computers become less expensive and more powerful. Sources for the bibliographic data being loaded include the Library of Congress (LC) MARC Distribution Service, the utilities, and commercial vendors. The process is likely to be accelerated now that computer-to-computer linking is a reality via the Linked Systems Project (LSP).

Ensuring effective and comprehensive bibliographic control continues to be the profession's overreaching concern. Bibliographic control is central to the functioning of any library or information center. Material that is not accessible is in effect rendered useless; cataloging provides access to that material. A core group is needed to discharge this function; catalogers constitute this core group of library personnel. To be effective, they must be well-trained, in addition to being well-educated. Any investment in their training is an investment in the future enhancement of comprehensive bibliographic control in this country, and indeed, the world.

It is some times incorrectly assumed that the advent of automation in libraries has lessened the need for well-prepared cataloger.   Nothing could be further from the truth. Automation has merely given us the ability to manipulate bibliographic data more efficiently.   The same principles that have governed bibliographic control still obtain for ordering the data for effective control and display now that the data are in machine-readable form. In fact, no matter what the format and type of library catalog, the catalog's function remains the same, namely to identify each person or entity uniquely, to collocate the works of each, to establish bibliographic item (book, serial, etc.) only once, and to show what is in a particular library's collections.

Among the many advantages that automation has brought to libraries is the potential to give a virtually unlimited number of access points in records for items. I might point out that this is mot a novel capability, however; any catalog format is capable of offering an infinite number of access points. It was only the practical constraints of the size of the book and card catalogs that imposed a limitation on the number of access points listed in them. What the machine allows that these previous formats lacked is the means to manipulate and display data in inordinate ways, so that diverse end-user needs are met.

Automation, and machine-readable cataloging, have done something else; with their advent, any catalogers may catalog for the nation. As I stated earlier in introducing my theme, a cataloging record produced at the local level stands a strong chance of being contributed not only to the local catalog for which it was prepared, but also to a national or even international file. With the enhancement of LSP to encompass the transmission of bibliographic records in addition to authority records, this likelihood becomes greater. Efforts are currently under way by the LSP Application Committee to achieve this capability. In tandem with this development, the Committee's energies are being devoted to drafting plans for linking local systems to the LSP partners. i.e., LC, the Research Libraries Information Network (RLIN), and Online Computer Library Center (OCLC). If local systems such as Geac and NOTIS, which are used in many research libraries in the United States, were able to link using LSP, these libraries could share data in ways heretofore impossible. Needless to say, standards assume a renewed significance in this expanded cataloging environment.

We must impress upon catalogers a sense of the importance of their work, because it affects the finished products and the ease with which they can be amalgamated into our growing bibliographic network. While concentrating on the specifics and mechanics of cataloging, catalogers must remain mindful of the broader view and the far-reaching impact their work may have.

One solution to overcoming the insulation, and sometimes isolation, that cataloging librarians may experience is for institutions to encourage and support their staff's attendance at and involvement in professional meetings and symposia. Benefits would accrue both to staff and the institutions. They could come to view their contributions in fuller perspective, in the process shedding some of the provincialism that sometimes creeps in. Institutions also have the option of establishing programs that give catalogers the chance to work in reference areas where they can see at first-hand how their cataloging records are used by the public.

Coming from a large institution, I have further concern about communication within a library. Increased concern about communication should take place both horizontally and vertically through meetings and written documents. It is important that all processors of materials be aware of what other units are doing and how their work fits into the whole.

PROPOSALS FOR ON-THE-JOB TRAINING: THE LC EXAMPLE

If it is axiomatic that on-the-job training is a requisite for good performance and productive output, we are faced with the question of how best to accomplish such training. Is there any one best way? I am convinced that the solutions and answers are varied and the avenues to be taken need to be modified from library to library. As head of the Processing Services department at the Library of Congress, I have responsibility for the training of more than 400 cataloging librarians. It is a daunting obligation. Our system for training has been less than perfect through the years and has been impacted by much of the same flux affecting other libraries--changing cataloging rules, freezing of card catalogs, and adoption of performance standards. We have, however, taken steps to improve our training process. Some of our remedies may serve as solutions for other institutions as well.

LC is a massive institution, regularly processing materials in some 70 languages and occasionally in about 400 additional ones, plus collecting in all subject areas. For this reason, the cataloging process at LC is akin to at scholarly assembly line. The vast size and complexity of operations within the department make the cataloging functions very specialized. Professional cataloging responsibilities are divided among descriptive catalogers, subject catalogers, and decimal classifiers;1 paraprofessional duties are assigned to preliminary catalogers, shelf listers, and MARC verifiers. Among these categories of staff, additional complexities are introduced by the requirements to catalog LC items using several systems: LC's internal systems for cataloging most materials, the RLIN systems for cataloging Chinese, Japanese, and Korean (CJK), Hebrew vernacular materials, and *National Union Catalog of Manuscript Collection* records, and the OCLC system for creating CONSER records.[1]

The career ladder for professional catalogers is GS-9 (entry level) through GS-12 (senior level). The one-on-one method is used for on-the-job-training. A new cataloger is assigned to a senior staff member who revises the catalogers work until he or she attains a level of proficiency suitable for independence and promotion to the next GS-grade.[2] Review of a cataloger's output continues until he or she reaches the senior level.[3]

Performance standards are in place to measure a cataloger's progress and against which he or she is measured for promotability. The nature of the work is such that a minimum of two years is required for a cataloger to advance through the career ladder. Even after reaching the top of the ladder, some form of review occurs to ensure that adherence to rules and procedures is maintained and that the quality of LC's cataloging products--distributed throughout the nation and the world--does not deteriorate.

Classroom training has existed at LC for many years. Training for catalogers in a classroom setting was formerly under the Cataloging Instruction Office, disbanded in the early 1980s. When I assumed my position as department head in 1983, I used the transition as a time to rethink the formalized training procedures within the department. My deliberations

Automation Instruction Office (TPAIO) to meet Processing Services' needs for an ongoing program of in-service training in technical processing, including automated technical processing systems.

The philosophy behind the creation of the Office can be summed up as follow: The Office staff are acknowledged as the training experts in the department. they are consulted automatically by any of the department's 17 divisions when a division realizes that it is embarking on a new program or change in procedures that will result in the need for training. With the creation of TPAIO, which reports directly to me, the department is underscoring its commitment to the training process and to the importance a training unit plays in producing competent catalogers.

It is unreasonable to assume that any one unit is capable of providing all the instruction that will be required of an institution as large as LC. As the unit specializing in the function, its staff should provide training whenever possible. When that is mot feasible, the training unit staff should coordinate the instruction to be done, thus ensuring consistency in approach. This means relying on the talents of others who may have the requisite expertise, but not necessarily the teaching skills. Staff chosen to train should first be trained for this function. The importance of instructing those who will be doing the training should not be minimized. Being trained by an inexperienced and unimaginative instructor can be a detrimental experience for an employee.

TPAIO has devised a course geared to such training, entitled "Training the Trainer." Its purpose is to teach individuals to train staff in highly technical subject areas related to processing materials. Four tasks for a successful instructor are impressed on them: (1) preparation; (2) Instruction; (3) evaluation; and, counselling. And, for these who are both trainers and supervisors, the course will help distinguish between the two roles. A by-product that can be used for future courses and by staff as they embark on future training assignments.

Recent years have witnessed changes in the way cataloging is performed at LC. Some of these changes gave stemmed from LC's expanding role in cooperative cataloging ventures, such as the National Coordinated Cataloging Operations (NACO) for the contribution of authority records, and the National Coordinated Cataloging Programs (NCCP) for the Contribution of both bibliographic and authority records. Each has occasioned additional training needs. To cope with these and to guarantee that appropriate training concerns are addressed early on, staff from the training unit are always appointed as members of the planning and implementation team of the project concerned.

Two experiments that have relevance for other libraries and that generate training requirements similar to those of other institutions are the Online Cataloging and the Whole Book Cataloging experiments. The former will allow LC catalogers for the first time to input their cataloging data online rather than typing worksheets. Whole Book Cataloging will test the concept of one person or team of persons performing the full complement of cataloging activities rather than just one aspect. There is nothing new about this approach to cataloging for most libraries, since it is a practice already followed by the majority. But, for LC, it raises the question of whether it is practicable, given all the additional work required to create name and series authorities, subject thesauri, and classification schedules. Is it reasonable to expect that one person can absorb the LC guide lines needed to function optimally when performing the full spectrum of cataloging in the LC environment?

LC's long tradition in resource sharing is well documented. In that same tradition, as a solution, or at least an aid, to satisfying the training requirements of other institution, LC should explore the feasibility of sharing its training tools with other libraries, just as it has shared its cataloging expertise and products. As a large institution, even though its bounty of resources has diminished in recent years, LC can still do what may be impossible for smaller libraries by devising training courses and developing training manuals that can be used by others. TPAIO has engaged in preliminary exploration involving the marketing of its training packages. If the market is receptive, various formats such as manuals, video tapes, and compact disks could be adopted to distribute these instruction tools.

CONCLUSION

As I thought about the problems of training catalogers and what solution could be offered, I became convinced that there is no quick fix or easy panacea. The immediacy and broad concern of training will require a commitment and outlay of resources that are commensurate with the need. Training of cataloging librarians will continue to be the domain of libraries, buttressing the education dispensed by library schools. An to reiterate, that education must concentrate on bibliographic control and what it means, especially how it is supported by automation and standards. Catalogers should come to the job knowing these aspects of technical services.

Training must become more structured, whether in one-on-one or classroom form. There are no shortcuts. Thorough initial planning and preparation of materials are time-consuming endeavors, but they can be the cornerstone of any future requirements and make the difference between success and failure.

Training techniques and materials can be shared in the manner I have proposed. Because Processing Services is part of th de facto national library, its training program should play a major role in on-the-job training beyond the department and the Library of Congress. We at LC can work to that end. I wait with keen anticipation to hear the proposals of others who are participating in the training segment.

NOTES

1. CONSER stands for Conservation of Serials, a program designed to establish a comprehensive database of bibliographic data for serial titles in machine-readable form.
2. Revision is the process of checking a staff member's cataloging by comparing the bibliographic and accompanying authority records against the item being cataloged. It involves the trainer following each step in the routine of creating the records, retracing the searching in the catalog and reference sources.
3. Review is the process of monitoring a staff member's cataloging by checking the bibliographic and authority records for accuracy, but without the trainer verifying them against the item or retracing the searching done.

The Role of Training in the Changing Cataloging Environment

Kathleen Bales

We deal with change as part of our daily lives, whether at work in libraries or at home with family. Much has been written about the effect of computers on the rate of change in our lives. Since our work lives are changing rapidly, the image of a cobweb-covered cataloger toiling away at a desk should have gone the way of the manual typewriter and the electric eraser. Then why, if the role of the cataloger has been transformed from the library caterpillar to the library butterfly, are there not enough librarians eager for flight? Why is there a shortage of librarians for cataloging jobs? Has the training we offer catalogers been inadequate for completing this career metamorphosis, or worse, not been sustaining enough for those who begin work as catalogers and then transfer to another part of the library? This article will examine technological change as a factor in cataloging activities and the training processes necessary to best manage change. It will also look at how computers impact library work, particularly cataloging. In addition, it will suggest training tools and techniques to use resources most effectively, enhance catalogers' job satisfaction and expand flexibility and career growth.

CHANGE

Peggy Johnson, writing about technological change, begins her article with a quote from Machiavelli on the difficulty of initiating "a new order of things". She goes on to say,

> "Automation is probably the most difficult change to implement, because it may alter virtually every library function ... The internal changes resulting from technological innovation are legion, as are the number of staff who resist them."[1]

Change in the work environment has a neutral value in itself. It can have both positive and negative effects on individuals and institutions. The attitude of an institution to change profoundly influences how the individuals in that institution react to change. Frank Hutchinson and Greg Gilber maintain that if an institution generally values and looks forward to change, the personnel will do a better job of coping when changes are required.[2] The effects of change on an institution may include a loss of productivity as the staff adjust to new ways of doing things. This can be minimized with a well-planned and implemented training program. Automation may enable a supervisor to monitor staff progress and productivity with less effort. On the other hand, increased access to information about production levels may cause staff members to take a less flexible approach to their work.

An individual can experience an increase in job satisfaction because of a change in the tasks that he or she does.

An ability to deal with change enhances an individual's flexibility, a benefit that reaches beyond the immediate job situation. At the same time, an individual may feel threatened by a change to tasks or workflow. According to Sheila Creth, training has traditionally been task-oriented in libraries, but rapid changes in the environment mean that the training must now serve two purposes: training for the task at hand and learning to accept change. "In the future, individuals will need to develop a dual attitude toward their work; they will need to have commitment and respect for the way work is currently performed combined with a willingness to alter and to let go of current practices when change is required."[3]   Managing the day-to- day work in institutions uses information about what already is. "But change efforts have to mobilize people around what is not yet known."[4] Desired or necessary changes can be accomplished much more easily if those in the organization internalize the need for changes, buying into the process.

It is ironic that the process of training to accommodate changes introduces change in turn; training is a change agent. Edward Jones states, "Education means change. If there has been no change, there has been no education. Unless there has been change in the participants in the cognitive area (knowledge), the affective area (attitudes, values), or the psychomotor area (skills), there has been no education. There may have been a lot of teaching activity and effort, but no learning or education."[5]

TRAINING

A large body of literature is available on training theory; much of it originates with theories developed by the U.S. Army to further the immense amount of training done by the armed implementation are 1) needs analysis, 2) design, 3) development, 4) delivery and 5) evaluation. Needs analysis and design should take about fifty percent of the total time spent on preparing a training program.[6] These five tasks are discussed below.

A needs analysis must uncover which competencies are needed, the existing level of skills in these competencies, an assessment of the deficiencies, and a decision as to whether they are correctable by training. Methods for ascertaining this information could include interviews, questionnaires, work samples, tests and guessing. (Guessing is probably the most widely used methodology in libraries.) It is during this process that the trainer begins to develop behavioral objectives.

The design stage includes deciding how the tasks can be best learned, discovering whether qualified trainers are available within the institution, and finding out whether a suitable training program already exists for these tasks, and if so, whether it is available.

Training for self-paced learning must be very well-designed, but this method is suited to adult learning. Group instruction is best when many people must learn the same thing in a short time, or when the training focuses on changing behavioral patterns. It is easier to learn the behavior wanted when it can be observed. It is clearly appropriate to combine these two learning styles for some situations.

Competent in-house trainers need a combination of content expertise and delivery expertise. Trainers will find that both types of expertise can provide career development for them. The use of in-house trainers can, however, be very expensive because of loss of productivity in the normal assignment. Outside trainers may also be expensive but such personnel may be able to help with the analysis and design tasks. Such trainers are also unbiased and uninvolved in an institution's politics; conversely, they may be too independent and insensitive to the institution's needs.

Prepackaged training programs may be available for some library training needs, but they will seldom be a perfect fit with the wanted content. If the program covers at least 80% of the content, it may be worthwhile to investigate customizing the program to include the remainder.

Developing a training program involves deciding how much material is needed, how the material should be presented (e.g., as a reference manual or as a handbook) and settling on the best way of approaching the material. A package for the leader must also be created, including exercises, handouts and audio-visual aids. The development stage is the most visible one of the planning process and is probably where most institutions begin work on their training programs.

The trainee should not be overloaded with information, but only be presented with what can be assimilated during the training period. The "why" of a task must be included as well as the "how." In choosing the approach to the material, the trainer must know how the material will be used. If the trainee will need to refer to a manual often in the course of performing the task, a reference manual should be designed, and instruction in using the manual should be incorporated into the training.

The trainer must make decisions about sequencing, considering whether to organize the material as general-to-specific or specific-to-general, referencing desired workflows and logical steps. The sequencing should follow the performance of tasks. When the first draft of the training materials is done, the trainer should organize a pre-training session to test it.

Decisions must be made about the equipment needed and the physical environment, as well as whether the training will be a team effort. It is typical for the developer, whether in-house or outside, to do the actual training. The line manager has traditionally done the training of employees s/he supervises. It is necessary, however, for a trainer to have strong presentation skills, strong conflict resolution skills and good ability to lead a group. If a manager does not have all of these skills, it may be better to have someone else present the training material.

The evaluation process includes deciding whether the goals have been met and whether the trainees perform better after the training. Discrepancies between objectives and results must be taken care of with further training and follow-up. This step will also help reinforce what was learned. Enjoyment of the training by trainees is not necessarily a measurement of effectiveness. There is no way to measure effectiveness accurately unless measurements of skills or competencies were done as part of needs analysis. Unless this first measurement step is included, materials presented are just that, and cannot be called training.

These theories, illustrated by the five training steps above and the resulting practices, were developed to deal with training personnel to push levers, pull knobs and generally run machines. Applying these theories and practices to the kind of work that catalogers do takes some creativity and adjustment. It seems less important to subscribe to a rigid methodology for training than to decide on what aspects of a methodology are right for a particular situation and then to apply them from beginning to end.

Knowledge of adult learning modes is also necessary in order to devise effective training programs to manage change. Alexander Stark indicates that motivation is very important and that the adult prefers learning by doing to listening to a lecture. The training program should build on experience and clarify how expectations will be met. Standards are needed to insure meaningful feedback. Protecting the adult learner's self esteem is central to the plan.[7]

COMPUTERS AND LIBRARY WORK

The term "computer-mediated" has been applied by Shoshana Zuboff to work done at a terminal,[8] where the computer literally comes between the worker and the task. The terminal operator may find it hard to believe that the computer will actually do what is reported on the screen. The computer gives feedback about the task; the task becomes an electronic manipulation of symbols, more abstract than the concrete manual task that it replaces. It may be difficult to gain the sense of accomplishment felt from finishing a manual task, such as revising the filing in a card drawer. As a result, the person sitting at the terminal can become more distant from the work.[9] The terminal operator may lose sight of the importance of the task and where it fits in to the workflow; the terminal session begins to be a contest to increase speed, to the exclusion of meaning. Admittedly, catalogers may not currently experience this degree of dislocation common to those sitting at a terminal all day. At this point in our use of the technology, the clerical aspects of the tasks have been diminished, leaving catalogers more time to solve problems.

It is important for future planning, however, to understand how the computer affects those using terminals in their jobs. Any loss of meaning resulting from increased automation must be compensated for in structuring the work and developing training programs. Providing an understanding of what the computer does with the information keyed in at a terminal becomes paramount. When trainees understand the process, they learn to trust the computer; this understanding should also make the abstract more concrete. (To be sure, the cataloger physical item examined while doing the work. When a cataloger keys in original cataloging in batches, however, the connection with the physical item may fade as attention is fixed on the system in use.) Ways must also be found to allow flexibility when the actual task is more structured as a result of automating it. In addition, when that structure is abruptly withdrawn if the system becomes unavailable, employees must be trained to cope. If a change to cataloging workflow introduces a personal cataloging workstation, this may allow a cataloger more control over the work, but it may also produce a sense of isolation. Those structuring the work must allow for methods of electronic networking to replace the personal contact lost in the new environment. Training in using this aspect of the system becomes very important, but it is not enough merely to teach catalogers to use an electronic mail system; some exploration of when to use it and for what purposes it may be useful is also necessary. Otherwise, problems that formerly would be addressed simply in person may easily escalate into electronic "memo wars." This mode of communication is appropriate for some situations, but not for all. Further, some individuals are made very uncomfortable by the absence of face-to- face dialogue in problem-solving.

CHANGES FOR CATALOGERS

An aspect of automation that directly affects catalogers is the USMARC format, whether in "pure" form or as adapted by a vendor or utility. Changes to the MARC format generally mean changes that catalogers must cope with, whether they input records or fill out worksheets. These changes fall into three main categories, requiring somewhat different approaches to training: those supporting changes in cataloging rules or practices, those enhancing the format to accommodate new types of materials or new ways of handling materials, and those resulting from efforts to make the format more logical and consistent. The degree of impact on the cataloger will depend not only on the size and scope of the change, but on whether the cataloger works online or uses worksheets to tag the records.

When a change is implemented by a utility or a vendor, the cataloger has probably had no direct influence on how this MARC change will be seen. If the change is manifested in a local system, however, the cataloger may have a chance to influence how the system presents the change. This latter case offers more cataloger control (buying into the change) and possibly more lead time, both of which are positive factors in creating a training program that will be successful.

Another type of change is that affecting the general rhythm of the workflow through a department. This change occurs most often when a library automates a process for the first time, changes from one system to another, or refines the way a system is being used. In this case, the work itself may change. The tasks may become more interactive or more batched and training for the new workflow must emphasize the rationale for the changes. Workflow changes will normally involve all levels of staff, not just catalogers, and this must be reflected in the training plans.

A third category of change is organizational, which may or may not be the result of automation. When a library reorganizes a department or a unit, the staff must receive at the very least an orientation that gives them information about what will be different and what will be the same. When a reorganization includes any change in tasks or responsibilities, the staff must receive training in those.

Of the types of changes cited above, the latter category is the most difficult. Johnson says, "It is usually easier to master a new task than a new technology. Adopting a new technology is often easier than altering the organizational structure. Changes in the cultural fabric are the most threatening and are resisted most."[10]

TRAINING IN LIBRARIES

The possible formats for presenting material during training are numerous. Larryetta Scholl and James Douglass list the following: audio-only, video-only, audiovisual, printed, programmed instruction, lectures, self-teaching exportable packages, supplementary instruction, adjunct programs, job performance aids and formal on-the-job training.[11] For reasons of costs and appropriateness, some of these will drop out of a list of possibilities for most libraries. The very nature of the changing environment discourages the creation of programmed texts, for instance, since this material must be very carefully designed to be useful. Most library training is done using printed manuals and exercises, with overheads added for group instruction. This type of material can be very effective so long as it is structured using a consistent methodology.

It is a challenge to add the testing and evaluation steps to library training. Gregory Kreiger observes that the test objective should be very specific; "finding out how much" a trainee knows will not give useful measurements. Tests measure either process or product. Tests-for-process measure the ability to perform against a standard; product tests measure a product against a standard.[12] Most cataloging work produces a product; however, the issue of measuring this product against a standard is a thorny one. Tests may need to allow for more than one "right" answer and should be pre-tested for correct answers by more than one expert.

Catalogers who are open to change have a clear advantage in the arena of work automation. Although the need to develop this attitude may be a behavioral change called for as the result of a needs assessment, planning and evaluating training for such a change may seem overwhelming to those in charge of ordinary library training programs. Fostering an open attitude to change may be approached, however, as an underlying part of all cataloger training. An examination of the groups or units in the library that are more flexible than others may provide information that can be used to do this. Serials catalogers must accept change by definition, since so much of their work is re-cataloging items that they or others have handled at least once before. Change is "part of their job description." It would be useful to make sure that all catalogers understand this aspect of their job, and is might be worth considering rotating some of the serials cataloging among monographic catalogers.

Another way of making change more attractive is to include cross-training in other library units as a normal part of career development. It may be enlightening for catalogers to use their own product (the catalog) when assisting library patrons. This type of training may need to emphasize behavioral changes in addition to learning a new skill set.

Giving all catalogers training in creative problem solving techniques, such as brainstorming, would encourage individuals to add to the rule-oriented approach that is so necessary for cataloging, and to use their considerable analytic skills in new ways.

Management support is essential for effective training programs. Those planning the training can use various techniques to obtain and maintain management support for the needed effort.   Staff and management alike will respond more positively if personnel with talent and enthusiasm are used in the planning process. The planning team should be aware of costs and work to minimize them, while maintaining a quality program. Pooling resources with other libraries for specific training efforts may be a possibility, particularly for those changes originating in the larger cataloging environment. Cooperating with the Human Resources department can help spread the costs of training. This is especially important when significant behavioral changes are desired. Human Resources personnel may also be able to help with technical aspects of training or with training trainers. If a library is automating a function for the first time, those planning the training could investigate the possibility of optical scanning of printed manuals to get the information in machine-readable form. It then becomes easier to link the new ways of doing tasks to current practice and to incorporate current documentation into the training.

MARC format changes lend themselves to the use of exercises and templates. The trainer will need to have examples of "before and after" to reinforce changes to existing practice. A series of self-paced exercises can be a cost-effective approach for routine MARC maintenance changes. A core group of trainers can build a file of unusual or difficult MARC coding examples by collecting them from problems encountered in normal work. These can then be used in future training programs. If the cataloging input system features validation of codes and values, the system itself can be an excellent training tool to reinforce what was learned in excercises. No input system currently in use explains the "why" of MARC coding, however, and trainees do learn more quickly if the changes have been explained and the benefits shown. For example, it is easier to accept coding new fixed field values if retrieval possibilities are pointed out.

For rule or practice changes, the cataloging and MARC aspects should be taught together. Catalogers need to understand the rule change before they learn to tag it. When the format is changing to include a new physical format, trainees must learn how this material will benefit the library. Catalogers should be asked to study the material as it passes through the department, to collect retrieval needs and problems. Training could include making plans to consult with the users of this material in order to assure the best possible service to them. It is a lot easier to be cheerful about assigning coded values and constructing special access fields if a cataloger knows that the fields will be used by people he or she has actually talked to.

Computer-assisted instruction is a new tool that can be effective for training. The use of software to provide system tutorials or simulations has been slow to gain acceptance in libraries, but some systems now offer such packages and other are considering this tool. OCLC, for example, has programs for basic system use, interlibrary loan, and CD-ROM cataloging. They plan to create similar programs for their new system, to cope with the large amount of training that will have to be done in a short period of time. They produce the CAI packages in-house, using authoring software.

Consumers of library systems should insist on such tools from their vendors or utilities. It is a waste of resources for each library to devise training for automated systems, when computer- aided instruction could provide all of the training except that which relates to use of the system in a specific library. CAI is very resource-consumptive to produce; one estimate is 200 hours of preparation time for each hour of instruction. This kind of investment may only be appropriate when the system module is stable and when the "mainstream" or "vanilla" use of the system is covered.

It would also be useful to investigate the possibility of a CAI package that would be a template, e.g., for MARC changes. The basic approach would be stable; only the details of new or changed fields would be updated for each release. One such package issued from each utility would save considerable resources in libraries across the country.

CONCLUSION

Change is inevitable and is happening rapidly in cataloging work. The ability of catalogers to be flexible in this environment will directly affect not only the work situation of individual catalogers, but will influence the way other librarians and management perceive the role of the cataloger in the environment. When we train catalogers to cope with changes, the training program must include not only the content of the change itself, but must also address attitudes to change. Bringing catalogers into the planning process for change increases their ability to buy into the change and accept it. This is the first and most important step in training for change.

Catalogers who are flexible and accepting of the change process can also become skilled in solving problems outside the cataloging department. It has already been demonstrated that their role in library automation enables them to exhibit important leadership in their institutions. Management must be prepared to accept catalogers in expanded roles, with new viewpoints. As Herbert White says, "The best and the brightest are also the least docile, and they are the ones who demand explanations and justifications of why certain procedures are followed."[13]

The opportunity is at hand to use the changes in the cataloging environment to develop better catalogers and flexible, forward-looking professionals. Training is the key to seizing this opportunity to keep and improve the cataloging staff that we have and to attract new catalogers to open positions. Save the endangered cataloger butterfly!

REFERENCES

1. Peggy Johnson, "Implementing Technological Change," *College & Research Libraries* 49 (January 1988): 38.
2. Frank Hutchinson and Greg Gilber, "Readying Your Company for Change," *Training & Development Journal* (August 1984): 28.
3. Sheila D. Creth, *Effective On-the-Job Training: Developing Library Human Resources* (Chicago: American Library Association, 1986), p. 6.
4. Rosabeth Moss Kanter, *The Change Masters: Innovations for Productivity in the American Corporation* (New York: Simon and Schuster, 1983), p. 304.
5. Edward E. Jones, Jr, "Training for Changes: Guidelines for the New Practitioner," *Training & Development Journal* (October 1984): 73.
6. Jerry L. Sellers, "Scientist and Engineer Development," in *Human Resources Management and Development Handbook*, ed. William R. Tracey (New York: AMACOM, 1985), pp. 954-958.
7. Alexander T. Stark, "Conducting Training Programs," in *Human Resources Management and Development Handbook*, ed. William R. Tracey (New York: AMACOM, 1985), p. 1414.
8. Shoshana Zuboff, *In the Age of the Smart Machine: The*

Future of Work and Power (New York: Basic Books, 1988),p. 6.

9.   Ibid., pp. 80-83.
10. Johnson, "Implementing Technological Change,"40.
11. Larryetta M. School and James F. Douglass, "Developing Training Systems," in *Human Resources Management and Development Handbook*, ed. William R. Tracey (New York: AMACOM, 1985), p. 1369.
12. Gregory M. Kreiger, "Test Construction and Validation," in *Human Resources Management and Development Handbook*, ed. William R. Tracey (New York: AMACOM, 1985), pp. 1373-1375.
13. Herbert S. White, "Catalogers--Yesterday, Today, Tomorrow," *Library Journal* 112 (April 1, 1987): 49.

Training and Continuing Education for Catalogers: The Electronic Environment of the 1990's

Nancy L. Eaton

Increasingly, cataloging is done via a combination of national bibliographic networks and local integrated automated library systems. Electronic formats such as CD-ROM discs, online data bases, and software pose new problems in bibliographic description and control. Libraries now are mounting indexing and textual databases on local mainframes along with their online catalog, which suggests the need for new responsibilities in database maintenance. New document delivery services may require bibliographic control at the article and chapter level to be effective. This paper will explore the implications of these changes for the training and continuing education of catalogers in the 1990's. It will not deal with other aspects of cataloging expertise, such as changes in cataloging codes or subject expertise, though those are also important training issues.

With the emergence of OCLC's online cataloging system in 1971, which had the express purpose of reducing the rate of rise of library per-unit processing costs,[1] the use of automation in cataloging has increased to the point that only in the smallest libraries would a cataloger function without using an automated cataloging system, whether it be OCLC, WLN (the Washington Library Network), RLIN (Research Libraries Information Network), UTLAS (the Canadian bibliographic utility), or one of the commercial cataloging systems such as Brodart, Gaylord, the Library Corporation, General Research Corporation, or Marcive.

Generally, the early versions of these centralized bibliographic databases used either online terminals for searching and cataloging, or optical character recognition forms for sending cataloging data for batch update to a central file. The MARC-II formats for bibliographic data became the standard for coding data for all of these systems. Once the system was installed and staff had been trained on that specific system, procedures could remain fairly stable for long periods of time. In recent years, however, a plethora of new systems and system enhancements have appeared, including linkages between national networks and one's local online integrated library system, microcomputer-based enhancements such as OCLC's Micro Enhancer Software (which saves time by batching routine cataloging work, which allows records to be edited offline, and which allows update or produce transactions during non-prime time when rates are lower), and use of CD-ROM discs attached to microcomputers for searching catalog records or authority records at the local level, followed by online access to the larger centralized database when the record is not found on the local CD-ROM database. A cataloger is now faced with understanding the differences between different systems and the various optional features of each, and how best to make all these systems function for maximum design efficiency.

For instance, a cataloger who uses OCLC as a bibliographic resource database and NOTIS as the local integrated library system might catalog on OCLC, reformat the OCLC MARC-II record for compatibility with the slightly different NOTIS MARC-II record format and local equipment requirements (e.g. eliminating delimiter w subfields and adjusting for fewer lines per screen on Telex terminals), download the record into NOTIS, do authority control using authority records in the NOTIS system, and create the index entries on NOTIS for the online public access catalog. In the process of doing this, the cataloger might also utilize OCLC's Micro Enhancer functions, might access the cataloging and authority databases first on a local CD-ROM version of the OCLC databases and, if the records were not found, then search the full online system. The cataloger has, in this increasingly common scenario, used four different interrelated automated cataloging products to produce the final catalog entry and associated authority records. This requires considerable flexibility and sophistication in the use of automated systems. In addition, these and other systems undergo continual evolution, and require ongoing training for use. For example, OCLC is totally redesigning its technical services functions to take advantage of the New System design with key word and Boolean logic and new telecommunications capabilities.

The increasing use of local integrated library systems for cataloging, authority control, and online public access catalogs has produced a need for database maintenance routines within a catalog department. Implementation of online public access catalogs in libraries requires that catalogers work closely with systems librarians and public service librarians in determining specifications between the cataloging and authority subsystems and the online public access catalog, since cataloging practice has repercussions in online catalog displays. These two developments are leading to reorganization within some catalog departments and changes in routines. Database maintenance units are appearing in some catalog departments; and administratively technical services and systems offices are being merged into one division in some libraries. Catalogers need to stay abreast of such administrative and procedural changes brought about by the use of automation for cataloging.

Many libraries (for example, Georgia Institute of Technology, California Institute of Technology, and Carnegie Mellon University[2]) that have implemented online public access catalogs are taking a further step and mounting other indexing/abstracting databases on the same campus system. Prime candidates are databases such as Medline, ERIC, Magazine Index, and IEEE indexes for engineering journals. The use of additional MARC-II bibliographic formats for audiovisual materials, archives and realia (for museum holdings, for instance) is also increasing, as holdings of online catalogs are enriched for campus access to other than the book collections. Faculty members at UCLA are beginning to apply for small grants under a Council on Library Resources funded project administered by Robert Hayes to utilize the library's ORION library system for personal or departmental databases.[3] It is not illogical to think that database maintenance for all MARC-II or library-related databases might fall to technical services, specifically cataloging staff, due to their experience and expertise with maintenance of bibliographic and authority databases. This might be most likely to occur in a library where technical services and systems have been merged

An extension of this logic pertains to the emergence of full text databases which, in addition to the bibliographic description, might contain key words or subject headings or abstracts for use with key word or Boolean retrieval software. Specific examples of this are the University of Vermont's Higher Education Act Title II-C grant on Acid Rain and the National Agricultural Text Digitizing Project (NATDP), in which full text materials are being scanned, digitized, and produced on CD-ROM discs for distribution to land grant libraries. The five full text databases being produced in these projects will include both bibliographic and indexing information. In the case of the acid rain documents from Canada, the cataloger on the project is both cataloging and indexing, with cataloging performed on OCLC and indexing information being submitted to NAL for input into AGRICOLA. In order for electronic document delivery to work effectively in the future, identification of articles and chapters of books may be critical in the same way that bibliographic item description in the national databases is critical to effective online interlibrary loan systems today. The expertise and outlook used for cataloging also applies to indexing, and I believe we will see a blending of these talents in some cases. These directions argue for future catalogers who are very flexible and who are interested in a broad range of cataloging, indexing, classification, and database maintenance issues. While this has important implications for recruitment and library school curricula, it has even more import for the retraining and retention of existing catalogers who did not enter the field with these expectations.

Several key elements in combination appear, from personal experience, to be most useful in helping catalog librarians to stay current and creative in using automated cataloging systems.

1. *Resource person(s)*: It is extremely important to identify one or more persons within a catalog department, who are not necessarily the head of the department, who are excited about automation and will make the extra effort to learn system(s) capabilities in detail, so that they will know the ramifications to processing and access when such things as as function tables or implementation decisions are executed. For example, within the NOTIS system, a decision has to be made whether to set up the catalogs as one integrated database or multiple databases. That decision affects how data displays in the online catalog, how reports sort (including exception reports for the catalog department), and how indexes are constructed. Having one or more resource persons in the department who can interpret the implications for such decisions and aid other less facile staff members through the thought process will make all staff more receptive to the system and to changes in procedures.

2. *Release time for experimentation*: A major error that can be made is to underestimate the amount of time needed for individuals to instruct themselves and to experiment with new systems or products in order to understand their features in depth. Release time from the daily press of cataloging must be provided to allow each individual time to read documentation, talk to co-workers, and practice with the system or systems. If this kind of time is not provided, people will be frustrated, will make mistakes, and will be much less receptive to creative adaptation of the system and to making changes in procedures.

3. *Network training sessions*: Most regional networks have taken on the responsibility for technical training sessions for member libraries. These may be workshops held at a central location, or the network may be willing to send a

trainer to an individual library on a per diem basis if the staff is sufficiently large. For example, NELINET (New England Library Network) has just completed a long-range planning process using the consulting expertise of Peat Marwick Main, the result being a new focus on providing technical training in the New England region as one of its priorities.[4] These training sessions or workshops are often designed to introduce new products or features of the OCLC system, which is the predominant network utilized in New England, and they can result in considerable savings of staff time spent deciding whether and how to incorporate new capabilities at the local level. Tagging workshops for various formats are also offered, and can be used to train new catalogers who join the staff, and thus minimize in-house training. For example, the University of Vermont has sent catalogers from the Media Library and the Fleming Museum to workshops at NELINET for training in audiovisual materials and realia tagging before they begin to enter their collections into the NOTIS system.

4. *Users groups and discussion groups*: One of the most useful feedback mechanisms for catalogers is to attend users groups, or discussion groups with their peers who are using the same automation systems. Most vendors have their own discussion groups or users groups. The NOTIS Users Group, for example, has grown into a three-day annual meeting held in Evanston, Illinois, near NOTIS headquarters, and includes system updates, various tutorial sessions for librarians and programmers, and has discussion groups centered around specific topics such as serials cataloging or use of the NOTIS/MARC-II formats for archival collections. Divisions of the American Library Association, particularly the Library

and Information Technology Association (LITA) and the Resources and Technical Services Division (RTSD), have a variety of discussion groups formed around such concerns as database maintenance, retrospective conversion methodologies, CD-ROM technologies, etc., which allow small groups of interested individuals to compare experience at a detailed level. These, in my experience, are extremely popular sessions, and are most useful when the group remains small, within the fifteen to thirty person range, although larger groups can hold lively discussions if the topic is controversial or vexing enough.

5. *Interdepartmental planning*: Implementation of an integrated system affects both public and technical services. Planning for system implementation most frequently is an interdepartmental process, with committees or task forces which cut across departments. This process should be encouraged for several reasons. First, it makes for better utilization of the system if all repercussions of a decision are known for all departments. Second, catalogers are made an integral part of the overall library planning or implementation process and feel part of the team. One of the things that automation can accomplish is to make clear that both reference librarians and catalogers are, in fact, working from the same theoretical framework in terms of how information is organized and described and that their differences are in the application, not underlying concepts. To the extent that such joint planning can help reduce the artificial divisions between public services and technical services which have existed historically in many libraries, it can make catalogers feel less isolated and the cataloging specialization more desirable. It is important that all catalogers are allowed to participate in this process at

some level if they are to be encouraged to take the broadest possible view of their roles.

6. *Documentation*: A crucial element for training and continuing education of catalogers who are adapting to or implementing upgrades to automated cataloging systems is adequate documentation. The networks tend to do a good job with documentation, as they have specialized in producing documentation for the bibliographic utilities for over fifteen years. Documentation from vendors is much less consistent and much more frustrating to staff who are trying to implement very technical systems with incomplete or inaccurate information. Often, because of inadequate documentation from the vendor, catalogers must participate in writing internal documentation for the department to clarify inadequate outside documentation. And even when documentation is excellent, the department will have to adapt that material to different jobs and tasks within the department to recognize local practice and specific position tasks. Again, adequate time must be allocated for this task.

7. *Computer-Aided-Instruction (CAI) and expert systems*: At times the change to an existing system is of such magnitude that workshops, documentation, and personal training may not be an efficient mechanism for retraining a large group of people. OCLC has concluded that this is the case with implementation of their New System, which is a major rewrite of the OCLC cataloging system that has been used in libraries with minor changes for over fifteen years. OCLC staff have therefore produced a CAI package which will be distributed through networks to all member libraries. Early estimates are that it will take a person about twenty hours to complete the entire training package. The package is being produced in sections, so

that selected sections pertinent to specific jobs can be used without going through the entire package. CAI packages of today's vintage typically use windowing techniques, graphics, etc., and may also include elements of expert systems, which can emulate systems and some logic processes. These packages are very sophisticated compared to the CAI packages of the 1960 and 1970's. The OCLC package, as of the writing of this paper, has not yet been distributed; thus, it is not clear how successful this mechanism for mass retraining of catalogers and other technical services personnel will be.[5]

CONCLUSION

This paper argues for a broad interpretation of the role of a cataloger as automated library systems bring cataloging and indexing systems within the same operational framework, and as implementation of automated cataloging systems, authority control systems, and online public access catalogs require joint decision-making in the implementation of these subsystems. As additional databases are added to the library's online system, the distinctions between the library's catalog and other information databases become less obvious. Catalogers may, in fact, find themselves in the roles of advising how to set up databases which will use the MARC-II structure of the library system. Training and continuing education for catalogers must, therefore, take into account this broader role. Even in the largest libraries, where the volume of materials continues to warrant large staffs of dedicated catalogers, the individual cataloger will still function best if s/he understands the overall system and the context in which s/he is operating. Thus, even in such an environment, it is important to bring the individual effective decisions to be made at the lowest level of the departmental hierarchy.

REFERENCES

1. OCLC Online Computer Library Center, Incorporated. *OCLC Code of Regulations, Article III*. February, 1988.
2. Various conversations between Nancy L. Eaton and Glyn Brudvig (Director of Libraries, California Institute of Technology), Miriam Drake (Director of Libraries, Georgia Institute of Technology), and Thomas Michalak (Assistant Vice President and Director of Libraries, Carnegie Mellon University), 1988.
3. Conversations between Nancy L. Eaton and Robert Hayes (Dean, UCLA Graduate School of Library Science) and Gloria Werner (Assistant Director for Technical Services, UCLA Libraries), August, 1987.
4. New England Library Network (NELINET). *Long-range Planning Study*, conducted under contract by Peat Marwick Main, Incorporated. Newton, MA: 1987, (Unpublished) Priorities were validated by the NELINET Board of Directors during bi-monthly board meetings, 1988.
5. Presentations on the OCLC New System Implementation by OCLC staff to OCLC Users Council. Dublin, Ohio: September 29, 1988.

Training the Cataloger:
A Harvard Experience

Michael Fitzgerald

A major investment for any cataloging department is the training of the newly hired cataloger, because, given the variety of humanity, the most efficient method of training in the last analysis is the individual apprenticeship.[1]

This apprenticeship has as its goal the production of a cataloger able to work independently, and so it is conditioned by assumptions, usually unspoken, about what the work of the cataloger is.

We like to think that we are working in a time of accelerated change, but I believe that it is the kind of change, not the fact of change that distinguishes us from our predecessors. Catalogers have always had to cope with changing rules and technologies from Panizzi's *91 Rules* to the *Anglo-American Cataloguing Rules* second edition, from the book catalog to the card files to the database, and from the typewriter to the computer terminal.

What is the kind of change that awaits today's new cataloger? Nancy John, writing about descriptive cataloging in the United States in *International Cataloguing*, has observed:

> Between 1960 and 1980 we can see the rise of the forces which resulted in American libraries changing from the supremacy of local cataloguing practice to willing subjugation under the yoke of national and international cooperation.[2]

At Widener Library, the central research library of the Faculty of Arts and Sciences at Harvard University, the last two decades have seen the evolution from union and public card catalogs and the use of local descriptive practice, subject headings, and classification to an online catalog based on national cataloging standards and practices.

AUTOMATION AT HARVARD UNIVERSITY LIBRARY

Widener's cataloging experience with automation began in July, 1974, when we joined the New England Library Network, NELINET, and gained access to the OCLC database. In 1981, the University Library's OCLC archive tapes were used in the production of a computer-produced microfiche (COM) catalog, the Distributable Union Catalog. The first cumulation included 236,479 monograph titles, 19,545 serials, and 105,909 order records from the University Library's Computer Assisted Processing System (CAPS).[3]

In 1983, the Harvard University Library entered into a cooperative agreement with the Library of Congress (LC), and so the College Library's Cataloging and Processing Department now contributes monograph records with their related authority

(MUMS) for distribution as part of the weekly LC MARC tapes. The catalogers must follow LC's descriptive and subject cataloging policies and practice as completely as any unit at LC and have been provided with equipment, training, documentation, regular review, and support by LC.

In 1985, the Harvard Online Library Information System (HOLLIS), the University Library's modification of the NOTIS system, was implemented.[4]   At first, HOLLIS was primarily an acquisitions and processing system, consisting chiefly of books and serials records from CAPS and CONSER[5] serial records. In 1987, the system was expanded by the merging into HOLLIS of the Bibliographic Master File, which contained catalog records from OCLC, RLIN, and LC, a major step forward in the realization of a single database for acquisitions and catalog records and an online public catalog.

Simultaneously with the development and planning for the Distributable Union Catalog, a Subcommittee for Bibliographic Standards, reporting to the Harvard University Library Union Catalog Planning Committee, had been established to develop a University Library bibliographic standard to be followed by all units contributing to the Distributable Union Catalog. The standard agreed upon had three main features: First, catalog records were to be created according to the *Anglo-American Cataloguing Rules* as implemented by LC with subject headings according to one of two national systems, *Library of Congress Subject Headings* or *Medical Subject Headings*; second, acquisition records were to have description based on the International Standard Bibliographic Description and access points in agreement with those in use in the Distributable Union Catalog (with the form of entry used on catalog records having priority over the form used on acquisition records); and third, duplicate records were

From its beginnings, the Distributable Union Catalog contained a number of conflicts. For example, because of the change in headings resulting from changed corporate body entry rules, the Distributable Union Catalog had more than 1,200 split files with some files representing several hundred occurrences of the heading. In addition to the consciously split files, there were countless conflicts of entry. The task of recognizing and reporting conflicts had been placed on all Distributable Union Catalog users, both librarians and the public. The burden of conflict resolution and file maintenance was divided between individual cataloging units and a Union Catalog Services Office. Topical subject authority control was centralized from the beginning. With the tapeloading of files from institutions affiliated with Harvard as well as from retrospective conversion projects, file maintenance has become increasingly more challenging.

IMPLICATIONS FOR THE NEW CATALOGER

The beginning cataloger at Harvard is now confronted with a file of more than two million records in HOLLIS, including 1,513,024 bibliographic records and 134,680 authority records.[6] The cataloger has available a variety of ways to create, control, and maintain the file, including the OCLC database and the LC MUMS file.

Stated in more abstract terms, the novice has embarked on work that has as its goal the service of the library's users through the imposition of bibliographic control on the library's materials.

Because of Widener's commitments, the library's users are, in fact, a diverse group extending far beyond Widener Library. In addition to Harvard faculty, students, and libraries, it includes users of the OCLC and RLIN databases, CONSER participants, and even staff members of Processing Services at the Library of Congress.

Service must be construed broadly as the creation of bibliographic and authority records for Harvard University Library, OCLC, and the Library of Congress, authority work and file maintenance for all Harvard libraries, as well as work on national and University Library committees.

Finally, bibliographic control takes a variety of forms in Widener moving along a spectrum of increasingly more complex records. At one end of the spectrum library assistants upgrade existing order records by searching the name heading to see that it is in the established form and by editing the title field to insure its accuracy. Newly received serial analytics and monographs in series are given brief temporary records with title and at least one name access point. Standard bibliographic records for monographs may range from minimal level cataloging to cataloging in full agreement with LC standards.

The novice cataloger must be brought to an appreciation and mastery of this complexity in the most expeditious way while contributing to the accomplishment of the Department's production goals for the year. In other words, the cataloger is no longer in a classroom setting where a greater degree of control over the materials presented can be accomplished, but in the workplace. Further, the novice is competing not for a grade, but for a reappointment on a career track.

THE TRAINING METHODOLOGY

As managers of the cataloging process, we have the goal of bringing the beginner to full or nearly full productivity as quickly as possible. Over the years, we have used a variety of ways to do this.

First and most essential is an apprenticeship with an experienced senior cataloger-reviser who builds upon the knowledge of the trainee to teach the creation of bibliographic and authority records and file maintenance. Although knowledge of individual rules or the details of tagging are useful, the primary goal of the reviser at this point is to develop the habit of research in the cataloger, so that s/he will become skilled in the use of the documentation. The oral traditions of an earlier day have largely disappeared, but in their stead have appeared looseleaf binder after looseleaf binder filled with USMARC tag tables, LC rule interpretations and manuals of practice, and local formats and policies. New catalogers must learn quickly that, although some of these details become second nature, it is important to know when and where to look for the information needed to handle new situations. The cataloger has to appreciate the importance and magnitude of the task of assimilating the flow of documentation--virtually an impossibility--that comes at us from within Harvard University Library and from without.

Under the supervision of a skilled reviser, the beginner soon learns to understand the meaning of rule-governed creativity.

Where should the novice begin? We have always begun with descriptive cataloging. When all Widener cataloging was original because we had our own descriptive policies, subject heading list, and classification schedules, the beginner, working with searching slips prepared by library assistants, edited the descriptive cataloging on LC printed cards or cards prepared very skillfully in our typing section. In recent years, we have introduced cataloging with the editing of OCLC member copy, the writing out of original worksheets, or LC copy cataloging. No one method proved obviously more effective than the others. LC copy cataloging, however, has become more a matter of what the library assistant is to overlook, and so it has proved confusing to original catalogers to be trained following the guidelines used by the library assistants. Original cataloging, on the other hand, assumes a broad familiarity with standards and policies and so can be slow and frustrating to the beginner, who becomes bogged down in the documentation.

Most recently, we have started the novice cataloger with books that have LC copy, so that s/he can see the relationship between the encoding and the bibliographic content of the record, the link between authority and bibliographic records, and the connection between the one record in hand and the bibliographic entity it represents and the rest of the HOLLIS universe.

At the same time, the orientation of the newcomer to the library and the university begins. With the increased sensitivity to individual needs that is a beneficent legacy of the sixties, the university has an orientation session for new staff, where personnel staff in the library explain benefits and rights, and the University Library also has a standing committee on communication and orientation. Within Widener, the reference staff has weekly tours of the library. We encourage participation in all these activities.

Further, as the automation of Harvard University Library has progressed, the number of consultative and advisory committees has grown, and it is common for these groups to hold public meetings to explain and review their recommendations. Attendance at these meetings is fostered, and their reports are widely available. The observant newcomer will become quickly aware of the diverse, demanding, changing, and sometimes bizarre world s/he has entered.

To make the workings of the Department more familiar, the beginner usually spends at least two hours a day on cataloging support activities. First, the cataloger searches and inputs at an OCLC terminal to gain extended hands-on contact with that database and learns how to use HOLLIS. (In the past some catalogers easily forgot the catalog for which they were preparing records, leaving the coherence of the catalog to a catalog maintenance section, but with HOLLIS, the direct involvement of the catalogers is necessary.) Finally, the beginner may review lists of headings on LC copy identified as new to the file, doing authority work and identifying necessary file maintenance. With these assignments, we hope to instill in the beginner an appreciation for the contribution of the library assistants to the accomplishment of the Departmental mission.

I noted earlier that training has to meet the needs of the workplace, but some accommodations to the beginner are made. For example, although foreign language skills are of primary importance to us when hiring, we begin training with English language materials, adding foreign language works as soon as possible. The reviser will sort through incoming materials trying to begin with single volume works by personal authors, moving on to multivolume monographs and corporate bodies as soon as it is deemed reasonable.

As the cataloger gains proficiency and develops an ability to recognize problems, the reviser will allow the newcomer to forward materials without revision.

Meanwhile, the novice serial cataloger follows a parallel path, beginning with a concentration on descriptive cataloging.[7] At first, the cataloger works with printouts of LC copy, 50 percent of which require modification because of the nature of serials. S/he is encouraged to study the documentation, including the serials format, the *CONSER Editing Guide*, and the Harvard University Library holdings format, the local implementation of the USMARC Holdings Format. The cataloger must also prepare the related authority and holdings records for HOLLIS. Then, the beginner moves on to handling OCLC member copy. The University Library is a self-authenticating CONSER participant, and so the cataloger soon finds it necessary to prepare NACO records for many headings. As soon as it is feasible, the novice begins original cataloging. Throughout this process, revision is done on a daily basis.

Additional activities include training in both OCLC and HOLLIS, so that the cataloger understands the nature of the databases, search strategies, and file maintenance. Because of a limited number of terminals the inputting of records is done by library assistants in the batch mode.

Not only does the beginning serials cataloger work with automated files, but--a major difference between serial and monograph cataloging--s/he also has to understand the earlier manual catalogs in order to deal with title changes. These older records reflect decades of different standards and local practices. A serials cataloger also must learn to interpret the related acquisitions records, such as the Visible Records of receipts and the serials authority records.

Because the Section is responsible for establishing numbered series, beginners are trained to make series authority records as soon as they have enough experience with HOLLIS. After the novice cataloger, whether working with serials or monographs, has spent three or more months focusing on descriptive cataloging, s/he joins other new catalogers in two series of classes conducted by the Chief Subject Cataloger, Peter Lisbon.[8] Meeting four times a week for over a month, the group first progresses through the LC classification schedules. Mr. Lisbon begins with Q (Science), R (Medicine), S (Agriculture), T (Technology), U (Military science), and V (Naval science), because he considers these classes more straightforward. In the meetings, he points out the scope of each class, its special features, problems, and pitfalls. Trainees are asked to spend 20-30 minutes a day looking up numbers in our shelflist to familiarize themselves with their construction. Then he moves on to D, E, and F, the history classes. C (Auxiliary science of history), G (Geography, Anthropology, etc.), J (Political science), and K (Law) follow. (As the Library of Congress has published its K classes, each has been adopted in Widener and the corresponding local class has been discontinued.) With the study of H (Social sciences), the group has reached a halfway mark, and after a brief introduction to subject heading practice, actual classification of some books is begun. Next M (Music), N (Fine arts), and L (Education) are discussed, followed by B (Philosophy and religion). Four sessions are devoted to the P classes (Philology and literature) because of their complexity and their importance to us. The survey of the LC classification concludes with A (General works) and Z (Bibliography and Library science). A general review with a discussion of shelflisting matters and the strategy of classification follows. A brief summary of the Old Widener classes still in use (for reference books, government documents, restricted access materials, and deposit library items) completes this first series of meetings.

The second series consists of one hour meetings for six to seven weeks. Trainees are assigned readings in the LC subject heading manual, which most people find a chore, and they do the classification and subject analysis of books which they have descriptively cataloged. Revision of their work continues for a year, gradually tapering off. Mr. Lisbon finds that it may take several weeks for a basic misconception to surface and so considers the extended revision necessary.

PROGRESS AND EVALUATION

Clearly, progress is a matter of individual ability. The principal reviser must constantly evaluate and report progress both to the individual and to the departmental administration, which depends heavily on the reviser to manage the development of its new member. Most people are not eager to evaluate others, and I have found that the less suited a person is for a job, the less likely the person is to recognize the fact. In cataloging, the performance evaluation is particularly difficult because of the terms in which it must be presented, the details of the cataloging process and its products. It is hard for a trainee, an administrator, or a personnel officer not to see the criticism as nitpicking. The most effective measure for all parties in the process is regular and open communication about overall performance and progress, both the successes and the failures. Because cataloging is such detailed work, it is easy for a reviser to focus on individual mistakes and assume that the novice will be able to deduce the quality of the overall performance from a recital or terse written record of single errors. The novice has no context in which to place these errors, and so it is the job of the reviser to do it.

The focus of the first year is the mastery of the basic activity of cataloging, the creation of bibliographic records describing, classifying, and analyzing the works added to the collection, and the related authority and file maintenance tasks. During this first year the groundwork, however, is laid for the larger task of the cataloging professional, the bibliographic control of the library's materials. Beginners must develop the understanding that will enable them to use limited resources of personnel and time to the greatest benefit of the library's users. Issues such as analytic practice, microform processing, minimal level cataloging, and series treatment must be addressed. With the increased participation in the creation and use of a shared database by staff from all quarters of the library, the professional cataloger is called on to define, explain, and maintain standards. The habits of mind that enable the professional to carry out this mission successfully are developed during the first year.

Finally, in the first year, the beginner should come to take pride in membership in an anonymous community of artisans who work to give the public greater access to the library's riches.

NOTES

1. I wish to acknowledge my appreciation of the training given me by my first revisers, Edith Clitheroe, formerly Chief Serial Cataloger at the John Hay Library, Brown University, and Alfreda Williston, formerly Chief Cataloger in the Harvard College Library.

2. Nancy R. John. "Descriptive Cataloguing in the USA." *International Cataloguing* 14 (October/December 1985):42.

3. "Second Edition of DUC." *HUL Notes,* No. 643 (March 4, 1982):1.

4. "Introduction to HOLLIS." *HOLLIS Reference Manual,* 2d ed., rev. (Cambridge, Mass.: Harvard University Library Office for Systems Planning and Research, 1988), pp. 1.1-1.2.

5. CONSER stands for Conversion of Serials, a cooperative project begun in 1976, sponsored by the Council on Library Resources, for the purpose of creating a database of bibliographic records for serial titles.

6. "HOLLIS Summary Statistics, April 1, 1988." *HOLLIS Newsletter* 3 (May 1988):8.

7. Interview with Ellen Andersson, Chief Serial Cataloger, Harvard College Library, October 25, 1988.
8. Interview with Peter Lisbon, Chief Subject Cataloger, Harvard College Library, October 21, 1988.

Standards, Volume, and Trust in the Shared Cataloging Environment: Training Approaches for the Smaller Library

Barbra Buckner Higginbotham

The cultural history of American library cataloging includes a long and honored tradition of meticulous training. In the latter part of the previous century and the early years of the present, before Library of Congress card distribution introduced the possibility of copy cataloging, every cataloger required careful schooling in the code, classification, and subject headings the institution employed; this process also included tutelage in a generous amount of local practice. An 1894 survey of 58 American libraries showed that, while Cutter's *Rules for a Printed Dictionary Catalog* was the guide "'most generally followed,'" few libraries employed a single code; rather, most combined one or two, making many adjustments for local needs.[1]

With the advent of the Library of Congress' (LC) card distribution service in 1901 and the rapid increase in quantity and availability of LC cataloging copy, many libraries greatly reduced their emphasis on the cataloger's painstaking education. Most bibliographic records were developed in Washington, D.C., and those few exceptions created by local staff were done fairly quickly, by imitation. The only consumers for the library's handiwork were its own readers, a group with little awareness of bibliographic standards. In this environment where LC copy predominated, authority work often did not exist; the local library relied upon the national library to provide consistency in headings and might or might not acquire and file its cross references.

In libraries doing a significant amount of original cataloging, the need for thorough training of personnel continued; however, like the libraries primarily dependent on LC copy, these institutions had no one to please but themselves and their own clientele. As a result, a great deal of local custom continued to influence cataloging practice, even when national standards generally were followed. It was the advent of the bibliographic utilities and electronically shared cataloging which introduced a training problem heretofore of little significance. Suddenly, one's original cataloging was not only instantly available to others for their use, but also subject to certain standards.

THE NEED FOR STANDARDS

Even the library happy with its own bibliographic eccentricities might find these unacceptable to the network requiring adherence to national standards, or to member institutions who are potential consumers of its product. Hafter points out that catalogers in libraries which are network participants are keenly aware of their work's visibility to peers across the nation, and of blacklists of libraries whose work is considered substandard; network quality-control staff and catalogers in sister institutions also search for and report cataloging errors.[2] How then can the smaller library which produces a considerable amount of original cataloging (perhaps a special library of some sort) ensure that its staff is thoroughly versed in standard cataloging and authority work, and thus a welcome contributor to the network?

Training new original catalogers has never been a serious problem for the larger library. This is not to say it is not a costly process, but at least staff proficient in cataloging practice and accomplished at training (these being two different skills) are present and can provide the breadth and depth of instruction needed even by those whose library education included a first-rate course in the control of library materials, and perhaps a cataloging internship as well. But in the smaller library which employs only a handful of catalogers, it is very difficult for a beginning librarian to get the intensive, thorough tutoring he or she needs. Of course, such libraries can resort to hiring only seasoned staff, but current library literature points to a shortage of catalogers, making such a solution both costly and impractical.

Perhaps those most aware of the problem of training original catalogers in smaller libraries are cataloging administrators in larger libraries that belong to the same network. Just as these larger libraries produce quantities of original work, they seek to identify and use even greater amounts of copy cataloging. When so-called member copy is of such poor quality that it must be referred to highly paid professional staff for evaluation and revision, rather than routinely processed by supporting staff as Library of Congress records are, the real effects of the smaller library's training problem are felt. It seems appropriate, then, that these larger libraries play a part in finding a solution.

A NEW WAY TO TRAIN QUALITY CATALOGERS

Networks, such as OCLC (Online Computer Library Center), RLIN (Research Libraries Information Network, WLN (Western Library Network), and UTLAS (University of Toronto Libraries Automated System), should coordinate internships in the original cataloging departments of larger libraries for staff from smaller institutions. There is evidence that some networks have recognized and made efforts to address the problem of the underprepared cataloger. Hafter cites one OCLC regional affiliate which assigns "master catalogers" in member institutions to review and critique the work of new or struggling libraries, and Intner notes another that has considered offering basic training sessions for copy catalogers or professionals wishing to refresh their skills.[3] The NACO training Library of Congress provides for libraries contributing authority records to the Name Authority Cooperative Project shows that cataloging internships work. Under the program proposed in this paper, while the home institution would bear the costs associated with sending its staff member to intern, including transportation, housing, meals, and other incidentals, the host library would provide the training at no direct cost to the trainee's organization. The network could compensate the host library for each intern either through some sort of direct payment or through a reduction in network charges.

There are certainly difficulties with this approach, not the least of which is that no library can afford to support a staff member at another institution for the six months minimally required to train an original cataloger, nor are there many libraries that can host a continuing stream of interns for this period. So, it is a given that the training period would have to be shorter (perhaps two months), highly structured, and very intensive. Even then, only the library producing a significant amount of original cataloging could afford to invest in such a program, and only for such a library could another network member justify providing such a training program.

How could such a series of internships be developed and administered? Within the Research Libraries Group, this work should occur at the network level, while the much larger OCLC network would probably choose to organize such a program within the regional networks, where a variety of more modest training programs are already planned and conducted. Criteria for host institutions might include the production of a significant amount of original cataloging that meets both network and national standards as well as good cataloging productivity. Those being sent to intern should learn in an environment which displays not only excellent cataloging practice, but also a solid appreciation of the economics of the cataloging process. Most networks already have several potential sources of host institutions, including those libraries whose staff may serve on network advisory councils, act as "approved revisers" of other members' records, or appear in the information banks maintained by some utilities of skilled catalogers willing to act as consultants.[4] Conversely, it would be wise to eliminate institutions that submit disproportionately large numbers of cataloging error reports, thereby avoiding libraries whose staff seem to spend considerable amounts of time scrutinizing and redoing the work of their peers, perhaps out of some unprofitable sense of competition.[5]

A commitment should also be required from libraries sending staff to intern. In addition to providing financial obligation should include the contribution of a certain number of original records to the database in the year following the internship, said records to meet network and national standards. Ideally, a board of evaluators should be established within each network (or, in the case of OCLC, regional network) to identify potential host and guest institutions, review applications from both types of libraries, and arrange suitable matches. This board should also develop the precise criteria by which participating libraries will be selected, and publicize them. Guest libraries whose records are of importance to the network, either in terms of quantity or subject coverage, should receive priority consideration. The board might or might not attempt to match host and guest libraries' subject specialties; normally, this should not be necessary (and might be unduly limiting in assigning host libraries), since one should be able to assume that the guest library has hired the staff member whom it sends to intern because he or she has relevant subject skills.

BENEFITS OF INTERNSHIP PROGRAMS

The benefits of this internship program go beyond those accruing to the library which, for the cost of air fare, lodging, and meals for two months (on the average, excluding salary, perhaps $3,000), buys excellent cataloging training. The network and each of its members benefits in that the quality of member copy is enhanced; if the program succeeds in placing interns in libraries that exhibit good productivity, the quantity of records in the database will also increase. The program will promote adherence to national bibliographic standards, and curb local idiosyncrasy (which, one excellent cataloger noted, took her "longer to learn than the [expletive deleted] code"). Arguably, excessive emphasis on complex local practice not only makes the utilities' databases less generally useful but also inhibits productivity and even career growth, as librarians become less easily interchangeable and more uncertain about the boundaries between national standards and local custom.

A more subtle benefit will be the evolution of a body of librarians whose cataloging reflects an understanding of the spirit of the code, and the ability to generalize from that spirit and the rules which exemplify it to those hundreds of bibliographic problems for which there is no specific rule. While this approach to cataloging was prescribed by Cutter ("No rules can take the place of experience and good judgment, but some of the results of experience may be best indicated by rules") and underscored recently by Intner (if librarians "are taught how to solve problems, what ideas drive the rules and are embodied in the tools they use, then they can handle real life cataloging"), those denied proper training often slavishly search for example when the rules fail them.[6] Catalogers who can conceptualize are more productive and feel greater confidence in making a decision and moving on to another title; conceptualizing works against the literalism and fear of error which characterize the cataloger whose productivity is low. In a smaller environment, where there is little opportunity for the revision and intensive cataloging necessary for the development of a fine cataloger, it is very difficult for this appreciation of the vitality of the code to develop.

DEVELOPMENT OF TRUST

Such a training approach will also serve to enhance the sense of trust catalogers feel in the work of others. Even in today's era of electronically shared cataloging, an unsettling and unhealthy parochialism still characterizes many catalogers' approach to their work. There remains a great deal of revision by one library's original catalogers of the work done by similar staff at other institutions. This lack of trust in the work of others hinders the growth of the database, the growth of individual library catalogs, and the professional growth of catalogers, as they dissect and redo the work of others, rather than create new records themselves. An internship program such as the one suggested has much to contribute in promoting that vital atmosphere of trust necessary for the development of a large body of quality cataloging records. It will help to alleviate the time- consuming accumulation of self-justifying documentation which Hafter describes as some librarians' response to network error reports.[7]

SPECIALIZED INTERNSHIPS FOR RARE BOOK CATALOGERS

Even though the internships described in this paper are designed for smaller libraries doing original cataloging of mainstream library materials, some variation on this program could be useful in training rare book catalogers. It is important to consider, however, that the balance among the three elements in the major goal of cataloging (the timely creation of records which accurately represent the item and provide adequate access to it) is different for rare books than for general materials. When cataloging rare materials, the matters of timeliness (productivity) and access undoubtedly take a back seat to the objective of creating a record which accurately represents the item in hand. Thus, placing rare book interns in libraries where productivity is high will be unimportant (or inadvisable), since what one technical services librarian calls the "Take no prisoners!" approach to cataloging is inappropriate for such materials. Likewise, while rare book catalogers should certainly be trained in authority control and rules governing the development of access points, there are often many ways, other than the library's catalog, of providing access to special materials. It is the rare book cataloger's mandate to produce a record which mirrors and captures the essence of the book in hand, in many cases to the copy level, which is most important for the rare book intern, who should create a shadow of the item that will live on, whatever becomes of the book itself. For this reason, criteria both for host and guest institutions will be different when rare book internships are arranged.

FUNDING A PILOT PROJECT

A network whose members are interested in exploring such a program of internships might well find foundation or other grant support for a pilot project whose effectiveness the entire membership could assess. During the project period, host libraries should receive heavier subsidies than would be the case were the program subsequently to be incorporated by the network. Likewise, the grant should partially support the expenses guest institutions incur when they send staff to intern. In this way, the network should be able to find both host and guest institutions willing to participate in the pilot program.

A SECOND APPROACH

While not so personal and direct as the internship program outlined above, a second useful approach to the training problems experienced by smaller libraries would be electronic access to a merged version of the cataloging code, its revisions, and the Library of Congress' rule interpretations. Large libraries have large staffs and thus find it easier to keep up with the rule interpretations issued in LC's *Cataloging Service Bulletin (CSB*--ruefully dubbed by one cataloger as "those quarterly jolts from the Library of Congress"). As a result, their cataloging is more consistent with that done by the de facto national library. Also, larger libraries often have the luxury of a principal cataloger, one whose job includes complete familiarity with the code and its many interpretations; such a resource is invaluable to other catalogers. In smaller libraries, however, catalogers generally juggle the code and the *CSB*'s as best they can, not always doing a thorough job of searching for the applicable rule, or its latest explication.

For such libraries (indeed, for almost any library) an electronic version of the cataloging code with the rule interpretations merged appropriately would be a godsend. Hours of frustrating cutting, pasting, interfiling, and searching could be eliminated if such a product were available and searchable by keyword. The appropriate electronic format is debatable. Since most catalogers now have network access to LC's subject and name authorities, online access to this augmented code-plus-interpretations product would have appeal. However, since such access is expensive, perhaps a CD-ROM product, updated and reissued quarterly, would be a more cost effective approach. Regardless of which approach is chosen, the point remains that, so long as catalogers rely heavily on a lengthy and complex code, as well as external interpretations of its various rules, their work is made much easier by quick, convenient, integrated access to both.

FURTHER EXAMINATION OF THE PROBLEM

This paper has been written within the context of cataloging as we know it today, and has sought to address a given training problem within the framework of the cataloging code, subject control, and classification systems currently in place in libraries in the United States. Nonetheless, thinking about the specific training problem addressed here, as well as the additional problems our current system presents for educating, recruiting, and training catalogers, ends by creating a sense of doubt about the validity of this approach. As White notes, we tend to seek solutions within "existing protocols of descriptive analysis, rather than look at opportunities to reexamine the premises initially developed" for the cataloging process.[8] Perhaps we may choose the wrong solutions because we are isolating and addressing the wrong problems. Perhaps, rather than asking ourselves how we might best solve problems associated with the way we do things now, we would better push the debate back to an earlier point by asking ourselves to what end we are cataloging, and whether or not we ought to be cataloging differently from the way we now elect, in order better to meet those ends.

For example, if we believe the purpose of cataloging is the timely creation of records which accurately represent the item and provide adequate access to it, perhaps a more useful expenditure of our efforts would be an exploration of the ways in which we presently attempt to achieve this goal, and a reassessment of their effectiveness. In many ways, to undertake so great a task is frightening; at the very least, the reevaluation of the ways in which we provide description and access to library materials would be enormously time-consuming, and it could indicate major changes to our present, familiar mechanisms. One fundamental question identified by White as not yet fully addressed is that of analysis versus retrieval, and which merits the greater attention; similarly, Hafter highlights "the growing doubts of many professionals about the validity of traditional cataloging standards in the new online environment."[9] Were our profession seriously to occupy itself with either of these questions, cataloging as we now know it could be completely transformed, along with the education, this one which calls upon some of our profession's major thinkers to address the relevancy of contemporary methods of description and access to the modern scholarly approach would certainly have merit, and command the attention of researchers, library administrators, and technical specialists alike.

NOTES

1. Kathryn L. Henderson, "Treated with a Degree of Uniformity and Common Sense: Descriptive Cataloging in the United States--1876-1976." *Library Trends* 25 (July 1976):225.
2. Ruth Hafter, "Born-Again Cataloging in the Online Networks." *College & Research Libraries* 47 (July 1986):361.
3. Hafter, p. 363; Sheila S. Intner, "Debunking More Cataloging Myths." *Technicalities* 7 (April 1987):10.
4. Hafter, p. 361-63.
5. Ibid., p. 363.
6. Charles A. Cutter. *Rules for a Dictionary Catalog*, 4th ed. (Washington, D.C.: U.S. Government Printing Office, 1904), p. 6; Intner, p. 9.
7. Hafter, p. 362.
8. Herbert S. White. "Catalogers--Yesterday, Today, Tomorrow." *Library Journal* 112 (Apr. 1, 1987):48.
9. Ruth Hafter. *Academic Librarians and Cataloging Networks: Visibility, Quality Control, and Professional Status*, Contributions in Librarianship and Information Science, No. 57 (Westport, Conn.: Greenwood Press, 1986), p. 129.

Dollars and Sense: Training Catalogers

Karin A. Trainer

A myth has crept into our profession that in some golden age, catalogers emerged from library school like Athena from the brow of Zeus, perfectly shaped and fully armed. My previous experience as a technical services administrator, as well as my reading of the historical record, suggests that this is not so and that we are deluding ourselves in regarding cataloging training as something that our predecessors did well, but for which we unluckily have lost the knack. In any case, hankering after the past, whether real or illusory, is rarely a productive activity. It makes more sense to look forward: to try to determine the skills our catalogers will need in the future, to find methods by which those skills can be developed, and to locate the resources required to support the skills development.

TRAINING CATALOGERS: WHAT DO THEY NEED?

Looking ahead, I expect our definition of a good cataloger will be expanded to require the mastery of four distinct skill groups, which I refer to as technical, theoretical, supervisory, and strategic. The need for technical skills is the least controversial, having been around the longest in one guise or another.

Catalogers traditionally have taken responsibility for learning to employ technical systems, from the early library script to the modern network terminal capable of displaying Chinese, Japanese, and Korean characters. On the one hand, they have been charged to understand and stay abreast of complicated national practices, as revealed in successive editions of cataloging rules (red, green, and orange), classification schemes, subject headings lists, bibliographic utility newsletters, and bulletins from the Library of Congress. At the same time, catalogers have been expected to learn very detailed local practices, such as local rules for shelflisting, call number marking, and serials control.

There is no sign that the amount of technical information falling under the purview of the catalog department will decrease with passing time. On the contrary, the growing number of formats in which information is published, and the addition to library catalogs of descriptions of materials owned outside the library (e.g., numeric data files residing in someone's office), are adding to the complexity of daily work. The installation of online catalogs and integrated library systems has further increased the technical complexity of cataloging functions. It is reasonable to assume that, as in the past, libraries will continue to look to their catalogers for mastery over the technical procedures and detail necessary to keep collections organized and accessible.

While expected to possess these technical skills, catalogers in the future will be using them in a different way than their predecessors did. The change is already underway. More and more libraries are discovering that they can no longer afford to have professional catalogers be mostly catalogers.

With the decrease in the amount of original cataloging to be done locally, and because of economic pressures, cataloging is being turned into an activity for non-professionals--and someone must train them in the technical aspects of cataloging and supervise them. This responsibility typically is falling to the professional cataloger, who is becoming a cataloging manager, whether formally called that or not. It is this trend that leads me to cite supervisory skills as a necessary unit in the professional's training program.

"Supervisory skills," as I use the expression here, encompass all of those human resources abilities necessary to keep a work group moving forward. A cataloging professional's own development will, therefore, be incomplete if it stops with the acquisition of technical skills. Rather, the person must be able to teach those technical skills to others in an effective way, to communicate, to motivate, to make good hiring and evaluation decisions, and to create the kind of climate in which good work takes place.

A good grasp of the theoretical underpinnings of bibliographic organization is the third kind of competency we will demand of cataloging professionals. Training in this area used to be a routine part of the library school curriculum, but my experience with recent graduates suggests that in some schools it now gets short shrift. This is ironic, because the need to have a sound theoretical basis for devising effective access systems for information has never been stronger. For one thing, local machine-readable files are being created everywhere--for example, in faculty offices, community agencies, and commercial firms--and the combined forces of user demand and advancing technology will result in these files becoming available for searching through libraries' systems. The usefulness of these files would increase were catalogers to begin working with the file designers to insure that they incorporate reasonable principles of descriptive and subject control. We should also be mindful that the present generation of online catalogs will seem obsolete in five to eight years, and catalogers must be prepared to serve as expert advisers on the caliber of the proposed replacements.

Finally, the cataloger of the future must be conversant with techniques for planning and research. As libraries move toward the twenty-first century, surrounded by more and more information technology and many extra players in the information marketplace, the demand for research pertaining to bibliographic control, including catalog use, will become more pressing. While I would not go so far as to argue that every cataloger needs to possess all of the skills necessary to conduct a methodologically and statistically sound study of, say, patrons' use of subject headings, I do think that some should, and that the others must have at least enough training to be intelligent evaluators of other librarians' research. Similarly, modern catalogers should be knowledgeable about strategic planning and forecasting in order to be in a position to provide the level of leadership their institutions need.

TRAINING CATALOGING LIBRARIANS--HOW DO WE DO IT?

The skills outlined above are such a varied lot that it is hard to imagine encompassing them in a single curriculum with a single method for training. They also are not the kind of skills that can be taught once for all time: cataloging rules change, formats change, automation constantly opens up new options, theories of human behavior are revised, and innovations are incorporated in research technique. The issue of providing adequate training for professional catalogers, therefore, has two components, namely laying the basic foundation for cataloging work and then assuring that catalogers' skills continue to grow.

I know I speak for most library administrators when I say we believe that the responsibility for laying the foundation should rest with the library schools. I imagine the library schools believe this, too, but we seem to part ways when it comes to defining the skills that make up the foundation. Perhaps, the most serious problem emerging from our existing system for library education is that it is not a system at all. For a variety of reasons, library schools do not produce graduates with a predictable set of skills or skills that prospective employers feel are relevant. One way to break through this impasse is to work together to arrive at what other professions call their common body of knowledge. Graduates are expected to leave school having mastered all of the topics outlined in the common body of knowledge, and the accreditation process for the school themselves includes an assessment of the match between their curriculum and the common body of knowledge. Since our professional accreditation process already is thought to be at a crossroad, this may be exactly the right time to lobby for a common body of knowledge agreement.

Providing opportunities for catalogers to further their training is a responsibility shared by employing institutions, professional associations, and the librarians themselves. Many different models for accomplishing this extra training have been found to be effective, including internships, professional institutes, one-on-one training, enrollment in courses at local universities, participation in conferences, job exchanges, and self-directed study. The problem in extending these opportunities for development is not that we cannot find workable training methods, but, rather, that we tell ourselves we cannot afford them.

TRAINING CATALOGERS: HOW CAN WE AFFORD IT?

The best answer to this question is really another question: How can we afford not to do it? Library cost cutting campaigns frequently begin with reductions in the lines for staff training and travel, but that method of "saving" money is wrongheaded, a fact that is easier to demonstrate in the cataloging arena than in any other realm of library operation.

As every library budget officer knows, cataloging departments are big cost centers; they are also operations with good track records for keeping output statistics in categories of work that are easy to define (e.g., titles searched, titles cataloged, authority records created). If cataloging professionals, indeed, were skilled in the four fields I cited earlier, they would be in a strong position to help their departments achieve measurable improvements in output, eliminate waste, and contain or reduce unit costs; they could engage in long-range planning and generate businesslike predictions for capital, staffing, and equipment needs. We should remember, too, that there are human costs associated with not training our catalogers: The first cost is the catalogers' diminished feelings of job satisfaction; the second is borne by the patrons, who are less well served when the cataloging professionals are incapable of taking on the research and design roles I suggested.

Financial support for training cataloging professionals after library school can be drawn from a number of sources, either separately or together, beginning with the cataloger's own pocket. There is a faction that holds that people derive most from a learning experience, whether a supervisory skills course or a therapeutic hour, when they are required to foot the bill themselves. This is not always practical in librarianship, one of the least lucrative of the so-called professions, and it puts young librarians with educational loans outstanding at a particular disadvantage. Determining the circumstances under which it is reasonable to expect a librarian to contribute to the cost of his or her own development is a fine art and a frequent subject of policy review.

Many kinds of training can be implemented with little or no direct financial outlay by either the cataloger or the library. Bringing in local experts to speak, promoting internal job exchanges, providing facilities for study groups, and sponsoring research forums are examples of steps libraries can take to foster catalogers' development without spending much hard cash. Of course, these activities do involve spending other kinds of resources, but they generally are easier resources for libraries to acquire.

When hard cash is needed for a project, administrators typically try to find it through internal budget reallocation, through proposals to government agencies and private foundations, or through new money coaxed out of the parent organization. In the current climate of rising prices for library materials and automated services, convincing parent institutions to add extra money to the training budget may be tough. The most promising strategy for winning this kind of extra money likely lies in conducting cost benefit analyses to demonstrate the financial wisdom of investing in broadening catalogers' skills. Where circumstances prevent the parent organization from making this kind of commitment, training proponents should scrutinize the cataloging department's own budget. Building a larger training fund through reallocation of departmental resources is an especially viable option for cataloging units, because their large size relative to other sections of the library gives them special flexibility. It is not pleasant to make choices about which piece of equipment to eliminate or which student hours to shave, but refusing to consider such measures implicitly reinforces the status quo at the expense of the future.

Seeking grant funds to support special training for cataloging librarians is rarely done, but seems a fruitful avenue to investigate. By the time the Simmons College Symposium takes place, I hope my Yale University colleage Gerald Lowell, Associate University Librarian for Technical Services, will be available to describe an innovative training program he is implementing with the help of the Council on Library Resources. His experiences may suggest productive new directions for other institutions to explore.

CONCLUSION

Finding the means to give cataloging librarians the training they need for the years ahead is a shared responsibility. Employers have it, library schools have it, professional organizations have it, and so do the cataloging librarians themselves. The rate at which we progress will be determined in large part by the degree to which we cooperate with each other and look for common solutions to our common problem.

Using Management Tools
for Cataloging Discussions

D. Kathryn Weintraub

INTRODUCTION

In 1981, the Library at the University of California, Irvine introduced a series of workshops in order to review the provisions of the then new catalog code and other national standards with members of the Catalog Department. These workshops were succeeded by two series of continuing meetings: One for some upper level library assistants (the Greater LAs, as they call themselves); and the other for the catalog librarians. This latter group kept their original name, "The Librarians' Workshop".

The purpose of these continuing meetings is to review the provisions of newly published standards such as the Library of Congress (LC) rule interpretations for descriptive cataloging, the LC subject manual, shelflisting manual, etc. There is considerable overlap of content between the two series of meetings, but as principal librarian, I spend more time in exposition with the Greater LAs and more time in discussion with the librarians.

There are already some reports in the literature on problems of structuring workshops in a cataloging department, e.g. those of Judith Hudson,[1] Catherine Ann Carter,[2] and Lois Kershner.[3] I have also reported elsewhere on some of the criteria upon which our program was based.[4] These reports have generally emphasized the need for careful preparation, clear exposition, and the opportunity for participants to prepare, review and practice new techniques.

When ongoing discussions are planned for experienced, knowledgeable and practicing catalogers, the emphasis shifts from formal presentations to discussions where participants share what they have learned from their own work and where they sometimes reach conclusions that no one of them (including myself as convenor of the meeting) would have reached independently. In order to facilitate such discussions, it is necessary to provide a formal framework for the discourse, a means for recording and organizing the findings of these meetings, and, ultimately, a means for evaluating the program. My purpose here is not to give a detailed prescription for how to do this; indeed, I am not sure such a recipe is possible, but rather to describe some tools I have developed that have proven useful for our discussions. These tools are a set of flow charts, a dBASE datafile, and a Lotus spreadsheet.

USING FLOW CHARTS

Some flow charts are available in published form,[5],[6] but our flow charts are mostly handwritten and include some information that is not otherwise available. Not only do such charts provide a well defined sequence of steps for beginning catalogers; they also provide a formal framework for disciplined discussion of specific aspects of cataloging. The fact that they are handwritten also makes it easier, I think, for participants to propose changes. For example, after reading the new version of Chapter 23 of the *Anglo-American Cataloguing Rules*, second edition (*AACR* 2),[7] it has become clear to everyone that the charts for place names need extensive revision.

Flow chart analysis, however, has at least two other advantages. First, it helps to clarify a complicated procedure by emphasizing underlying similarities in operations that are superficially different. In the case of description of the item, for example, every area begins with a similar series of questions: What is the source of information for the area? How is it transcribed (i.e. is it copied as is the case for an edition statement or is the form of the statement code defined as is the case for statements in the physical description area)? If copied, what are the required modifications for that area? (i.e. Do *AACR* 2 Appendices A, B, or C apply to elements of this area?) What elements of this area should be recorded for this item? In what sequence? What is the prescribed punctuation? What notes are required in relation to the elements of this area in order to describe this item fully? The most immediate effect of this discussion in our department was to change the organization of the introductory workshop so that each area was introduced together with the rules for notes that relate to that area.

Flow chart analysis also clarifies dependencies between one area and another. For the most part, our analysis of *AACR* 2 has led to the conclusion that the code is defined in a logical sequence. The main problems we have found are those that relate to horizontal and hierarchical relationships. Horizontal relations are those which link versions of an item (e.g. printings, reprints, editions, translations, etc.) and hierarchical relations are those which link the whole to its parts (e.g. the relation between a series and its monographs).[8]

So far as hierarchical relations are concerned, once we understood the problem, our solution was to change the sequence of steps in our flow charts and ask catalogers to do all work relating to description and access for a series first before they do anything relating to the description of the individual item. This solution also applies to other items where hierarchical relations are involved, e.g. supplements or sequels, but we have had less difficulty with items that exemplify these other types of hierarchical relation.

Horizontal relations have proven far more difficult. While we generally manage to work through these problems as they arise, the solutions are largely ad hoc in character and, therefore, theoretically uninteresting. Catalogers are repeatedly admonished to re-read rule interpretation 1.0 and rule interpretation 1.4F6. The flow chart for determining the date of edition of an item (and therefore, in many cases, for determining whether it is a printing of an already cataloged edition or a new edition) is one of the more complicated charts. It is more-or-less routine to work through this chart several times with beginning catalogers. Sometimes, it is even necessary to repeat the description of these decisions in later discussions with experienced catalogers. Eventually, the catalogers reach a point where their solutions are consistent. Nevertheless, I think this is a topic where further research and code revision are needed.

USING dBASE DATAFILES

For a discussion to be useful, it is necessary to use examples that will help the participants solve the problems they deal with in their everyday work. Exercises, made-up title pages and worksheets have one important advantage: they ensure the organizer that a given body of material will be covered in a systematic manner. But such tools are rarely more than busy work when you are dealing with practicing catalogers who are both knowledgeable and experienced. What they need is to discuss how a given standard relates to the work they are actually doing.

Accordingly, I usually ask the participants to bring items and/or catalog records with which they have worked during the week and that also exemplify the type of problem addressed by the standard currently under review. These examples are invariably good. They truly represent the workflow of our own library. The fact that no one person has selected all of the examples to be discussed ensures that the meeting will be a discussion and not just a formal exposition of one individual's insights. The process of thinking through and explaining to one's peers the way in which a given record illustrates a solution to a particular problem helps the individuals to gain an understanding of specific problems. Once they have been able to think this through and explain it in their own words, they can then repeat the process in informal discussions with other catalogers within the department.

We do not want to lose such examples, but organizing the paper printouts of these records was a problem. Instead, I have developed a set of dBASE files to store the information. Each record includes the OCLC bibliographic or authority record number, the Library of Congress card number or authority record number (LCCN or ARCN) if the record is an LC record, a brief statement of the problem and the appropriate index term. The index terms, so far, are *AACR* 2 rule numbers, LC subject manual numbers, LC shelflisting manual numbers, or LC classification numbers. Figure 1 is a printout of a small sample from the file for bibliographic records indexed by *AACR* 2 rule number. This is our largest file since all catalogers participate to some degree in the discussions of descriptive cataloging. While the files do not differ greatly in principle from some other sample collections,[9,10,11] they do have some very specific advantages. First, the fact that it is an in-house file means that we can add, edit, or even delete as necessary. A standard exercise in an introductory workshop is to review the examples for a given rule and then say "something" about the examples. The "something" can be to suggest a change in the brief statement of the problem, or to suggest that it would be more appropriate to index the example under another rule number, or even, perhaps, that the record be deleted because the example is repetitive. Occasionally, a participant might simply elect to explain why an example is useful for clarifying the rule in question. It is even possible that the new trainees will supply additional examples that illustrate different situations. More recently, as the files have become more inclusive and therefore more useful, catalogers throughout the department have begun to supply additional examples from their workflow even when there is no discussion.

The arrangement by rule numbers emphasizes the need for catalogers to follow a prescribed sequence of steps and verify their decisions by consulting published standards. The examples consist of entire catalog records and this often clarifies the use of a particular note or emphasizes the relationship between different parts of a record. For example, if a record describes a new edition of a work with a changed title, there should be both a note and a title added entry as well as cuttering in the call number to bring the editions together. Similarly, if a work is a facsimile reprint, there should be a note, a small letter 'a' added to the date in the call number and some specific values in the fixed fields of the record.

Finally, these files are only an index to a volatile database and, therefore, the records can change as standards change. This is true especially if the standards affect the national authority file. Thus, the authority records that illustrate the rules for British place names still illustrate these rules, but the rules have changed and so have the authority records. Other changes are not so predictable. I had an excellent example of a contents note for a multi-volume set where volume 9 had two works and no collective title for the volume. After using this example many times, one day a cataloger came to me and said it was not much good. It is still an example of sorts, but the set has grown to 18 volumes and it now illustrates the fact that LC does not always supply contents notes for large sets.

USING LOTUS SPREADSHEETS

A formal system of evaluation is a necessary part of any program. It tells the participants that they are getting better; it tells management that something is happening; it tells the organizer what is and is not effective. One aspect of such a review is an analysis of the quality of work of individual catalogers. Figure 2 is a printout of a Lotus spreadsheet I have developed for recording the results of periodic reviews of the quality of work for individual catalogers.

The system is set up in such a way that a blank template appears on the screen and the inputter selects from a menu the cataloger whose figures are to be posted. At that point the name, date, file names, etc. are inserted into the blank template and into the relevant macros for the spreadsheet. After the new figures are entered, a second macro adds these values to the previously stored data for that cataloger, stores the file, prints an updated sheet for the cataloger's information and returns the screen to a blank template with a menu.

I collect the data for these sheets by revising all of the work of each cataloger for a given period of time. After revising each catalog record, I return it to the cataloger together with a sheet listing whatever comments I have on the cataloger's work. At the same time I keep a set of pencilled hash marks for entry into the spreadsheet at the end of the week.

The advantages of a spreadsheet for these records are that the sheet reduces certain possibilities for human error and prints out a clean copy of the data. There are, however, two obvious possibilities for human error in this system: First, the judgment that a given portion of a catalog record is in error may be wrong; and second, it is possible to make mistakes in the entry of data. However, since the cataloger gets the individual catalog record back for review (and since the cataloger knows that errors are being counted), it is likely that any mistakes in judgment as to what is or is not an error will be discussed and negotiated promptly.

The other possibility for human error in record keeping occurs when data is entered into the spreadsheet. At present, the macros freeze the column and row captions during entry so that it is fairly easy to verify that data is being entered into the correct cell. Apart from that, I usually do some cross checks of data when I enter the figures for the week such as comparing the number of records revised (upper right hand corner) and the total number of errors (lower right hand corner).

All of the arithmetic is done either through cell formulae or macros, which greatly reduce the possibilities for computational error. All of the row and column totals and all of the percentages are calculated by means of formulae recorded in the relevant cells. Furthermore, after the data for a week is entered, a macro is used to add the values from the previous spreadsheet to the new values. This ensures that the correct pairs of cells are totalled each week. Finally, the cataloger sees the spreadsheet each week. The purpose of this is either to encourage them to keep up their good work or, if appropriate, to correct whatever practices may be causing trouble. But it also means that there is an additional check on the data recorded in the sheet and, if there was a mistake, it is that much more likely to be noticed.

The real questions have to do with the way in which data is defined and recorded. The statistical categories would probably vary in other libraries. In our library, we have found that such characteristics as whether copy is *AACR* 2 or pre-*AACR* 2, or whether it is or is not based on an LC record are rough predictors of the probable difficulty of editing a record. The column captions on this template reflect these categories of record. However, one of my concerns in developing these sheets was to discover which aspects of cataloging were causing the most trouble, so that I could tailor the training program to these problems. Accordingly, the row captions enumerate several of the component parts of the cataloging process.

While the sheets are useful, they are also problematic. I will describe some of the problems first, then some of the advantages and finally explain why the sheets are more useful as a part of the evaluation of a library assistant than of a librarian. Problems with statistics are of two types. First, the statistical categories may not include all possibilities. Even though this sheet has been developed over a period of years and even though many categories have been added, it is still not complete. Only last week, one of our catalogers enhanced a minimal level record that had been entered into the OCLC database in 1983. He did many fine things to improve this record. He added a call number and subject headings and corrected the series entry, but he never noticed that the description of the item was a fine example of the 1908 catalog code. Of course, it is a requirement of the database that all records entered in 1981 or later conform to the current catalog code. There is no way to record this error until I modify the spreadsheet because there is no row herein for correct choice of code for description of the item.

The other type of error with statistics is that numbers, like words, can be used to distort reality as well as to describe it. In this sheet, the error rate is computed as a ratio of the number of errors to the number of records reviewed and this can lead to several types of distortion. If there are many errors in a single record, it will look as though a cataloger is generally careless although, in fact, the only problem may be that the cataloger failed to notice that one item in a hundred was a *tete beche* book. I generally try to reduce the impact of this type of error by revising records in the same fixed sequence of steps defined in our flow charts. If I uncover a major error, I first count it, then stop, return the item to the cataloger to rework and resubmit for a second revision.

A second type of distortion occurs if the cataloger makes the same mistake on several records. In such cases, I usually go over the spreadsheet with the cataloger in order to show them that, while their work is generally quite good, there is a fairly easily definable problem that needs to be worked on. Despite all of these problems, the sheets do have value. Although I have never put it all together into a single chart, I have learned some general things about cataloging which I did not know before. For example, the most difficult part of cataloging is determining how to record the dates in the publication, distribution area (i.e., *AACR* 2, Area 4). Authority problems may take more time than any problem of descriptive detail and they may require more knowledge of reference sources and code provisions, but mistakes in authority work are far less common than mistakes in the date element of the publication, distribution area.

Another thing I have learned over time is that the higher the level of the cataloger--i.e., the more experience the cataloger has, the more knowledge of cataloging that the cataloger has, the greater their level of language skills, the greater their knowledge of subject areas, etc., etc.--the higher the error rate. If you think about it, it makes sense. How many mistakes can a cataloger make if they only attach to current LC records where there are no changes to be made. The Greater LAs work with any record in the database and, under some circumstances, even prepare new records for the database. They have to correct any or all elements of the description, be prepared to do authority work, correct call numbers, revise outdated subject headings, and so on. Clearly, they have far more opportunity to make mistakes.

The sheets are especially useful for reviewing the work of new catalogers or catalogers who have been recently trained for a new task. For example, the sheet reproduced in Figure 2 shows that that cataloger had more difficulty revising pre-*AACR* 2 copy (first two columns) than with other work. As a matter of fact, this particular cataloger had only begun to edit such records two weeks before the review was undertaken and, when compared to other beginners, her work was quite good. A second value of these sheets for our library is that they show changes in the quality of work of a section over time. A few years ago the error rate for the Greater LAs centered in the 30 percent range and now the figures for this section are much nearer to 10 percent. Even though the precise figures may not be exactly representative because of the many reasons given above, it is, nonetheless, a fact that there has been improvement in the quality of work for this section.

A third value, when the same system is used for all members of a section, is that the percentages make it possible to rank the catalogers within the section in terms of the quality of their work even though the number of items reviewed for different catalogers may vary. For example, at one time I had the impression that one of our catalogers made an unusually large number of errors. However, when I began to review her work more carefully, I discovered that she was a very fast cataloger and that her error rate was low when compared to that of other members of her section.

Yet another value of this sheet is that it provides an objective basis for discussion of individual problems in cataloging. The percentages and the error rate may be distorted but it is still possible, with a sheet like this, to make specific statements such as, "Two-thirds of your errors have to do with problems in describing series." In some instances this is a more effective statement than one to the effect that, "You seem to have a lot of problems with series statements."

SPECIAL VALUE FOR LIBRARIANS

As I have already indicated, the sheets have been used far more consistently as a part of the overall evaluation of copy catalogers than librarians. This is true because many of the real values of this sheet are not applicable to librarians. First and foremost, librarians are not being trained in cataloging. Cataloging librarians, at least in our library, have all studied cataloging in library school; they have all had cataloging experience of some type; and, at least at the present time, they have all been catalogers at Irvine for some years. It is useful for them to meet and discuss a new set of LC rule interpretations but, having done so, they usually know how to relate this information to their own work.

Secondly, librarians are not reviewed as a section; instead the University has a peer review system. This means that the percentages would have no value for comparative purposes. The work of each librarian is reviewed separately with input from a varying group of other librarians. Thus, an error rate for a librarian could not be used to rank the individual within the group or to measure the changes within a group over time. Instead, it would appear out of context and, because of the problems involved in defining the error rate as a ratio of the number of errors to the number of records, it would have no real meaning. Frankly, when out of context, statistics lie.

The one reason for using such sheets with librarians is to bring to the attention of the individual librarian the fact that there are some specific problems with that librarian's work. And that is the only way I have used these sheets for librarians. One of my tasks is to revise all of the original records that we input into the database. By doing this, I am usually able to spot any problems that individual librarians have with one of the current standards. Usually, such problems can be handled with individual discussions or, if the problem is common to more than one librarian, we might go over it in a meeting. However, I have used the spreadsheet in cases where I thought it would be useful for the librarian to see the overall effect on their work of specific problems. We have one librarian who is quite competent in a particular subject field, but who honestly thinks that description of the item is not very interesting. This person was always very glad to correct any errors that I might point out after revising a catalog record, but somehow the same mistakes would appear on the next record.

We had several discussions of this problem and after awhile, it developed that this person was very anxious to see a spreadsheet that summarized the quality of the work. There were some ups and downs--by mutual agreement I destroyed all copies of one floppy disk--and I have yet to prepare a sheet that I am willing to share with anybody other than the librarian in question. Nevertheless, from my point of view, the attempt to prepare this sheet has been very successful. Nowadays, whenever I point out an error on a worksheet, this person appears in my office with catalog code, authority records, or whatever applies in hand and we have a lengthy discussion of the appropriate application of these standards. I have learned a lot about the type of material with which this librarian works-- information that I did not have before--and, whenever I score a point, I notice that the particular mistake does not recur.

CONCLUSION

My conclusion is that you can make more friends when you build a database or reference tool that helps people to do good work, but sometimes you have to use more than one tool to reach your own objectives.

NOTES

1. Judith Hudson. "On-the-Job Training for Cataloging and Classification." *Cataloging & Classification Quarterly* 7, no. 4:69-78.
2. Catherine Ann Carter. "On-the-Job Training for Catalog Librarians: A Case History of a Formal Approach to Training." *Cataloging & Classification Quarterly* 7, no. 4:79-92.
3. Lois M. Kershner. "Training People for New Job Responsibilities: The Lesson Plan." (Unpublished typescript)
4. D. Kathryn Weintraub, "Quality in Copy Cataloging at Irvine." in *Managing Copy Cataloging at ARL Libraries,*

5. Malcolm Shaw, et al. *Using AACR2, A Diagrammatic Approach.* (Phoenix, Ariz.: Oryx Press, 1981).
6. Peter Enyingi, Melody Busse Lembke, and Rhonda Lawrence Mittan. *Cataloging Legal Literature: A Manual Based on AACR2 and Library of Congress Subject Headings for Legal Materials.* Appendix B. 2nd ed. (Littleton, Colo.: F.B. Rothman, 1988).
7. *Cataloging Service Bulletin,* no 41 (Summer 1988):35-50.
8. Paula Goossens. "Hierarchical Relationships in Bibliographic Descriptions." in *Hierarchical Relationships in Bibliographic Descriptions, INTERMARC Software-Subgroup Seminar 4, Library Systems Seminar, Essen, 25 March 1981,* herausgegeben von Ahmed H. Helal, Joachim W. Weiss. (Essen: Gesamthochschulbibliothek, 1981), p. 14. (Vero fentlichungen der Gesamthochschulbibliothek Essen, Bd. 2.)
9. Florence A. Salinger and Eileen Zagon. *Notes for Catalogers: A Sourcebook for Use with AACR2.* (White Plains, N.Y.: Knowledge Industry Publications, 1985).
10. Nancy G. Thomas and Rosanna O'Neil. *Notes for Serials Cataloging,* ed. by Arlene G. Taylor. (Littleton, Colo.: Libraries Unlimited, 1986).
11. Jim E. Cole, David E. Griffin, and Dorothy E. Cole. *Notes Worth Noting: Notes Used in AACR2 Serials Cataloging.* (Ann Arbor, Mich.: Pierian Press, 1984). (Current Issues in Serials Management.)

Figure 1:
Some Records from the Database

SAMPLE CATALOG RECORDS
ILLUSTRATING AACR2 RULES
AND ARRANGED BY AACR2 RULE NUMBERS

PAGE NO. 1

RULE #	OCLC #	LCCN #	COMMENT
1.0A1	11841729	83-234988	Stamps, seals, etc = pt. of sour
1.1B1	13437672	85-751907	...and waken green
1.1B1	16802187	87-409075	Title = [author, title]
1.1C2	11979671	84-740005	Note GMD for coll w/o coll. titl
1.4C7	11681452	84-223896	Street address includes zip code
1.4D5	12644460	85-50610	2 Am. entities in PDEA
1.4F8	8591521	82-145620	Open entry for loose-leaf
1.5E1(c)	13785577	86-61238	Note for accompanying material
1.6G	12618670	81-192608	Numbering for 1rst parallel titl
2.5B11	11443857	84-172928	1 portfolio (2 folded sheets(10p)
2.5B19	4358058	78-903637	4 v. in 1 (Reprint of 4 vol. worl
2.7B4	9283174	83-173	Title on verso of t.p.:
2.7B7	11622843	85-1492	Reprint of two wks orig. pub. sej
2.7B10	7653818	81-474047	Note for a mounted photo
5.5B1	8633154	82-770310	Multiple scores in lieu of parts
21.1B2(b)	13601274	86-752993	Liturgy added to para. b in LCRI
21.4	11467887	84-26930	As told to
21.4C1	16070182	87-172930	Scott Montgomery is not 'real'!
21.9	8708007	81-175226	Adaptation
21.12B	8915234	82-213933	Rev. ed. by a different author
21.30G	15489	87-6371	Supplement to #'d issue of serial
22.2C2	13913269	86-224230	Compatible "pseud"
22.17A4	10442761	83-181447	Prince Consort
24.13(5)	14165012	86-149389	Conference as subordinate body
24.27C3	16981492	86-755294	Catholic Diocese
25.2B	11727095	84-670041	No UT for a rev. ed.
25.31B6	15144024	87-752888	Liturgical work in Latin language
A.40	1423074	86-752952	g-Moll but F-Dur

PROGRAM PREPARED BY
D.KATHRYN WEINTRAUB
EXAMPLES CONTRIBUTED BY
MEMBERS OF THE CATALOG DEPT.
UNIVERSITY OF CALIFORNIA, IRVINE

Figure 2:
Sample Cataloger Evaluation Sheet

Name: Amanda Sue Cataloger   Date: 03/21/88

Type of change	Desc: Blank LC & LC Based	Contri.	Desc: i LC & LC Based	Contri.	Desc: a LC & LC Based	Contri.	New Records K-level	LC & LC Based	Other	TOTALS	PERCENT
No. of Records	21		1	2	5	68		1	3	101	100.0%
Choice of rec										0	0.0%
Descri. of item											
TSRA						1				1	1.0%
Edit. area					1					1	1.0%
PDEA	1					6				7	6.9%
Phys. desc.#										0	0.0%
Extent										0	0.0%
Series Area										0	0.0%
Notes Area*						2				2	2.0%
Subtotal	1	0	0	0	1	9	0	0	0	11	10.9%
Descri. Access											
Choice						2				2	2.0%
Form of Name	2									2	2.0%
Subtotal	2	0	0	0	0	2	0	0	0	4	4.0%
Subject Analysis											
Choice	1									1	1.0%
Form of Ent.										0	0.0%
Subtotal	1	0	0	0	0	0	0	0	0	1	1.0%
Classification											
Class No.						1				1	1.0%
Book no.										0	0.0%
Subtotal	0	0	0	0	0	1	0	0	0	1	1.0%
Record Format*										0	0.0%
Significant Error Total	4	0	0	0	1	10	0	0	0	15	14.9%
Percentage	19.0%	0.0%	0.0%	0.0%	20.0%	14.7%	0.0%	0.0%	0.0%	14.9%	

*These rows are not included in the significant error total.

APPENDIXES

About the Participants

Alexandra Herz and Sheila S. Intner

ROBERT M. HAYES, SYMPOSIUM KEYNOTE SPEAKER

Robert M. Hayes is Professor at the Graduate School of Library and Information Science, University of California, Los Angeles, where he teaches courses in information science and related topics.

In 1959, Dr. Hayes founded Advanced Information System Company, a consulting and research firm, and in 1964 he joined the faculty of the University of California at Los Angeles. From 1965 to 1970 he directed the School's Institute of Library Research. He became Dean of UCLA's graduate School of Library and Information Science in 1975, a position he held until 1988, when he returned to full-time teaching.

Dr. Hayes earned three degrees in mathematics at the University of California at Los Angeles, the bachelor's in 1947, master's in 1949, and doctorate in 1952. He was President of the American Society for Information Science in 1967-68, and of the American Library Association's Information Science and Automation Division (later the Library Information and Technology Association) in 1968-69.

Dr. Hayes was co-author of *Information Storage and Retrieval: Tools, Elements, Theories* (1963), and the landmark work in automation, *Handbook of Data Processing for Libraries* (1970, 1975). He also edited a series of books on information science for the John Wiley Publishing Company. Among his most recent publications are "The Management of Libraries: An Assessment of Library and Information Science Curricula" (*Library and Information Science Education*, 1987), and "Strategic Planning for Information Resources in the Research University" (*RQ*, 1986).

In 1985, Dr. Hayes received the Beta Phi Mu Award for distinguished service to education for librarianship. According to the citation, though Dr. Hayes specializes in mathematics and information science, he is "also a keen student and avid supporter of the profession of librarianship."

PART I: SESSION ON RECRUITING CATALOGING LIBRARIANS

JAMES M. MATARAZZO, SESSION KEYNOTE SPEAKER

James M. Matarazzo is Professor at the Graduate School of Library and Information Science of Simmons College, where he teaches in the areas of special library management and science and technology literature. As Associate Dean from 1974-1988, he was closely involved in the recruitment, admission, and placement of students in the Simmons College program. Prior to joining the Simmons Faculty, he practiced at the Libraries of the Massachusetts Institute of Technology, where he served as Assistant Science Librarian (1965-1967), Government Documents Librarian (1967-1968), and Serials Librarian and Head of Technical Reports (1968-1969).

A Fellow of the Special Libraries Association, Dr. Matarazzo received the SLA Professional Award in 1983 and the SLA President's Award in 1988. He served as a member of the SLA Board of Directors and also as a member of the Council of the American Library Association (1979-1987).

Dr. Matarazzo is the author of *Closing the Corporate Library* and *Library Problems in Science and Technology*, chairperson and editor of the *SLA Task Force on the Value of the Information Profession*, and co-editor of three editions of *Scientific Engineering and Medical Societies: Publications in Print*, as well as authoring numerous articles.

LIZ BISHOFF

Liz Bishoff, who is currently Manager of Cataloging and Database Services at the Online Computer Library Center, Inc., was Principal Librarian for Support Services of the Pasadena Public Library. She specializes in library automation cooperatives and technical services management.

She chaired the Cataloging and Classification Section of the American Library Association's Resources and Technical Services Division in 1983-84, and was a member of the Resources and Technical Services Division Catalog Code Revision Commission. In 1984, she received the Esther J. Piercy Award. Ms. Bishoff was just reappointed the American Library Association representative to the Dewey Decimal Classification Editorial Policy Committee.

Among her most recent publications is "Who Says We Don't Need Catalogers," appearing in the September 1987 issue of *American Libraries*.

Ms. Bishoff received her bachelor's degree from Western Illinois University and her master's in library science from Rosary College.

D. WHITNEY COE

D. Whitney Coe, Anglo-American Bibliographer at Princeton University's Firestone Library since 1983, has also served as Acting History Bibliographer, Team Leader of the Humanities Cataloging Team, Principal Cataloger, and Head of the Descriptive Cataloging Section, all at Princeton.

Mr. Coe received his bachelor's degree from the University of California at Berkeley, a master's degree in Russian History, and a master's degree in library science from Syracuse University. He co-authored "AACR as Applied by Research Libraries for Serials Cataloging," and "AACR Chapter 6 as Adopted, Applied and Addressed by Research Libraries," both of which appeared in *Library Resources & Technical Service*.

ELIZABETH FUTAS

Elizabeth Futas is Director of the Graduate School of Library and Information Studies at the University of Rhode Island, where she is also professor, teaching Reference and Collection Development.

Dr. Futas received her bachelor's degree from Brooklyn College, a master's degree in library science from the University of Minnesota and the doctorate from Rutgers University. Her varied career in teaching and practice included posts at Emory University, Queens College, the University of Washington at Seattle, Rutgers University, and the Ford Foundation.

Editor of *RQ*, Dr. Futas has served on the Council and Executive Board of the American Library Association and on the Women's Task Force of the Social Responsibilities Round Table. Her many publications include: *Library Forms: An*

Illustrated Handbook, and *Library Acquisitions, Policies and Procedures*. In 1983, she edited an issue of *Library Trends* devoted to collection evaluation.

HEIDI LEE HOERMAN

Heidi Lee Hoerman is Assistant Dean for Technical Services at Montana State University. Previously she served as Original Cataloger at Indiana University, as Head of the Cataloging Department, and later as Head of Technical Systems and Bibliographic Control at Teachers College, Columbia University.

Ms. Hoerman received her bachelor's degree from Bates College, her master's degree in library science from Indiana University, and is working on a Doctorate in Education at Montana State University. Chair of the Resources and Technical Services Division's Cataloging and Classification Section Committee on Education, Training and Recruitment for Cataloging, she is also the Association for College and Research Libraries' representative on the Library of Congress Cataloging In Publication Advisory Group. A member of the Association of Library and Information Science Education, and the Northern Rocky Mountain Educational Research Association, she has held many local and regional offices, and was a member of the American National Standard Institute .Z39 Subcommittee on Language Codes.

THOMAS W. LEONHARDT

Thomas W. Leonhardt is Dean of University Libraries at the University of the Pacific in California. Previously he was Assistant University Librarian for Technical Services at the University of Oregon, Head of the Acquisitions Department of

Duke University, and Head of the Acquisitions Department of Boise State University.

Editor of the *RTSD Newsletter,* and editor also of the forthcoming publication *Foundations in Library and Information Sciences*, Mr. Leonhardt is a member of the American Library Association and its divisions, the Association of College and Research Libraries, Library and Information Technology Association, and the Resources and Technical Services Division.

Mr. Leonhardt has written on "The Place of Special Collections in the Acquisitions Budget" for *Library Acquisitions Practice and Theory*, and produced the *Spec Kit on Approval Plans in ARL Libraries* (Washington, DC, 1982). He received his bachelor's degree and master's degree in library science from the University of California at Berkeley.

JAMES G. NEAL

James G. Neal is Assistant Dean and Head of Reference and Instructional Services at Pennsylvania State University. Prior to that he was Assistant Director for Public Services at the University of Notre Dame Libraries, and a Council on Library Resources Academic Library Management Intern.

An active member of the American Library Association, the Association of College and Research Libraries, the Library Administration and Management Association, and the American Society for Information Science, Mr. Neal speaks frequently at conferences and has published widely in the areas of library automation, personnel management and library history. Recent publications include "User Support in Online Library Information Systems," in *Information Communication and Technology* (1987), and "The Turnover Process and the

Academic Library," *Advances in Library Administration and Organization* (1984).

Mr. Neal received his bachelor's degree from Rutgers University, a master's degree in history, a master's degree in library science, and a certificate in advanced librarianship from Columbia University.

JILL PARCHUCK

Jill Parchuck is Head of Original Monographs Cataloging at the Columbia University Libraries. She was also Director of the Hudson Area Association Library in New York.

Chair of the Ad Hoc Committee on Uniform Titles of LITA/RTSD Authority Control in the Online Environment Interest Group, Ms. Parchuck is also a member of the American Library Association's Resources and Technical Services Division, the Association of College and Research Libraries' Rare Books and Manuscripts Section, and the California Poetry Bibliographers.

Ms. Parchuck is the author of the *Manual for Online Maintenance of Monographic Set Records*, the *Manual for Online Maintenance of Microform Set Records*, and *Guidelines for Cataloging and Classifying the Poetry Collection* (Buffalo, 1983). *A Bibliography of the Works of Carl Rakosi* is in progress. Ms. Parchuck received her master's degree in library science from the State University of New York in Albany.

MARION T. REID

Currently Associate Director for Technical Services of the Louisiana State University Libraries, Marion T. Reid previously served as Acting Associate Public Services Director, Assistant Director for Technical Services, and Acting Assistant Director for Collection Development at that institution.

Ms. Reid's publications include chapters on "acquisitions" in *Technical Services Operations in Libraries*, and in the *ALA World Encyclopedia of Library and Information Services* (2nd. ed). She has also written a chapter entitled "Evaluating the Work of a Vendor" for *Acquisitions Art and Science* (ALA).

President of the American Library Association's Resources and Technical Services Division for 1987-88 and currently its Immediate Past-Chair, Ms. Reid is also a member of the Association of College and Research Libraries. A Fellow of the Council of Library Resources in 1974-75, she also won a Louisiana State University Executive Program Scholarship for 1980-83. Ms. Reid holds a master's degree in library science from the University of Illinois.

FAY ZIPKOWITZ

Fay Zipkowitz is Associate Professor at the Graduate School of Library and Information Studies of the University of Rhode Island. Previously, from 1981 to 1987, she was Director of the Rhode Island Department of State Library Services.

Her career has included practice in technical and public services in all types of libraries. She has also been an archivist.

A Fellow of the Council on Library Resources in 1974, Dr. Zipkowitz is active in state, regional, and national library associations, and is especially interested in legislative issues, demographics, training, and standards.

Dr. Zipkowitz received her bachelor's degree from Long Island University, a master's degree in library science from Western Reserve University and a second master's degree from the University of Massachusetts. She holds the Doctor of Arts from the Graduate School of Library and Information Science of Simmons College.

PART II: SESSION ON EDUCATING CATALOGING LIBRARIANS

JANE B. ROBBINS, SESSION KEYNOTE SPEAKER

Jane B. Robbins is Director at the School of Library and Information Studies of the University of Wisconsin-Madison, where she teaches, also, in the areas of research methods and education for library and information science.

Born in Chicago, Dr. Robbins received her bachelor's degree from Wells College, her master's degree in library science at Western Michigan University, and her doctorate at the University of Maryland. Her early career in library practice included positions cataloging in Washington, D.C. and Evanston, Illinois. She served as reference librarian in Colorado and as a consultant in Wyoming, as well as teaching at the Universities of Washington, California, Berkeley, Pittsburgh, Denver, and Louisiana State and Emory Universities.

Dr. Robbins is editor of *Library and Information Science Research*, a quarterly international journal. Her most recent research activity relates to evaluation of public library adult literacy programs.

MICHAEL CARPENTER

Michael Carpenter is Assistant Professor in the School of Library and Information Science of Louisiana State University. Prior to that he was Secretary and Treasurer of Carpenter &

Smallwood, Inc. in Los Angeles for many years as well as a Serials Cataloger, Special Recruiter, and Pilot Preservation Project Searcher, all for the Library of Congress.

Dr. Carpenter received a master's degree in business administration and a master's degree in library science from the University of California in Los Angeles, and his doctorate in librarianship from the University of California at Berkeley. He is a member of the Library Association of the United Kingdom, the American Library Association, the American Society for Information Science, and the Association of Special Libraries and Information Bureaus.

Dr. Carpenter's publications include "No Special Rules for Serial Entry," (*Library Resources & Technical Services*, 1975), *Corporate Authorship; Role in Library Cataloging*, and *Foundations of Cataloging: A Sourcebook*.

CAROLYN O. FROST

Carolyn O. Frost is Associate Professor in the School of Information and Library Studies of the University of Michigan. Her career in teaching and practice has included positions in the University of Oregon's Medical School Library, the University of Oregon's School of Librarianship, and the University of Chicago.

Dr. Frost received her bachelor's degree from Howard University, a master's degree in German Language and Literature from the University of Chicago, a master's degree in library science from the University of Oregon, and the doctorate in library science from the University of Chicago. She is a member of several national library associations, including Online Audiovisual Catalogers, the Michigan Library Association, the Association for Library and Information

Science Education, and the American Library Association's Black Caucus. She chaired the Resources and Technical Services Division's Education Committee from 1982 to 1984.

Dr. Frost has published numerous articles and books on the subject of cataloging, most recently "Nonbook Materials in the Online Public Access Catalog," in *The Collection and Control of Nonbook Media* (1987), and *Media Access and Organization: A Cataloging and Reference Sources Guide for Nonbook Materials* (in press).

SUZANNE HILDENBRAND

Suzanne Hildenbrand is Associate Professor at the School of Information and Library Studies of the State University of New York, at Buffalo, where she teaches cataloging and classification and online bibliographic retrieval.

A native of New York City, Dr. Hildenbrand received her bachelor's degree from Brooklyn College of the City University of New York, her master's degree in library science from Columbia University, and her doctorate in the history of education from the University of California, Berkeley. Her varied career includes experience as a high school and college librarian and as a Cultural Affairs Officer (Librarian) with the United States Information Agency in Africa and Great Britain.

Among Dr. Hildenbrand's recent publications are "A Data Base to Analyze Women's Press Titles in the Online Computer Library Center (OCLC) System" in the *Proceedings of the Fifth International Conference on Data Bases in the Humanities and Social Sciences* (1988), "Women's Studies Online: Promoting Visibility," in *RQ* (1986), and *Women's Collections: Libraries, Archives and Consciousness* (1986).

SHEILA S. INTNER

Sheila S. Intner is Associate Professor at the Graduate School of Library and Information Science of Simmons College, teaching in the areas of collection development, cataloging and classification, and bibliographic instruction.

A frequent contributor to the literature of cataloging and technical services, Dr. Intner is editor of *Library Resources & Technical Services*, the journal of the Resources and Technical Services Division of the American Library Association, and she recently published *Circulation Policies in Academic, Public, and School Libraries* (Greenwood Press 1987), *Policy and Practice in Bibliographic Control of Nonbook Media* (ALA 1988), and *The Library Microcomputer Environment* (Oryx 1988). She also writes *Technicalities*' bimonthly "Interfaces" column.

In 1987, Dr. Intner founded the Special Interest Group on Technical Services Education of the Association for Library and Information Science Education and in 1988 became chair of the Cataloging and Classification Section of the American Library Association's Resources and Technical Services Division. Also in 1988, Dr. Intner received the Annual Award from Online Audiovisual Catalogers. Her doctorate, received in 1982, is from Columbia University.

BEATRICE KOVACS

Beatrice Kovacs is Assistant Professor at the University of North Carolina at Greensborough where she teaches cataloging and classification, collection development, literature of science and technology, and medical librarianship.

Dr. Kovacs is a member of the University Academic Cabinet at North Carolina, Greensboro, a charter member of the

North Carolina Library Association's Library Administration and Management Section, and Vice-Chair of the Library Development Committee of the Southeast Library Association. In 1987 she received a grant for "Microcomputer Software for Cataloging," from the R.J. Reynolds Foundation and for "Decision-making in Collection Development: Public Libraries," from the North Carolina Library Association's Public Library Section.

Among Dr. Kovacs' recent publications, several are forthcoming: The Decision-Making Process for Library Collections: Case Studies in Four Types of Libraries (Greenwood Press, Contributions in Librarianship and Information Science), "An Education Challenge: Teaching Cataloging & Classification (*Library Resources & Technical Services*), and "The Impact of Weeding and Collection Development: Sci-Tech Collections vs Academic and Public Library Collections" (*Science and Technology Libraries*). Dr. Kovacs holds a doctorate in library science from Columbia (1983).

JOSEPH R. MATTHEWS

Joseph R. Matthews is General Manager of GEAC Advanced Libraries Division in Honolulu, Hawaii. Prior to that, he was Vice-President for Operations at Inlex, Inc. He has over ten years experience as a consultant working with libraries to solve problems through applied technology and practical innovation and he has helped many libraries evaluate their needs, select computer systems, and negotiate vendor contracts.

Mr. Matthews has published widely in the areas of management, computers, and automated library systems, including, most recently, *Director of Automated Library*

Systems and *Public Access to Online Catalogs* (1985), and *Guidelines for Selecting Automated Systems* (1986). A participant in the Council on Library Resources Online Catalog Project, his papers in connection with it are well known.

A frequent speaker at American Library Association conferences and workshops, for several years Mr. Matthews was a member of the faculty of the Library Administration and Management Association preconference on automation of circulation control. Mr. Matthews received an MBA from the University of California, Irvine.

FRANCIS MIKSA

Francis Miksa is a Professor in the Graduate School of Library and Information Science of the University of Texas at Austin. His previous positions in teaching and practice have been at Louisiana State University, Northern Baptish Theological Seminary and Bethel College.

A member of the American Library Association, the American Society for Information Science, and the Association for Library and Information Science Education, Dr. Miksa was Visiting Distinguished Scholar, Online Computer Library Center, Office of Research, for 1986-87. Dr. Miksa received his bachelor's degree from Wheaton College, and his master's and doctoral degrees in library science from the University of Chicago.

Dr. Miksa's publications include: *Charles A. Cutter, Library Systematizer* (1977), *The Subject in the Dictionary Catalog, From Cutter to the Present* (1983), and *The*

Development of Classification at the Library of Congress (1984).

PART III: SESSION ON TRAINING CATALOGING LIBRARIANS

HENRIETTE D. AVRAM, SESSION KEYNOTE SPEAKER

Henriette D. Avram is Assistant Librarian for Processing Services at The Library of Congress, where she is responsible for the training of more than 400 cataloging librarians.

A leading figure in the national and international library and information science communities, Ms. Avram joined the staff of The Library of Congress in 1965 and held increasingly responsible positions culminating in her current appointment in 1983. She pioneered the development of the MARC format for machine- readable cataloging, now used worldwide for the exchange of bibliographic data.

A leader in the areas of library automation, standards, networking and bibliographic control, Ms. Avram was awarded the American Library Association's Lippincott Award in 1988 and received the became an Honorary Fellow of the International Federation of Library Associations and Organizations in 1987. She has published widely in the areas of automation and bibliographic control, and her books on the MARC Format are landmarks.

Ms. Avram received an honorary doctoral degree from Southern Illinois University in 1977.

KATHLEEN BALES

Kathleen Bales is System Analysis and Design Manager of Research Libraries Group, Inc., in Stanford, California.

Previously she served as Senior Systems Analyst, Library Systems Analyst, Profiling and Testing Manager, and Library Coordinator for Research Libraries Group, Inc.

Ms. Bales co-authored *Bibliographic Displays in the Online Catalog* (1986), and wrote "The ANSI Standard for Summary Holdings Statement for Serials-RLIN Implementation" (*Serials Review*, Vol. 6, No. 4). A member of the American Library Association, Ms. Bales specializes in library systems, systems analysis, and cataloging. She holds a master's degree in Librarianship from the University of California at Berkeley.

NANCY L. EATON

Nancy L. Eaton is Director of Libraries and Media Services at the University of Vermont in Burlington. Prior to that she was Head of Technical Services for the Atlanta Public Library, Automation Librarian at the State University of New York in Stony Brook, and Assistant to the Director, Head of the Machine Readable Cataloging Unit, and Cataloger for the University of Tapas at Austin.

A member of the American Library Association, Ms. Eaton is on the Online Computer Library Center's Board of Trustees for 1987-88, and has been Project Manager of the National Agricultural Text Digitizing Project from 1986 to the present. In 1987, she became a Senior Fellow of the Council on Library Resources, University of California at Los Angeles.

Author of *Book Selection Policies in American Libraries* (1972) and *CD-ROM and Other Optical Information Systems* (1988), Ms. Eaton holds a master's degree in library science from the University of Texas at Austin (1968).

MICHAEL FITZGERALD

Michael Fitzgerald is Chief Cataloger and Associate Head of the Cataloging and Processing Department at the Harvard College Library, a post he has held since 1971.

Mr. Fitzgerald received his bachelor's degree from Providence College and was a Fulbright Scholar at the University of Munich. He did graduate work at Brown University and received his master's degree in library and information science from Simmons College in 1964. Beginning at Harvard the following year, Mr. Fitzgerald served in an advisory capacity to the Library in the development of HOLLIS, Harvard's online catalog system.

Mr. Fitzgerald's American Library Association service includes terms as chair of the Committee on Descriptive Cataloging and liaison to the Committee on Code Revision as well as a member of the Cataloging and Classification Section's Committee on Cataloging: Asian and African Materials and chair of the 1987-88 Margaret Mann Award Jury. Mr. Fitzgerald also served on the Subcommittee on Language Codes of the National Information Standards Organization.

BARBRA BUCKNER HIGGINBOTHAM

Barbra Buckner Higginbotham is Chief Librarian at Brooklyn College of the City University of New York. Previously she served as Head of Access Services, Head of Original Cataloging, and Assistant Head of the Columbia University Libraries, and was also Technical Services Librarian at the United States Customs Service Library.

A member of the American Library Association, Dr. Higginbotham has expertise in medical databases and hospital library management as well as history of preservation and bibliographic control. She received her bachelor's degree from Centenary College (1968), and her master's and doctoral degrees in library science from Columbia University.

KARIN A. TRAINER

Karin A. Trainer is Associate University Librarian of Yale University. Prior to that she served as Director of Technical and Automated Services at New York University, and held numerous positions of increasing responsibility in cataloging and bibliographic control at Princeton University.

The holder of a master's degree in library studies from New York University, and a master's degree in library and information science from Drexel University, Ms. Trainer has been Book Review Editor of *Information Technology and Libraries* since 1983. She was Chair of Technical Services Directors of Large University Libraries for 1985-86, and is an active member of the Association of College and Research Libraries, the Resources and Technical Services Division, and the Library Information and Technology Association.

D. KATHRYN WEINTRAUB

D. Kathryn Weintraub is Principal Cataloger at the University of California at Irvine, where, among other duties, she trains catalogers in descriptive and subject cataloging. Previously she taught cataloging and classification, social science and humanities reference, library systems analysis and technical services in library schools at the University of Chicago, Indiana University, and the University of Wisconsin, Milwaukee.

Dr. Weintraub was President of the California Library Association's Technical Services Chapter for 1986-87, and is a member of the American Society for Information Science, the American Library Association, and its divisions Resources and Technical Services Division and the Library Information and Technology Association.   Her most recent publication is "Quality in Cataloging at Irvine," *Association of Researc h Libraries Spec. Kit., No. 136.*

Dr. Weintraub received her doctorate in library science from the University of Chicago in 1970.

Selected Bibliography

Cecilia Piccolo

American Library Association, Resources and Technical Services Division, Cataloging and Classification Section, Task Force on Education and Recruitment for Cataloging. "CCS Task Force on Education and Recruitment for Cataloging Report, June 1986," RTSD Newsletter 11, no. 7:71-78.

Based on the results of a survey of library schools to determine content of cataloging courses, a recruitment survey, and consideration of related issues, the Task Force recommends examination of curricula and related accreditation requirements, and the development of programs designed to present a more realistic picture of cataloging to students, including increased input from and contact with practitioners for those in library schools.

Auld, Lawrence W. S. "The King Report: New Directions in Library and Information Science Education." College & Research Library News 48:174-179 (April 1987).

Jose-Marie Griffiths' and Donald W. King's report New Directions in Library and Information Science Education (White Plains, NY: Knowledge Industry Publications, 1986) concludes that on-the-job training is needed to develop many of the competencies identified by the authors as necessary for professional library work. Educational programs should develop specializations which are functionally, rather than type-of-setting, oriented. Auld suggests that this report can be used both as a means of evaluating curricula and as an aid in library administration.

Carter, Catherine Ann. "On-The-Job Training for Catalog Librarians: A Case History of a Formal Approach to Training." Cataloging & Classification Quarterly 7:79-93 (Summer 1987).

A formal training program in cataloging has been designed at Penn State for use in training new catalogers and new members of the public services staff with cataloging responsibilities. This program is highly detailed, in part because the effort to decentralize cataloging resulted in the hiring of librarians who had completed only one cataloging course in library school, and had not intended to pursue a career in cataloging.

Dewey, Barbara I. "Selection of Librarianship as a Career: Implications for Recruitment." Journal for Education in Library and Information Science 26:16-24 (Summer 1985).

Surveys of incoming library school students at Indiana University were collected to determine the factors which led to the choice of profession and location for education. Because many students were influenced by direct contact with librarians, recruitment efforts of library schools should include increased contact with local librarians. Implicit in this conclusion is the suggestion that technical services areas may suffer due to lack of visibility. Location of the school was very important; three-quarters of the respondents applied to one school only.

Grover, Robert J. "Library and Information Professional Education for the Learning Society: A Model Curriculum." Journal for Education in Library and Information Science 26:33-45 (Summer 1985).

Nine objectives which should form the basis of the core graduate curriculum in library and information science, derived from current definitions of what constitutes an information professional, are articulated. This model presents a convincing method for successfully integrating theory and practice in information science education.

Hafter, Ruth. "Born-Again Cataloging in the Online Networks." College & Research Libraries 47:360-364 (July 1986).

Catalogers may regain professional status lost with the advent of shared cataloging by developing as "master" catalogers experienced at review and correction of network records and therefore acknowledged as experts on standards maintenance. This article suggests that catalogers' future success will be dependent on development of an understanding of the political issues in network participation, an item the author believes warrants inclusion in in-house training programs.

Henderson, Kathryn Luther. "Some Persistent Issues in the Education of Catalogers and Classifiers." Cataloging & Classification Quarterly 7:5-26 (Summer 1987).

The progress of the "theoretical vs. practical education" debate is traced through the first century of library education. Because cataloging courses in current curricula must be directed toward the needs of both those interested in cataloging careers and those not, theoretical discussions may best be presented early, with most practical applications reserved for later, more specialized, courses. Demand has always been higher than supply; however, current recruitment efforts should emphasize the creative role of the cataloger in exploiting new technologies and opportunities, rather than presenting all these systems as rigid limitations on creativity.

Hill, Janet Swan. "Staffing Technical Services in 1995." Journal of Library Administration 9, no. 1:87-103 (1988).

Changes in the nature of the technical services workplace brought about by automation have not resulted in vastly reduced staff numbers. Some tasks have been eliminated, while many others have been added or augmented due to the expansion of services possible under automation. Professionals assume increasingly managerial roles, and will be required to collect and interpret data available from local systems to analyze efficiency and effectiveness, select and evaluate vendors and systems, and plan for the future. These tasks require a high level of training, with greater breadth than previously provided by library education programs.

————. "Wanted: Good Catalogers. The Applicant Pools Seem to Have Dwindled." American Libraries 16:728-730 (Nov. 1985).

The current dearth of qualified applicants for advertised cataloging positions is tied to a negative view of cataloging conveyed in library schools. Recruitment efforts should include requests to library schools to review and modify their programs with a view to making cataloging more attractive. Practica have too often been limited to non-standard materials and methods, and should be redesigned to include more "mainstream" work in cataloging departments.

Holley, Robert P. "The Future of Catalogers and Cataloging." Journal of Academic Librarianship 7:90-93 (May 1981).

Four groups of catalogers will emerge following a period of change in cataloging departments caused by automation. These groups will be the catalogers at the Library of Congress who will continue to focus on original cataloging production; catalogers in large research libraries who will supplement the LC database in the bibliographic networks with original cataloging of specialized or unique collections; cataloging managers who will design and oversee department workflow and supervise non-professional staff; and subject specialist librarians who will perform all functions from selection and cataloging to reference within their area of expertise. Education foundations for catalogers in any of these groups will need to be stronger than ever, as cataloging expertise will have to be coupled with subject and/or management expertise to respond to the needs of these increasingly demanding positions.

Horny, Karen L. "Fifteen Years of Automation: Evolution of Technical Services Staffing." Library Resources & Technical Services 31:69-76 (January/March 1987).

A comparison of staffing levels in a technical services department just prior to the implementation of the NOTIS system and fifteen years later (1985) shows no reduction in the number of professional catalogers and only a small reduction in cataloging support staff. Many improvements to catalog quality and public service, such as an increase in access points, thorough and consistant editing, and the regular performance of database maintenance functions are possible in a automated library, and will probably place increasing demands on the organizational and technical skills possessed by the professional staff.

Hudson, Judith. "On-The-Job Training for Cataloging and Classification." Cataloging & Classification Quarterly 7:69-78 (Summer 1987).

A sample training program for copy catalogers and for original catalogers is outlined, showing a progression through problems of increasing complexity. Graduates of library schools intending to be catalogers should have a strong background in theory, as well as familiarity with *AACR2*, MARC, subject analysis and bibliographic utilities.

Intner, Sheila S. "Library Science Education in the Online Environment." ACM SIGCUE Outlook 19:49-59 (Spring/Summer 1987).

Librarianship has metamorphosed by annexing technologically-based information disciplines, broadening traditional concepts and transforming itself into library science. Educational programs responded slowly, but they continue to change by adding courses in computing and technology. Teaching cataloging has become more difficult because students differ in their knowledge of computing and because there is much more to be taught. The potential of computer-based catalogs makes cataloging more exciting to teach and learn, and demands the conduct of more sophisticated research.

Robbins-Carter, Jane and Seavey, Charles A. "The Master's Degree: Basic Preparation for Professional Practice." Library Trends 34:561-580, (Spring 1986).

The library profession has failed to formulate a definition of competence in information fields and therefore does not control its market to the extent that other professions, such as medicine and law, do. The master's curriculum is undergoing profound changes, leading to integration of information science topics into a largely theoretical core. Library curricula may also gravitate toward increased specialization and away from offering preparation for all types of library positions, although the demands on library schools to serve as regional centers for training has slowed this trend.

Saye, Jerry D. "The Cataloging Experience in Library and Information Science Education: An Educator's Perspective." Cataloging & Classification Quarterly 7:27-45 (Summer 1987).

A model cataloging curriculum, including identification of student groups taking cataloging courses and articulation of short- and long-term objectives of the courses for each group, is presented. Emphasis is placed on group interaction and hands-on use of unabridged standard cataloging tools, to instill an investigative, problem-solving attitude toward the practice of cataloging, and to encourage students to debate applications of rules and defend decisions.

Sellberg, Roxanne. "The Teaching of Cataloging in U.S. Library Schools." Library Resources & Technical Services 32: 30-42 (Jan. 1988).

The role of cataloging in library school curricula, originally restricted to practical, laboratory-type skills development, later grew to include greater emphasis on theoretical study. The decline of the relative importance of cataloging in curricula combined with the increasing complexity of cataloging practice results in few and poorly trained graduates interested in pursuing a cataloging career. Library schools associated with major research universities should develop second-year specialty programs in cataloging, exploiting their ties with the university libraries for recruitment of faculty, use of resources, and development of practica. Employers must express preferences for and be willing to pay more to, the graduates of these specialized programs.

White, Herbert S., and Paris, Marion. "Employer Preferences and the Library Education Curriculum." Library Quarterly 55:1- 33 (January 1985).

A survey was conducted of directors of academic, public, and special libraries to determine topics in library school curricula which they favored in prospective junior professional employees' backgrounds and to evaluate options for extending education beyond the one-year master's program. Results were examined according to size as well as type of institution. Although most favor increasing the content of existing courses, many also supported increased program duration; however, few were willing to commit themselves to increased compensation or favored consideration when making hiring decisions.

Williamson, Nancy J. "Education for Positions in the Subject Control of Information." Cataloging & Classification Quarterly 7:57-67 (Summer 1987).

The place of subject analysis in the curricula of graduate schools of library and information science and topics which should be covered to adequately prepare a student for a career in subject control of information are presented. The dichotomy between education for traditional librarianship roles and education for information management roles presents problems in goal definition for subject analysis curricula. One-year programs require condensation of course material, and students' objectives are not always clear at the outset of a program making the "generalist vs. specialist" debate underlying curriculum design difficult to resolve.

Young, J. Bradford. "The Teaching of Cataloging: Education or Training." Cataloging & Classification Quarterly 7:149-63 (Summer 1987).

The goals of cataloging education have been strongly influenced throughout the history of library education by recurring issues related to the field of cataloging. Training prepares the student to perform tasks as presently designed, education prepares for change. The apparent conflict between training and education is less a battle between mutually exclusive forces than it is a dialectic, the product of which is a dynamic response to current cataloging issues.

Index

Prepared by Katherine Graham, Terry Inskeep,
and Jeanne Walsh, under the supervision of
Associate Professor Candy Schwartz